BASIC PRINCIPLES OF PSYCHOANALYSIS

Basic Principles
of Psychoanalysis

BY A. A. BRILL, M.D.

With an Introduction by

PHILIP R. LEHRMAN, M.D.

Doubleday & Company, Inc., 1949

Garden City, New York

002540

Acknowledgment

ON BEHALF of the family of Dr. A. A. Brill I wish here to express our deep appreciation and gratitude to our friend Philip R. Lehrman, M.D., for carrying to final completion the editing of this book in accordance with my husband's plans and in fulfillment of his desire.

ROSE OWEN BRILL, M.D.

August 30, 1948

Prefatory Note

DR. A. A. BRILL had finished rewriting this book and had the manuscript with him when he entered the hospital on February 27, 1948. Most of the revision he had done prior to his last brief illness. Characteristic of his thoroughness, he felt that some more revision might be needed—but he died a few days later, on March 2, 1948. He left word with his wife, Dr. K. Rose Owen Brill, that I should complete anything he might have left undone in this book. However, there was little left for me to do. I have made some changes in psychiatric terminology, added a footnote or two, and selected from his recent writings several paragraphs for the concluding chapter.

For forty years in which Brill was actively functioning as an expositor of psychoanalysis he has profoundly influenced the medical profession. As the first American psychoanalyst, he was deeply esteemed as the teacher of two generations of psychiatrists and psychoanalysts. First to bring Freud's monumental discoveries to this country—and by his translations of Freud's major works to the English-speaking world—Brill's place in the history of twentieth-century psychiatry has been fully acknowledged here and abroad. Primarily a clinician, his main interest was the suffering human being, and he worked to his last days with patients not only in his private office but as consultant to the psychiatric departments of Bellevue Hospital, the Veterans' Administration Hospital Number 88, and the Manhattan State Hospital on Ward's Island, New York. On a Saturday afternoon a few weeks prior to his death I talked with him about the number of patients he had studied since he obtained his M.D. degree in 1903 from the College of Physicians and Surgeons, Columbia University. We covered his four years' psychiatric work in Central Islip State Hospital; his assistantship in Burghölzli, Zurich, Switzerland; his work at the Vanderbilt Clinic, the Neurological, Bellevue, Beth Israel, Bronx, and Post-Graduate hospitals as well as his consultantships with the Department of Correction and the Police Department of New York City; also his association with the Veterans' Administration and the Selective Service. Finally, we considered his own extensive private practice. When we reached the count of fifty thousand we had not yet covered all of his rich experience!

Brill was well prepared in psychiatry and pathology for his lifework in psychoanalysis. He was also master of half-a-dozen languages, a student of the classics, and had keen interest in nature, art and music. He was well oriented in anthropology, sociology, and education. His clinical presentations show a special talent for conveying to the reader of his works the distilled essence of the impressive accumulation of sound observations in the science of the mind. His examples are always alive and brilliantly interlaced with a critical digest of the heterogeneous storehouse of his knowledge. His candor and wit illuminate the tragicomic in many life situations which he reports. Like Freud's, his case histories read like interesting romances, and he has given to authors many a "plot" which came to his attention from patients. The universal human experiences which are instanced in this volume are of immense importance not only to psychoanalytic psychiatry but to sociology, aesthetics, pedagogy, and the allied sciences. Language, too, was enriched by Brill, for in translating Freud's works and in his profuse writings new expressions had to be coined and familiar words had to be invested with new meaning. "Brill" is now a word in the dictionary.[1]

Most of his efforts in furthering Freud's views were directed to the medical profession. Psychoanalysis not only has wiped out the demarcation between mental medicine and physical medicine, as may be witnessed by the upsurge of "psychosomatics," but also has extended its dynamic influence on the allied sciences. It has forced a union between them. To understand the neuroses one must have a grasp of biology, psychology, sociology, anthropology, philology,

---

[1] *American College Dictionary,* Random House, 1947: Brill, n. Abraham Arden, born 1874, U. S. psychoanalyst and author, born in Austria.

and pedagogics. Brill insisted that, conversely, students in any of these disciplines must also have a knowledge of "Freudian Psychiatry." Its findings proved that "there is no real gap between the child and the man, between so-called normal and abnormal, between the civilized and primitive man. The individual differences in their various adjustments or maladjustments to their group can only be explained by looking at the total personality from all angles."[2]

For many years Brill was associated with the department of pedagogics of New York University, where he gave regular courses and seminars to undergraduate and graduate students, teachers, psychologists, sociologists, and others. At the various hospitals where he was consultant he taught the medical staffs who eagerly awaited his "rounds." He was a lecturer on psychoanalysis at the College of Physicians and Surgeons, Columbia University, and Clinical Professor of Psychiatry at New York University, and was active in the psychoanalytic training program of the New York Psychoanalytic Institute. This book is primarily addressed to the "extraacademic" reader. Its scholarship is nowhere marked by pedantry and it reflects the all-embracing understanding of man by the good physician.

PHILIP R. LEHRMAN, M.D.

July 31, 1948

[2]A. A. Brill: *American Journal of Sociology,* 1939, Vol. 45, No. 3, p. 325.

Contents

I   THE CATHARTIC METHOD   1

II   THE SYMPTOM: ITS NATURE AND FUNCTION   21

III   THE PSYCHOLOGY OF FORGETTING   41

IV   PSYCHOPATHOLOGY OF EVERYDAY LIFE   65

V   WIT: ITS TECHNIQUE AND TENDENCIES   97

VI   THE DREAM: ITS FUNCTION AND MOTIVE   119

VII   THE DREAM: ITS FUNCTION AND MOTIVE (CONTINUED)   135

VIII   TYPES OF DREAMS   157

IX   TYPES OF DREAMS (CONTINUED)   189

X   COMMON FORMS OF PSYCHOSES   215

XI   THE ONLY CHILD   237

XII   FAIRY TALES AND ARTISTIC PRODUCTIONS   251

XIII   SELECTION OF VOCATIONS   265

BIBLIOGRAPHY   289

INDEX   291

Introduction to Original Edition

THERE ARE a number of misconceptions concerning psycho-analysis, some of which at least I would like to clear up. In 1908, when I first introduced psychoanalysis into this country, I addressed myself primarily to the medical profession, for psychoanalysis was developed by Professor Freud while he studied the border-line cases of mental disturbances, and my interest was merely that of a psychiatrist who vainly tried to help such patients and finally found in psychoanalysis the most valuable instrument for the treatment and exploration of the mind. But even then it was realized that the subjects treated by psychoanalysis went far beyond pure medical spheres, for when a human mind was scrutinized for the purpose of studying the origin of an abnormal manifestation, all normal mental and emotional expressions had to be considered. In the course of many years Professor Freud thus solved the mysteries of dreams, wit, mythology, fairy tales, and threw much light on the history of civilization and on the development of religion and philosophy,—subjects and phenomena which, strictly speaking, do not belong to abnormal states. It was therefore quite natural to expect that persons interested in the above mentioned subjects would be attracted also to psychoanalysis, and a review of the very extensive psychoanalytic literature shows that it not only drew to itself the attention of the medical profession but also that of the psychologist, educator, and serious-minded layman, and notwithstanding some uninformed individuals to the contrary, much good has already been accomplished. Last but not least it has also attracted many charlatans and quacks who find in it a medium for the exploitation of the ignorant classes by promising to cure all their ailments by psychoanalysis. This, as everyone knows, is nothing new in medicine; there is no disease which is not "cured" by quacks. One could therefore easily remain silent and think that any person who is foolish enough to entrust his mind to quacks deserves no consideration, but as I feel somewhat responsible for psychoanalysis in this country, I merely wish to say that, whereas psychoanalysis is as wonderful a discovery in mental science as, let us say, the X-ray in surgery, it can be utilized only by persons who have been trained in anatomy and pathology. As a therapeutic agent psychoanalysis at best has a very limited field, it can only be used in the treatment of special cases. It cannot cure cancer, it cannot make an adjustable citizen out of a defective "radical," it cannot return an arrant young husband to a neurotic elderly lady, it has no more to do with the separation of mismated couples than the microscope with the dissolutions of tissues; in fine it cannot make a normal person out of an idiot, and does not give a philosophy of life to a person who has not brains enough to formulate one himself. But it has already rewritten all the mental sciences, and in the hands of trained psychiatrists it can cure the most chronic psychoneurotic affections. Moreover, the knowledge gained through it is developing a prophylaxis, which will not only diminish nervous and mental diseases but will establish newer methods in our system of education. In brief, psychoanalysis aside from its therapeutic application, which is not the object of this work, is of interest to any person who wishes to understand human nature and know himself in the Socratic sense.

The material found in this book is taken from the lectures given in my elementary course at the department of pedagogics of New York University. This course was primarily intended for those who are occupying themselves with problems of education and psychology. But as it is impossible to talk about the normal individual without showing what would happen to a child if subjected to a peculiar or special kind of environment, I have given illustrative cases from abnormal spheres as well as brief, in no way technical, descriptions of some forms of mental derangements. I have also tried to avoid technical expressions as much as possible, and have not taken the trouble to clutter this volume with a lot of references, which a book intended for professional people would necessarily demand; but all who know of my activities realize that all my work is built on Professor Freud's foundations, and they are referred to his works for more detailed and more technical information.

Michael S. Fraenkel, one of my former students, has given me very valuable suggestions. I am very much indebted to him.

A. A. BRILL

November, 1921

BASIC PRINCIPLES OF PSYCHOANALYSIS

1. The Cathartic Method

". . . It is by utterance that we live . . ."

PSYCHOANALYSIS is a term that was fully developed by Professor Sigmund Freud and his pupils, and, etymologically, means mental analysis. We hear about all kinds of psychoanalysis, but the psychoanalysis that we are going to study is a mental analysis of a special kind that works with special instruments; it means the analysis of normal and abnormal activities by a certain definite method—through the analysis of dreams, psychopathological actions, hallucinations, delusions, and psychic attacks of all kinds which we find in the abnormal spheres. It was originally developed by studying the so-called borderline cases of mental diseases; that is to say, Professor Freud started with cases of so-called "nervousness" which the average psychiatrist of his time put under such headings as neurasthenia, hysteria, obsessions, and phobias. In order that we may understand fully how the subject of psychoanalysis was evolved, it seems to me desirable to say a few words about the early history of mental diseases.

Brief Survey of Nervous and Mental Diseases

The first scientific description of mental illness dates back to 460 B.C.; at that time Hippocrates considered mental disturbances as abnormalities owing to some abnormal condition in the brain. Following him there was a long period of intermission, but one may find clinical descriptions by such men as Aretaeus in A.D. 60, by Galen in A.D. 160, and by many others. During the Middle Ages the subject was not only neglected, but a great retrogression followed. The mentally sick were treated most cruelly, and, like criminals, were chained and put to death for being obsessed. But with the advance of civilization these sick people began to receive more and more attention, and in 1792 Professor Philippe Pinel of Paris brought about the abolition of chaining. He was the first person to recognize that the "insane" person was a sick person and not a demon or criminal, and since his time there has been a gradual tendency toward both ameliorating the condition of the mentally ill and understanding the nature of "insanity" generally.

Modern or present-day psychiatry dates back about fifty years or perhaps even less. But we may say that long before then individual efforts had been made to study the subject intelligently and scientifically, and we find accordingly a great many scientific contributions to catatonia and other mental diseases. Yet most of the textbooks then current talked about mania and melancholia as if they were diseases by themselves. Nowadays we know, of course, that melancholia and mania are not diseases; it would be just as wrong to call coughing a disease. We all know that coughing is only a symptom of a disease; it is not a clinical entity. That is to say, one may cough because he has tuberculosis, or perhaps an ordinary so-called cold. And so, too, with mania. Among the mentally ill there is no form of psychosis that may not show a period of that so-called mania. It is just a symptom. And so, as you see, symptoms were taken for diseases and there were a great many misunderstandings. I have seen on record at state hospitals how a patient has been diagnosed, say in 1880, as a case of mania, two years later as a case of melancholia, three years later again as a case of mania, and five years later the patient died of softening of the brain. This occurred simply because the doctors did not know any better, and this is still more or less true of some practitioners, particularly of those doctors who have received their education under the old regime.

It was Professor Emil Kraepelin, at that time of Heidelberg, who evolved modern mental science. He was a pupil of the great psychologist Wundt, and after observing some patients for three or four decades he discovered that these patients followed definite courses not only in the manifestations of their mental symptoms but also in their whole physical make-up. Kraepelin did for mental diseases what Virchow did for pathology. The latter held that we must know how the organs look in order to diagnose a disease.

He examined diseased lungs, for instance, and found that they showed certain characteristic features. But of course it was not until the microscope was used that real entities were established, for though a diseased lung may appear tubercular to the naked eye, it may not be that at all when studied and compared under the microscope. In mental diseases the microscope is psychoanalysis. Up to the advent of Freud and his school no effort was made to find out what the patient had in mind or, if he said anything at all, what it meant. It was sufficient to write in our notes that he was dull, stupid, and demented. What all that really meant made little difference. When I came to the state hospital I examined a patient's record of twenty years. I would read—1882, patient dull, stupid, and demented; then a few years later: patient demented, dull, and stupid; and so on, until they almost exhausted all possible permutations and combinations. Then, "the patient suddenly died."

With Kraepelin's work, however, which was introduced into this country mainly through the efforts of Adolf Meyer, there was a marked improvement. Psychological entries were regularly made, every history was comprehensively noted, and particular attention was paid to the general behavior of the patient. We noted, for instance, what the patient said and did, whether he showed any hallucinatory and delusional trends, such as imagining that he was an emperor of Japan and that he was robbed of his throne, or whether he was just indifferent to his environment. His intelligence, memory, and orientation were thoroughly tested, and last, but not least, he received a thorough physical and neurological examination. Only after such an examination did one venture the diagnosis. However, when one read a number of histories of the same disease entity, say, dementia praecox, one could readily observe that there were no two cases exactly alike. And Kraepelin and his school never asked why it was that patient A had hallucinations of hearing a woman calling him endearing names, and why patient B heard a little child crying "Mother," and why patient C heard a man speaking to her. No effort was made to find out why this was so until Professor Freud published his original studies of the so-called borderline cases of mental diseases.

When we began to examine the nature of hallucinations and delusions, we found, for example, that there is a definite reason why such and such a woman sat in a corner of the room at the hospital and fondled a doll made of rags and newspapers, talking to it as though it were her baby. When we investigated this woman's life, we found that she had had an only child and lost it, and thus became mentally ill. When a woman talks to herself, we often find upon examination that she misses the person to whom she talks. I have in mind at present a woman who continually conversed with her imaginary bridegroom. Upon investigation it was found that on her wedding day, when all the guests and relatives were assembled, he took short leave and did not come. Everybody, of course, went home and bitterly inveighed against him; she alone tried to defend him. She was stupefied and could not imagine that he would not come; she begged the people to wait, and they continued to wait for hours, but the man never appeared. Then, suddenly, she ran to the door and exclaimed that she heard him talking to her, and since then she has been in a hospital.

Before Freud developed psychoanalysis it was commonly held that if a person is nervous, there must be something wrong with his physical make-up, regardless of whether this could be substantiated by examination. Such patients constituted a very large part of office practice. They complained of all sorts of aches and pains, peculiar feelings, morbid fears and obsessive thoughts, for which there was no known physical basis. Dr. Beard, an American physician, concluded that as nothing wrong could be ascertained in the physical examination of such cases there was necessarily something wrong with their nerves, and he therefore designated this whole class of cases as *neurasthenia,* which means a weakness of nerves. As a matter of fact, these cases really show no more "weakness of nerves" than people who have no such complaints to offer. But Dr. Beard and others of his time thought that the nerve fibers must be weak, for apparently there was no heart trouble, nor lung trouble, nor anything else that was organically wrong, to account for the patients' complaints.

Various remedies were used in neurasthenia, but the treatment was purely symptomatic. Thus if the patients were excited, the medicine quieted them; if dull or depressed, they were stimulated. But whatever was the remedy, they did not recover; they kept on taking these drugs and returning to the doctor, much to the disgust of both physician and patient. I may say that fully 80 per cent of patients who consult doctors suffer from such complaints, as has been shown by the experience of numbers of consultants. They represent the largest class of patients that we find in clinics, dispensaries, and private practice. Of course they may be helped somewhat, but only temporarily by some current therapy. Years ago, when I worked in five different clinics and dispensaries in New York, I would come in contact with patients who had made the acquaintance of all of them. I would treat a woman in the Vanderbilt Clinic and then meet her in the Bellevue dispensary; she would look quite abashed and sorry, and declare apologetically that the medicine she received from me in the first clinic no longer did her any good. And so these patients kept on moving from one clinic to another, and, as a matter of fact, this is largely the case today.

About 1880 Professor Heinrich Erb of the University of Heidelberg discovered the therapeutic value of electricity. It soon became the rage; it was used in the diagnosis as well as in the treatment. Every nervous person was sooner or later initiated into the mystery of electrical shocks; when the ordinary ones proved ineffective, new forms of electrical currents were invented. But at best such treatment served only as a form of suggestion. In a few weeks the patient would come back with some new ailment. Electricity may do some temporary good, but it never cures. A little electricity, a dose of medicine, or a cold bath or massage may help somewhat, but I do not hesitate to say that I have never seen a case that was cured by such means. Like the other practitioners of his time, Professor Freud resorted to all the remedies at his disposal, but the results were very discouraging.

It was at this time that Freud read about Professor Charcot of Paris, who was experimenting with hypnotism. Charcot found that he could hypnotize a hysterical person and suggest to her the symptom of another person and the patient would have this symptom. In other words, he maintained that hysterical symptoms can be suggested through hypnotism, and if they can be suggested by hypnotism, they can also be removed by it. Let me say, in passing, that hypnotism is nothing quite so strange and mysterious as you generally imagine. Do not think that a person can be hypnotized *nolens volens* in the manner shown on the vaudeville stage. No one can be hypnotized against his will. But there is no doubt that if people are willing, they can usually be hypnotized. Charcot's experiments soon became widely known in the scientific world. Freud heard about these new studies when he went to Paris and became one of Charcot's pupils, and the translator of some of his work.

The "Talking Cure"

Before going to Charcot's clinic, Freud became friendly with Dr. Breuer, a man older than himself, who worked in the same laboratory with him. One day Breuer described what he considered an unusually interesting case. It was of a young woman whom he thought to be intelligent and refined who was suffering from a severe case of hysteria. She had been treated by some of the most prominent neurologists and psychiatrists in Europe and finally came back to Breuer, her family physician. One day while under hypnosis she said to him: "Dr. Breuer, if you would only let me talk to you and tell you how my symptoms started, I think it would help." Dr. Breuer was sympathetic and told her to go right ahead. She began to tell him of a paralysis she had, and presently she went into an intimate account of her life; she talked on and on, with much feeling about the symptom, and after many hours she felt relieved. This treatment continued for a long time with good results. The patient, Miss Anna O., liked the treatment and called it the "talking cure." She was hypnotized and questioned about the symptom. She would tell when a certain symptom came, how she suffered, and spoke about things that a doctor would not generally think of listening to. It meant quite a tax on Breuer's time, but he was anxious to help her. He became attached to her and sympathized with her emotional difficulties; gradually she was losing one symptom after another. It seemed strange to Breuer; he had given her before all sorts of medicines, another doctor had given her hot and cold baths, and another electricity, and now she came merely to tell him stories and was getting well.

Freud heard about this case before he went to Charcot in 1885 and was deeply impressed by it. When he returned from Paris and entered private practice he naturally started with hypnotism which he learned in Charcot's clinic, but, like others who used this therapy, he was soon dissatisfied with the results. For he soon discovered, first, that not every person can be hypnotized; second, the successes obtained by hypnotism were not lasting. A symptom was easily removed but it was soon replaced by another symptom or the same symptom returned within a few days or at best within a few months. Moreover, the whole method of hypnotizing and commanding the patient to give up the symptom did not appeal to Freud's personality. He preferred to investigate the causes and development of the symptom, and hence Breuer's method of hypnotism and tracing the origin appealed to him as a more rational method than mere hypnosis. He finally convinced Breuer to collaborate with him, and after years of investigation they published in 1893 a preliminary report about their new method entitled *The Psychic Mechanism of Hysterical Phenomena,* and two years later they published their classical work, *Studies in Hysteria.*[1]

Freud and Breuer worked together for some time and got good results. They were so impressed with this new procedure that they called it the "Cathartic Method," which means the purging of the mind, a sort of unburdening of the mind. In everyday life we all know the therapeutic value of expression; when a person tells you his troubles he begins to feel better; we say a weight has been removed from his heart. They took cases that had been resisting treatment for years and cured them. They finally formulated various theories. In the first place, they found that all hysterics suffer from the past. Every hysterical symptom represents some mental or emotional disturbance that has taken place in the person's life in the past; there were occurrences of a disagreeable and painful nature which every individual likes to forget. Their idea was that if a patient can recall the unpleasant situation which gave origin to the symptom and live it over, so to say, he loses the symptom; that words are almost equivalent to the action, and that in going over some painful experience in the past there is what they called an *abreaction,* German, *Abreagierung,* in which the painful emotions associated with the experience were liberated and thus ceased to create physical disturbances. Thus when the patient had a pain in the face it was treated as neuralgia; of course it may have been that or not. If it was neuralgia, it usually yielded to treatment; if not, it was psychic or a functional pain. It represented in concrete form the expression: "I felt as though he slapped me in the face." When

[1]Translated by A. A. Brill, topic title "Nervous and Mental Disease," Monograph Series No. 61, New York, 1936.

the painful situation was brought back to the patient and explained to him, the symptom disappeared.

Let me make all this a little clearer by an example. A woman has a pain in her arm; she consults the doctor, who examines her and asks her whether she was out yesterday.

She says she was, and that the weather was bad and she caught cold. He prescribes a medicine, but the pain continues. She returns to the doctor, he tries some other remedy, but the pain grows worse. The patient is discouraged and consults another physician; she now merely tells him she has rheumatism in her arm; she gives him the symptoms; he takes it for granted that she has rheumatism and treats her accordingly. She goes from doctor to doctor until some diagnostician pronounces it hysteria and not rheumatism. She consults a psychoanalyst and we find this story: She is a young woman who had made the acquaintance of a college student. As time went on they became more and more intimate and it was rumored that they were to be married; in fact she, too, thought so. Upon graduating, he left the city and kept up a long correspondence with her. He came and spent his vacations with her; but he did not propose. The general impression was that, as he was a young man, he wished to make his way in the world before he married. Thus for years he came, spent his vacations with her, and left without proposing. The last year he wrote her with manifest enthusiasm that at last he had reached the goal of his ambition: he had received an appointment with such and such a salary. All the relatives heard about the letter and were now quite sure he would marry her. He came for his vacation, as usual, spent some time with her, and took her out for a long walk the night before he left. But he did not propose.

Everybody was disappointed; the mother was disgusted; her brother threatened to punch him in the face when he came again; and the poor girl was terribly grieved. She was told to drop him and think no more of him; she was willing to do so but claimed that it was much easier said than done. She argued that he must love her or else he would not write and spend his vacations with her; she felt that she was his only confidant. She did not realize that there are men who are so inhibited in their love life that they cannot propose. She was experiencing a mental conflict. She wanted to drop him; but there was no mistake about his loving her. He was a serious, quiet, well-behaved man who came from a very fine family and whom no one could accuse of being a trifler. "He certainly is not an adventurer, because he does not act like one," she would think to herself; "but why, then, does he not propose?" I would like you to notice the human, emotional element that enters into all these cases. Gradually, however, she made up her mind that he did not love her and that she would have nothing more to do with him. In time she was even ready to write to him not to correspond with her, but she could not gather sufficient courage to do so. Gradually there came that pain in her arm.

When we go beyond the superficial aspects of this case we find that it goes back to a fundamental condition in the past. We discover that the patient is suffering from the past, that the pain in her arm is only a monument of the past; it is a memento, one might say, of her mental conflict. In other words, when she was emotionally arguing with herself whether the young man loved her or not and when she had to suppress all talk about him, and make herself believe that she did not love him, her feelings, her emotions, became converted into those of pain. The arm was the arm that he pressed on the night before he left. She would say to herself: "But what about that feeling? He pressed my arm"; for then she had hoped that he would say the expected words. Analysis reveals that it is that feeling that she wished to retain in memory that became a pain; it was a symbolic form of expression, for she could not talk about it in any other way. Without having to speak about the young man she could now unconsciously retain this episode through the pain in the arm. There was, in a sense, a morbid gain. She could now talk and complain about her pain and thus have some form of expression, though the fundamental and deeper phase of her condition was submerged and she knew nothing about it. We see here a conversion of past emotion into something physical.[2] When the patient realized this deeper aspect of her condition and when the painful past experience was brought to her consciousness, she was cured. It was after careful study and observation of such cases that the idea was then postulated, first, that one can convert psychic

[2]This conversion of mental into physical elements takes place in a certain definite way. This particular patient had the reminiscence of the arm, so it was in the arm; sometimes it is in the nose, hair, or any other organ or bodily function. It is hard to realize how many different complaints one hears from patients of this type.

energy into physical manifestations; second, that a cure is effected by bringing the submerged painful experience to consciousness, thus releasing the strangulated emotions. This new viewpoint meant an enormous step forward.

The Conscious, Foreconscious, and Unconscious

We may see from the above case that what Breuer and Freud brought to the surface by the Cathartic Method were those things that the patient found disagreeable and painful—things that she could not talk about. This young woman could not complain of the fact that the young man did not propose to her for so many years; and of course, if it is essentially a sexual situation, no sensitive person can speak about it openly, particularly a woman. In other words, they formulated the theory that the patient suffers from what we call strangulated emotions, certain feelings and ideas which one would like to give vent to but cannot. We say they finally become unconscious, and we postulate such a thing as an unconscious mind, that is, something of which the person is absolutely unaware and which he cannot, through any effort of his own, bring to consciousness. In the Zurich school, which I shall have occasion to speak about later, we thought of the emotions thus associated with a painful experience as forming a *complex*. We defined it as an idea or group of ideas accentuated and colored over by profound emotional feelings which was gradually relegated to the unconscious for the very reason that it was of a distinctly painful nature and so could not be kept in consciousness. We unconsciously run away from distressing thoughts: we say we wish to forget them. These strangulated ideas and emotions remain in the unconscious in a dormant state, and any association may bring them to the surface.

A woman, for instance, gets up one morning, feeling perfectly well; she sits down at her desk to write a note to her friend. She writes the date and stops; a feeling of sadness gradually grows upon her, and she decides not to write. All day she feels depressed. It so happens that she comes to see me and tells me about it. Upon talking to her, I find that the moment she took her pen and wrote the date the latter struck a complex in her mind which evoked a certain date that went back a great many years to a day when something extremely disagreeable happened to her. When she became depressed, she knew nothing about it. She did not consciously recall the original painful experience. She merely experienced the emotion that went with the episode. In this pushing out of what is painful from the field of consciousness we have an unconscious protective mechanism. We have to forget, so to say, a painful experience; if everything disquieting and troublesome were to remain in consciousness, life would be unbearable. But a word, an odor, a sound, a color, may plunge us right back into that state of mind of, let us say, ten or more years ago; we have completely forgotten the whole situation, but the emotion, like an old unwelcome visitor, comes up and depresses us. Sometimes the recurring emotions are pleasant ones, but usually they are unpleasant.

In studying such cases we find that the painful episodes sank into the unconscious because they could not be worked off at the time of their occurrence. An individual experiences a profound emotional shock and cannot give it expression; it remains in a repressed condition; and the only way to liberate the pathological energy it has accumulated is by bringing it to the plane of conscious expression. When the patient talks about it, he is living it over in a very vital sense. I have had a patient take a little statuette which was on my desk and throw it on the floor and break it, simply because he was intensely wrought up over a certain experience he recalled. I had a lady in my office who was greatly surprised at first and laughed, when I explained to her the reason why she could not walk. Presently she cried out: "Doctor, my legs are tingling." I told her she could now walk home with ease, and she did. There was an abreaction when we reached the crux of the emotional experience and the whole situation was brought back to her consciousness.

I would like you to notice that I am using the term "unconscious" and not "subconscious" or "co-conscious," which is used rather loosely by many people to denote so many different mental states. As we have already said, the unconscious, according to Freud, includes all those psychic manifestations of which the person is not and cannot be aware. It is made up of repressed material, that is, of the sum of those psychic experiences which have either been crowded out of consciousness because of their painful and unattainable content, or have been repressed from the very beginning of childhood. They represent the primitive impulses that have been inhibited and sublimated in the development of the child. For the child is originally a primitive being—it is like a little animal—and as it gradually gives up the gross animal impulses, it represses them; we say they are pushed into the unconscious. We usually try to make a child do what it would not do if left by itself. There are primitive impulses in every child which have to be curbed from the very beginning and which may form points of crystallization for future repressions. An occurrence in one's life at the age of fifty, for instance, may be traced back to some childhood repression; there is always some subtle and intimate connection in our present emotional experience with something that occurred in the past. Absorbed in the immediate synthetic significance of a present experience we cannot stop to realize the important part the past has had in molding it; in a very real sense it may be said that we are always elaborating upon old psychic material. But what is more, these past elements lie in the unconscious and are prevented from coming to the surface by the protective mechanism to which I have already drawn your attention.

Then, too, there are efforts at repressions which take place in our adult life; and because these experiences are not subjected to the same amount of repression as the earlier and more primitive ones, they remain in what we call the *foreconscious*. We have, then, an unconscious, a foreconscious, and a conscious plane, as it were. As we go along I shall try to show how different psychic manifestations, such as neurotic symptoms, or dreams, fall into one or another of these categories. We shall see that the psychoneurotic symptom is the function of two separate systems, or psychic streams, both striving for expression. One subjects the activity of the other to a critique, which results in an exclusion from consciousness. Now the criticizing system, or the foreconscious, is in closer relation to the one criticized, or the unconscious; it stands like a screen between the unconscious and consciousness. Both the unconscious and the foreconscious are unknown in the rational sense, but the unconscious is incapable of consciousness without external aid, while the foreconscious can reach consciousness after it fulfills certain conditions which we shall take up later on. We maintain that eight ninths of all our actions are guided by our unconscious and that consciousness as such is nothing but an organ of perception.

The Cathartic Method Elaborated

For some time Freud continued to treat cases of hysteria and neurasthenia quite successfully, but he was soon confronted by a serious difficulty: he found that a great many people who were sick and needed help could not be hypnotized. He was especially interested in a certain very intelligent woman whom he made every effort to hypnotize, but without success. Finally Freud took her to Bernheim in France, who was reputed to be able to hypnotize almost all of his patients, but he, too, could do nothing with her. What was to be done? Freud then thought of an experiment that he saw in Bernheim's clinic. In hypnotism, if you give the person what is called a post-hypnotic suggestion, that is, tell him that at three o'clock, Friday, January 25, he is to come to a certain place, and take, let us say, an umbrella there, precisely at that time he will experience a feeling of inner compulsion, and if no physical conditions intervene, he will try to carry out the suggestion. When the person is in the hypnotic state and receives such a suggestion, he is absolutely unconscious of it later; it is followed by what we call post-hypnotic amnesia: he forgets completely the entire experience. I once performed this same experiment with a nurse; a doctor was present to see how it worked out. Exactly at the stated time she came; she was under the impression that the doctor was one of my patients, and though she knew very definitely that no one was allowed to come into the office while I was being consulted, she nevertheless made an effort to enter. The doctor met her at the door and upon asking her what she wished, she replied: "I must go in and get an umbrella; it is raining." When he drew her attention to the fact that it was not raining, she felt quite embarrassed. Thus, without thinking, she carried out the idea she had received in the hypnotic state. In the same way, also, an alcoholic, for instance, will experience a feeling of nausea and will actually vomit whenever he tries to drink alcoholic beverages after he has received a hypnotic suggestion to that effect. Of course the matter is not quite so simple as it may sound.

After such a post-hypnotic suggestion Bernheim would ask the patient to try to recall what happened while he was not conscious. The latter would say that he remembered nothing; he was urged further, however, to concentrate and think until at first some vague reminiscence came to consciousness, and finally the very suggestion that was given during the hypnosis. Now Freud saw no reason why the same thing could not be done with his patient who could not be hypnotized; if it was possible to recall a post-hypnotic suggestion, why should it not be possible to recall the episode associated with her symptom? He set about questioning the woman; at first she could recall nothing; he would insist upon her telling him what came to her mind as she was concentrating her attention upon the symptom. She talked about many things that had no apparent connection with the particular situation; she went on and on, and he noted very carefully everything she said. In this way he finally reached the origin of the symptom. He then found not only that hypnotism was not necessary but that it was much better to treat the patient without it. For one thing, Freud never liked the commanding approach used in hypnotism, he felt that it did violence to the patient; second, by conscious questioning it was possible to trace all the forces that were responsible for the symptoms. But in following this method of "free association" he soon found that everything the patient reproduced was definitely related to the symptoms, that nothing could be ignored. As time went on he realized that besides obtaining associations he also had to interpret them, for every person has an individual way of expressing his thoughts. The combination of free association with interpretation and later with dream interpretation Freud called *psychoanalysis*. This method of procedure was the most significant contribution to the psychoanalytic technique.

I would like to draw your attention in this connection to a fundamental difference Freud pointed out between hypnotism and the psychoanalytic method. The former he said works, as in painting, by putting on things, *per via di porre,* as Leonardo da Vinci has so aptly expressed it; the latter method by removing all extraneous material, *per via di levare.* As the sculptor chisels pieces of marble into the ideal shape, so also in psychoanalysis we endeavor to bring the individual into complete harmony and unity of character by taking away all undesirable excrescences in the form of needless inhibitions imposed upon him by his environment. In hypnotism we disregard the individual's mental make-up; he is in an unconscious state and we simply impose upon him some suggestion in a bold, authoritative fashion. In psychoanalysis we learn to know the patient: we delve into the deeper mainsprings of his character; we gain his confidence; and when we have learned his personality and come into vital and intimate relations with it, we then remove, like the sculptor, all extraneous matter. We impose nothing; we merely eliminate and discard whatever is superfluous, obstructive, and cumbrous.

Following this analogy I may add that there is also a similarity in the relations that sculpture and psychoanalysis respectively bear to the material with which each works. Just as in the former the ultimate result of the artist's efforts, his consummate achievement, will depend in large measure upon the nature of the material he uses, so in the latter the physician's ultimate success in the treatment will be dependent to no small degree on the constitution of the patient. We are told that in creative work there is always a fine blending of form and idea, of substance and execution. We look upon Michelangelo's Moses in a spirit of profound awe; how sublime and terrible does this old prophet appear! But have you ever paused to consider for a moment how ludicrous this powerful statue would be if instead of that fine, white, clear marble the sculptor had used, let us say, some stone with black streaks running through it? And likewise in psychoanalysis the physician can attain the best results with the best type of individual only; by that I mean a patient of the higher type mentally, morally, and in every other respect. Psychoanalytic therapy can accomplish nothing with the defective; the individual must be at least of the average type to derive any benefits from psychoanalytic therapy.

When one attempts to discover the origin of the symptom through the free and continuous associations of the patient, such as we have noted above, one finds the way beset with countless difficulties. Many things have to be found out before one can judge from the productions obtained from the patient; one gets a mass of material and may soon lose his way in it; one has to know what it essentially means. If one examines the actual productions that a person gives when one asks him to tell what comes to his mind, one will find a very peculiar state of affairs; one will then realize that there is no such thing in the world as a clear thinker. A patient has a jumble of thoughts running through his mind and feels that he would appear ridiculous and stupid if he were to describe them; he is naturally embarrassed and finds refuge in silence. Moreover, there are certain perversities of nature that come to his mind— very delicate subjects indeed, that no one likes to talk about. Thus an enormous number of things emerge which he thinks are quite irrelevant, family skeletons, and little buried secrets that the doctor need not know. What is more, the very thing one is seeking is kept down and held in his unconscious by chains, as it were, because it is disagreeable and painful. As we have said, there is a protective mechanism on the part of his mind to prevent it from coming to the surface; he must not know it, because if he does, it will cause him pain. Another great difficulty is that the same words very often have different meanings to different people; no two individuals talk exactly the same language; everybody has his own way of expressing ideas; everybody has his own mode of reaction to this world. There are some expressions in every family that the un-initiated cannot understand; there is a sort of Freemasonry in every home. But the greatest difficulty is that the language which is found in the unconscious is different from that of everyday life; what I mean is that in the unconscious, conceptions are expressed in a different way than in conscious life, as I shall show more fully when I discuss the subject of dreams. Now all this had to be fathomed, analyzed, elaborated, weighed, and understood, before one could get at the heart of the situation.

In thus probing the unconscious, Freud became impressed with certain fundamental facts. For one thing, he began to see more and more clearly that impressions are imperishable, especially those received in early life. When we probe the mind we always find that the individual receives the most vital impressions that stand out for life and direct him in the beginning of his existence. The child's mind, when born, is, in the words of Locke, a *tabula rasa,* a blank slate. The child is indeed endowed with certain elementary mecha-nisms that will help him to sustain life; gradually, however, those impressions are formed which are so vitally necessary for proper adjustment. Whether the individual will become the so-called normal or abnormal person, whether he will be able to adjust himself to his environment or fall by the wayside, depends almost entirely upon the nature of these early impressions. Given an average amount of brains, every individual as he grows up has certain tracks laid out for him by his environment; he can follow those tracks and those only; if he attempts to get off the track, he finds himself in trouble; he finds himself incompatible with his environment, he collides with his environment. Thus it is of great importance to give the individual enough tracks to be able to move freely and at the same time not to come into conflict with his fellow beings. From a very broad experience with nervous and mental diseases I feel that if everybody would understand this, all mothers and teachers particularly, we could reduce nervous and mental diseases as much as we have reduced the diseases of smallpox and typhoid. We are not afflicted with these age-old diseases today because we know what produces them and have learned to prevent them. We can do likewise with a knowledge of the psychoanalytic principles. Indeed *the great service that psychoanalysis can render today consists chiefly of prophylaxis;* as far as curing patients is concerned, I feel rather pessimistic at present. We can cure few in comparison with the overwhelming numbers: the treatment can be carried out only by physicians of experience not alone in nervous and mental work but also in psychoanalytic technique; then, too, it requires so much time and money that very many people cannot afford it. I feel that it will probably take many, many years before we shall have enough institutions to afford needy patients the benefits of psychoanalytic therapy.

There was also another fundamental thing that very forcibly impressed Freud, as he continued treating and studying his patients. He found that when they began to dwell on their intimate personal experiences they practically all would invariably bring up matters appertaining to sex. He was so impressed with this fact that he asserted that *in the normal sex life no neurosis is possible.* Even before him neurologists of the old school had always suspected that sex played a part in nervous conditions, but to them it was just gross sex, it meant just the physical elements of sex. Freud formulated a new concept of sex. To him the sexual life of the individual meant his *love life.* He used the term in the broadest sense, as embracing not merely the gross sexual, or the physical elements, but all that we commonly associate with love. He found that the conceptions of sex in vogue at his time were practically all false. It was generally held that there was no manifestation of sex until the boy or girl reached the age of puberty, when, suddenly, and in some mysterious way, the sexual impulses appeared. Freud found, however, that there were sexual experiences, or feelings very much allied to sex, at the beginning of childhood. What many people consider as something other than sex is really an integral phase of it.

Love and sex are the essential components of the love life and they go hand in hand. Later on Freud used the term *libido,* which he defined as a quantitatively changeable and not yet measurable energy of the sexual instinct which is directed to an outside object. He explained that the sex instinct consisted of all those impulses that center about love in the broadest sense, that its main component is sexual love, and sexual union is its aim, but that it also includes self-love, love for parents and children, friendship, attachments to concrete objects, and even devotions to abstract ideas. Bearing in mind the libido theory one can easily understand the sexual life of the child, the pervert, and neurotic, each of which shows a different form of sexual behavior as will be demonstrated later. In other words, sex in our sense is not confined to the physical manifestation in the popular sense. To be sure the latter form is the *sine qua non* in marital relations. Let me assure you that I have seen a number of cases where all so-called love existed but there could not be normal sex relations, and there was a separation or a divorce. Consider, for instance, the case of a woman who marries a man after being in love with him for about six years; upon marriage it is found that he cannot consummate his marital agreement; we find very soon a separation followed by a divorce.

We maintain that sex is born with the individual just as he is born with every other organ, every other function. The child is born without teeth, but upon examination you will find that the primordia are there from which the teeth will later come. The child has all the partial impulses of sex, of love, and of the mechanisms that later go to make up the specialized function. You can actually see a child of a few weeks react to the feeling of like and dislike; observe an infant of say a few weeks, smile at it and it will respond, frown at it and it will make faces. What does a child of that age know? you ask. It has these partial impulses at birth and it reacts accordingly. This attitude toward sex has been subjected to a great deal of criticism, and Freud has been accused of laying an

undue amount of stress on sex; many have been and still are opposed to his theories on that very account. They declare that there
are a great many cases that show nothing irregular in their sexual
life and yet are nervous. Without going into details at present I wish
to say that my own experience very definitely corroborates Freud's
position.

Continuing to delve deeper and deeper into the recesses of the
mind, Freud also began to see more and more clearly the intimate
relation existing between the dream and the patient's innermost
thoughts and feelings. In dwelling on some significant emotional
experience the patient would very often say: "Just at that time I had
a peculiar dream. I was walking and a man came up to me and
attacked me; I was terribly frightened; I tried to run but could not;
I was just rooted to the spot." At first Freud paid no more attention
to these dreams than any other intelligent man of his time. But
gradually, as he listened to them, he began to see that they must
have some place in the vital economy of the mind, for everything in
the physical or mental spheres must have a function. In time he was
convinced that the dream is not a mere jumble, a senseless mechanism, but that it represents, frequently in symbolic form, the
person's inmost thoughts and desires, that it represents a hidden
wish. In brief, Freud concluded that a dream must be treated in the
same way as a symptom. He thus developed his monumental work,
the greatest in the century, in my opinion, *The Interpretation of
Dreams*. He found that the dream offered the best access, that it
was the *via regia,* as he put it, to the unconscious; that it was of
tremendous help not only in the treatment, but also in the diagnosis.

And finally, as Freud continued to observe and study his cases
more and more deeply, as his horizon widened and widened all the
time, he began to see more and more that everything in the psychic
life has meaning, everything has a cause, nothing that the individual may do or say is meaningless. Every slip of the tongue, or
mistake in writing, or some unconscious gesture or movement has
significance. I asked a friend the other day over the phone where he
had been since his marriage, and he replied that he went on a
"moneyhoon." He meant to say "honeymoon," but when a man
marries, money begins to play a rather significant part. If we pay
attention to what is being said and done around us, we find a
tremendous amount of material that is unusually interesting. We

will learn later on why we make these mistakes. Freud's fascinating book, *The Psychopathology of Everyday Life,* deals with this subject, and I would advise those who are anxious to read his work to begin with this one, for it is the simplest of all his writings. In probing the unconscious Freud thus discovered material that is of the utmost importance not only in the treament of patients but also in the development of normal people, in education, folklore, religion, art, and literature, and every other field of human interest.[3] We may say that he has practically rewritten all of mental science and created new concepts in every sphere of mental activity. With his work as a starting point, new fields of thought and investigation have opened all the time, and there gradually has grown up an enormous literature on psychoanalysis, swelling all the time in the variety and range of the subject matter, all growing out of the effort to help humanity, to treat those unfortunate people for whom nothing could be done in the past—the so-called "nervous" people.

[3]*The Basic Writings of Sigmund Freud,* translated with an introduction by A. A. Brill. The Modern Library, N.Y., 1938.

2. The Symptom: Its Nature and Function

Freud's Concept of Sex

IN OUR PREVIOUS discussion we noted that a neurotic symptom, such as, for instance, the pain in that young woman's arm, is really a monument of the past; that through the symptom the neurotic is able to dwell on the painful episode in the past, to complain, and weep over it very much like one who would shed tears today over the battle of Lexington, or over the Spanish Inquisition. I said that the patient had to repress certain ideas and emotions because they were intolerable and distressing; he had to forget a disagreeable situation to which he could not adequately react. We say that the ideas and emotions were strangulated; that they were pushed into the unconscious. It is different, of course, with the average normal person; if he is insulted and feels hurt, let us say, he will either try to retaliate, or if he cannot do that out of weakness, or cowardice, he will very soon manage to "get over," as we say, the whole affair, to shake himself free from it. Some people, however, by virtue of the fact that they are made of finer, more sensitive substance, of perhaps better clay—let us call it a special constitution—cannot forget the situation and they will dwell on it continually. They were commonly designated as nervous persons, or neurotics; they were generally considered as defective in one way or another, or as mental degenerates. From what I have already pointed out you can readily see that this conception is entirely erroneous; that, on the contrary, far from being mental degenerates, they are, as a class, high types of individuals.

This does not mean, however, that those who are mentally deficient do not have hysterical mechanisms. The crucial point is that they do not manifest a definite neurosis as we understand and describe it. When a young lady who has been well-bred experiences a sexual feeling, she will often revolt against it; and particularly if she has not been enlightened in matters of sex, she will make an earnest effort to crowd it out of consciousness, because she regards the experience of and by itself as something distinctly ugly, wrong, immoral. On the other hand, mental defectives who are never able to assume those inhibitions that society has imposed upon the average individual are thus able, by virtue of their deficiency, to commit all sorts of immoral acts. Only a woman who is a defective can be a prostitute in every real sense of the word; a normal woman might perhaps think of being one, but only a moral idiot or an imbecile can be one. The normal woman is so constituted that prostitution is altogether out of the question; she may, perhaps, have some sort of an affair with a man, but she will not resort to prostitution in the narrow sense of the word. Nor does a normal man become a habitual criminal. He may swear off the taxes, or take an occasional false oath, but he is not going to make a practice of committing crimes. The inhibitions that are imposed upon us by society are so strong and exacting that we revert of ourselves to the age-old conclusion that "honesty is the best policy": it is the most sensible, the most practical, the most pragmatic policy; it allows us a measure of freedom which we otherwise could not enjoy. Nevertheless, there is no doubt that civilization with its manifold inhibitions, impositions, and prohibitions makes it indeed very difficult for us to live. There is not a human being who does not feel the burden of civilization lie heavy on his shoulders; and though we all bear the cross as patiently as we know how, who of us in his heart of hearts does not find himself at times discontented and complaining? That is the price we have to pay for civilization. Sometimes the injustice heaped upon a predisposed individual is so great and overwhelming that, as his deeper sense of morality stays his rash hand from some criminal act, he becomes neurotic; and sometimes he goes even further, he becomes psychotic. That is the way he tries to purge his bosom of all "perilous stuff."

I am using the terms "neurotic" and "psychotic" and I wish you to note the difference between them. A neurosis is an emotional disturbance such as we have seen in the case of the young woman who had that pain in the arm, for instance. The neurotic or psychoneurotic is perfectly sane. What is more, he is usually above the average person in mental development. A psychosis is a mental disorder; the psychotic patient suffers from some form of mental illness. He need not necessarily, of course, have anything in common with the mental defective. While I am on this point, I would also have you distinguish functional from organic psychosis. The latter is owing to some physical disturbance like certain poisons, alcohol or syphilis, injuries to the brain, or abnormal growths. The functional cases are those whose brains are apparently normal; that is to say, if you examine the brain of a paranoiac and that of a brilliant man, you will find no difference between them; the former shows no pathological condition.

In mental diseases there are two important entities that were discovered by Emil Kraepelin toward the end of the last century, and as I shall have occasion to refer to them from time to time, in the course of this survey, it may be well to say a few words about them in this connection. Kraepelin found that some young patients whom he observed in the hospital, sometimes for years, and who were diagnosed as sometimes suffering from mania, and sometimes from melancholia, showed a definite form of psychosis which he called dementia praecox. It is usually a chronic mental disturbance, which, once developed, can rarely be entirely cured. Only on rare occasions do sufferers from it improve sufficiently to be sent home, in which case they cannot always adjust themselves completely; some usually require constant care and attention. Probably 75 per cent of patients of this type are between the ages of fifteen and twenty-five; when they become ill, they may show symptoms of mania or melancholia or both, but the principal feature is an emotional deterioration. That is to say, what we first notice is that they grow careless and indifferent about their personal appearance, their surroundings, and the people about them.

A very intelligent college student, for instance, loses interest in his work and does not care a farthing whether he passes his examinations or not. Listless and unconcerned, he sits and gazes into space; doctors and parents regard this at first as mere laziness. The condition may continue for years; he may be taken to a doctor, who often diagnoses it as neurasthenia. Some time later he may suddenly do something quite absurd, and the parents wake up to the seriousness of the situation; or he may commit some gross act in public and be arrested and sent to a mental hospital. Now this is one of the greatest entities in mental diseases. I may safely say that the bulk in the mental hospitals is made up of just this group of which the prognosis is usually bad. As I have said, patients of this type rarely recover; they sometimes improve sufficiently for the average laymen to consider normal, but the majority of them always retain a mental scar. Since 1912 we usually refer to this malady as schizophrenia, a name coined by Eugen Bleuler.

Another entity which Kraepelin discovered was the so-called manic-depressive group of psychoses; patients afflicted with this disease sometimes manifest symptoms of mania, a condition of marked excitement and exaltation, and sometimes melancholia, a condition of extreme depression and retardation of thought and action. Kraepelin found that cases of this type run a definite course throughout life. They may have attacks of melancholia followed by mania, with an interval ranging from a few months to a few years between or after the attacks, then they begin a new cycle. If you examine the life history of a patient who has such attacks, you find that they last a certain period, and then he recovers. Such patients are designated in common parlance as crazy, particularly when they have the manic attacks. They may have four or six or ten attacks of melancholia during their life, soon shake off the depression and recover, and not show the slightest mental scar.

When the first of these entities, schizophrenia, was investigated some years ago in the Manhattan State Hospital in New York, it was found that more than 70 per cent of the cases had open delusions of sex. If the investigation had gone a little further, and sex were taken to mean what Freud generally designates as sex, that is, the individual's love life, I have not the slightest doubt but that it would have been found to be 100 per cent. According to the common conception of sex, in other words, a woman fondling a bundle of rags as if it were her baby was not regarded as manifesting a sexual disturbance; we, however, look upon the case as being sexual because it deals with her love life. If people generally would regard sex in the light of libido, they would readily see that it is involved in all mental disturbances. Thus Freud's dictum that no neurosis is possible in a normal sex life holds true even for the psychosis. I once had the privilege of addressing a large gathering of laymen, and it was noteworthy that after I had explained to them in what broad sense Freud and his pupils use the term sex, their former resentment was gone; some of them declared that if by sex we thus mean everything relating and growing out of the love life of the individual, there was no question at all but that they were absolutely in accord with our stand.

We can lay it down as a fundamental principle that if a person's love life is adequately adjusted, his adjustment to life generally is normal. On the other hand, those who are unadjusted, suffering from a neurosis or psychosis, are maladjusted sexually. Let us not imagine for a moment that there is anything harmful in an individual who is thus imbued with conscious or unconscious sex cravings; we are all born with the sexual impulses, and it is only the person who does not possess them that is really abnormal; he is as unfortunate as those who are born deaf and dumb. The normal average person has a love life and it has to manifest itself in some way; it is just as essential for a person to have an outlet in his love life as to have pure air and food to sustain himself; if he has not, he eventually has to suffer for it. Now civilization has rendered the normal outlet very difficult; with the advance of civilization the struggle for existence has been more and more lightened, but as far as satisfying the emotion of love is concerned, man finds himself in a somewhat embarrassing and critical situation: with the advance of civilization, the outward expression of love has become more and more difficult.

Our sex impulses are most assiduously guarded; society is most severe in its censorship of all manifestations of sex: the sex impulses are continually subjected to a merciless criticism. In our Anglo-Saxon communities they have not even the aesthetic and social outlet because of the too great separation that we find between the sexes.[1] The result is that, owing to the matrimonial difficulties and the two-children system, the women especially, who have not been able to express themselves adequately for centuries and whose lot is growing harder and harder in our civilization, suffer from a marked need of love. If you find a woman depressed and out of sorts with herself and weeping, who cannot tell you what is ailing her, you may safely conclude that there is something wrong with her love life. She is not necessarily craving physical sex; give her the

---

[1] This was originally written more than a generation ago, but conditions are not very much better today.

necessary love outlet through happy marriage and children, and she will have no more crying spells. It is for this reason that hysteria has always been characterized by these crying spells, but no one ever made any effort to discover this underlying cause. A mother may suddenly lose her only child whom she loves deeply. If she is a sensitive woman who receives no love from her husband, she will often develop a neurosis, for now that the child has gone out of her life, she has been cut off from her only love outlet. There is nothing degenerate in this; it is no more degenerate than to have pneumonia, or tuberculosis, or a broken leg.

Some time ago a young woman consulted me, because, as she said, she was extremely nervous; she declared that she suffered from insomnia, that her appetite was poor, and that she entertained peculiar thoughts. When asked what she meant by peculiar thoughts, she replied that she simply could not stomach her mother, who was constantly "getting in her way." Whenever, for instance, she wished to do something, however trifling, her mother stood in the way. There was nothing of love or sex as we commonly understand these terms, so that to one who is not accustomed to our viewpoint it would have shown nothing wrong sexually. But as there is a very vital and intimate relation between child and parent, there was really a disturbance in the love life of this young woman. So you see how different our conception of sex is from that ordinarily held.

Some women will sometimes say to me with manifest feeling: "Now, Doctor, you don't have to ask me about love or sex, for I never experienced such a thing in my life, and, what is more, I never bother with such trifles." But let us remember that love is the very mainspring and breath of life, the *vis vitalis,* as it were. Indeed, everything in life may be reduced to two fundamental instincts: hunger and love; they are the supreme rulers of the world, as Schiller has put it:

> *"Einstweilen, bis den Bau der Welt,*
> *Philosophie zusammen hält*
> *Erhält sie das Getrübe*
> *Durch Hunger und durch Liebe."*

From a purely biological standpoint the instinct of hunger or self-preservation has gradually lost its importance with the advance of civilization; it has, however, not entirely been eliminated. We still have to work for the necessities of life, but it is no longer that bitter and dangerous struggle of primitive times when a man was compelled to forage and risk his life. Today no one need really starve from hunger; and, what is more, he is not permitted to do so, even if he should want to. How zealously do the authorities work to break a hunger strike! I myself have fed psychotic persons through the nose for as long as two and three years until they consented to take nourishment in the normal way. But the satisfaction of the sex cravings has become, as we have said, a more and more distressing problem with the advance of civilization. We find that in the whole range of the animal kingdom nature has made definite provisions for sex which begins to manifest itself at puberty. But in a state of civilization the human being cannot live like the animal, and instead of exercising his biological functions as destined by nature, he is forced by society to defer them to a later period of his existence. It means, of course, a tremendous amount of control and effort on the part of the individual; and it may be of interest for you to know that there is not a young man or woman with whom I have come into intimate contact who has not had trying and terrible struggles in thus controlling the sexual needs.

I wish to repeat here that our conception of sex applies also to children. This may sound a bit startling to you, so let me proceed at once to illustrate what I mean with one or two examples. A child of about three and a half years old absolutely refuses to do whatever it is bidden; it has been an angelic little creature, and suddenly a complete transformation occurs. It cries, resists every effort to make it do anything, and is absolutely unmanageable; the doctor has been called in, but medicines have proved ineffective. Here is the history of the case. It was the youngest of a few children in the home; the parents have separated; it was found that the mother carried on an affair with a certain man and she naturally had to leave the house; the children were placed in charge of a very fine governess. The mother was a woman of an emotional type and very much attached to her children. The governess was an English lady, undemonstrative and strict with the children. The older children, who were all past the fifth year, managed to get along quite well; if they resented anything at all, they registered their protests in the open and the affair was over. But this youngest child at once began to cry and behave in the strange fashion I have described. The symptoms surprised me; it behaved like a grownup suffering from schizophrenia. Of course I decided at once upon the nature of the cure. The child's love life was disturbed; it was accustomed to receive love from its mother, and suddenly a new environment interfered; this strange woman came into its life, who looked at everything objectively, impersonally; the child was pining for the mother's affection. It took quite a little effort before I had matters so arranged that the mother could see the child every other day. The little girl soon recovered and has been well ever since. We say that there was a disturbance here in the sexual or love life of the child.

Or consider the case of another child of four years who was perfectly well until the parents decided to send away the French governess. The little girl grew very depressed, was bitterly incensed at her mother, and remarked to her father: "If Mademoiselle will be sent away, I'll die herself." (She had not yet learned to say "myself.") The father, who was a physician, was very much alarmed; he came to me and declared quite frankly that he did not know what to do. I assured him that I had no doubt at all that if the child had been given enough attention by the mother, she would not behave in that way; that now that it was decided to send away the governess, upon whom she was depending for her love, she felt that she would be left all alone. Indeed how would an adult feel if he were separated from the one person whom he loves? The doctor assured me that that was exactly the situation; that he always felt that his wife neglected the little girl. I advised him to see that his wife take her place as mother to the child, play with her, and give her of her affection, and then dismiss the governess. Thus the problem was solved: the little girl received a normal love outlet.

We must remember, however, that the sexual life of the child is different from that of the adult. The sex life of the former consists of what we generally think of as love; the child likes to be petted and fondled and humored, especially if conditioned to it by doting parents. Later on, when the child grows into manhood or womanhood, there are other manifestations which we do not find, of course, in childhood. Yet these first and early emotional reactions are just as much a part of the sex life as the later ones. Whenever we find, then, an emotional disturbance in a child, let us not fail to examine the parental behavior; if in an adult, let us remember the words of Dumas, *père: "cherchez la femme,"* or *"l'homme."*

The Symptom as Outlet

In speaking about the neurotic, we said that the symptom represents some painful experience in the past which he tried to crowd out of consciousness, to forget. Thus it is in a very real sense an emotional outlet, and that is why patients intrinsically, though unconsciously, are loath to give it up; there is, as we have said, a morbid gain. It sometimes happens that there can be no normal, wholesome outlet for some loss or misfortune, from the very nature of things, we might say. Take, for instance, the case of a woman who has lost her husband and has no children, no relatives, no financial resources. She is also in no condition, by virtue of age and other factors, to think that she can go out into the world and find some normal outlet, such as marriage. She becomes hysterical and we find her in a hospital. She is intelligent and sensible, and when you begin to discuss her case with her, she will presently tell you that she really does not know what she can or will do when she leaves the hospital. When you assure her that you will cure her, she begins to worry about the awful void ahead of her, for indeed she has nothing to live for. In other words, the doctor who attempts to cure her is face to face with a herculean task. We had, of course, an altogether different situation in the case of the young woman who had the pain in her arm. One could see at once that she could and ought to be cured; there was everything in her favor; her complaining about the pain and her consulting doctors were really substitutes, I might say, for the love for which she was ardently craving; all that she had to do was to learn to face reality. In proportion, then, to the lack of normal outlet, the patient will continue to hold on to the symptom more and more firmly. Thus, given two young people who are equally sick, if one derives a greater morbid gain from the neurosis than the other, he will remain sick much longer than the other to whom fortune has not been so "kind." The time required to cure a patient is directly proportional, we might say, to the degree in which he is morbidly benefited by his neurosis.

In the same way there are persons who simulate insanity; it is in itself an outlet, a sort of morbid gain. In the olden times when an individual dissembled madness, he was brutally punished for it; the doctor would presumably cure him by the very simple device of turning a hose of cold water on him. If he survived the treatment, he was fired out of the hospital with very little ceremony. But let us not forget that even those cases who simulate are abnormal; no normal person will resort to such an outlet.

An individual who acts in this fashion is ill, and we should treat him as such. Today we impress upon him that we know he is feigning, but we do not treat him with brutality. The Commissioner of Correction asked me some time ago to examine a man of this type who was accused of a certain crime. There was a friend of mine with me who is not a physician and I told him that the case was a puzzle to medical men. When I examined this patient he played crazy and did all sorts of queer things. I gave him a thorough examination in the presence of my friend whom I addressed as doctor. I said: "Doctor, it is the rarest case I have ever seen," and I mentioned some medical name. "I am quite sure that in this case there is such and such a condition; just to corroborate the diagnosis, I'll wager that if I take the man's arm and stretch it out, he will hold it in that position indefinitely." Before I had the opportunity to do that, he did it himself; the poor fellow tried very hard to feign various conditions. I told him that there was to be no prevarication and he soon confessed that he was deceiving and begged me to help him. I made it very clear to him that I would help him on the condition that he be straightforward and honest.

No one can feign insanity. When a person tells the doctor he has pneumonia, it may be proven by just listening to the chest. Likewise in mental diseases there is nothing that has not been reduced to a definite form and condition. When a person is really psychotic, his psychosis is manifest. I have never found anyone who has succeeded in counterfeiting it, and I have seen malingerers here and abroad. They may succeed in bamboozling some doctors who do not know. You will occasionally read in the newspapers that some men have simulated insanity and then declared that they are not at all insane, but I know for a fact that a real psychotic person would be the last one to plead he is insane. Let us repeat that any individual who tries to pretend psychosis or hysteria, no matter in what difficult straits he finds himself, is abnormal, for no normal person would resort to such an outlet.

We see this mechanism very often in a less pronounced form. A patient informed me once that when she was young she found that she was treated well when sick, and so whenever she did not wish to go to school, she would say that she had a headache. That was her way of solving the problem. Now she really has those headaches and is unable to do important work that she even likes, though it is noteworthy that the headaches are far more severe when she has to attend to something she dislikes.

What we said about the neuroses applies also to the psychoses. Like the neurotic symptom, the mental condition serves as an emotional outlet—it enables the patient to realize his wish. Some individuals, upon experiencing some heavy shock or misfortune, cannot resign themselves to the actual reality. The problem is such a moot and difficult one that in order to solve it at all they have to tear themselves away from reality completely. When they become ill, the wish that they desire to realize is then fulfilled in their mental condition. Here, too, we see that there is an attempt at adjustment, there is a morbid gain. Let me give you an example.

A few years ago there was much discussion in New York City on the need for laborers upstate for the harvest. Many tailors and people in similar vocations were then out of employment. One of these men, who was quite poor, was very glad to take advantage of the opportunity, particularly since he heard he would earn from three to four dollars a day and free board besides. When he was put to work as a farmer, however, it was found that he was not at all fitted nor strong enough for the work. The result was that he was made a fool of by the farmer and his sons. He became quite sullen and morose and when once, upon provocation, he dared to retort, they gave him a sound thrashing and fired him. What is more, they would not pay him what was due him. He appealed for redress in the local court of justice, but everybody turned a deaf ear to him. He was about a hundred and sixty miles away from the city, and as he could not scrape up any money, he was compelled to walk home. He reached the city, fagged out and starved, crying for revenge. He consulted a lawyer, who asked him for ten dollars as a retainer; the poor fellow did not have a cent. He was at a loss. Wherever he turned he could receive no justice. Burning for redress, he would perpetually talk about it to his wife; he could not shake it from his mind. One day he became fearfully excited, he shouted, kicked at the bedsteads, tore the pillows, heaping all the while all manner of abuse on the farmer. The wife was alarmed and sent for an ambulance; he was taken to Bellevue Hospital, where I saw him. He hallucinated and raged continually against the farmer, who, he imagined, was right there before him. However, he soon quieted down, and after talking with him for a while I immediately grasped the true nature of his condition: the poor man behaved in that strange fashion because he had no other way of giving vent to his feelings. He *abreacted* what he could not assimilate.

I shall tell you right here the meaning of some of the terms I am using. By *hallucinations,* I mean *false perceptions, that is, apparent perceptions without corresponding external objects.* If a person sees things that do not exist at the time, he is suffering from hallucinations of sight; if he hears voices when nobody is talking to him, he suffers from hallucinations of hearing; if he mistakenly feels that an animal, for instance, is crawling in his stomach, he has a sensory hallucination. Thus all the senses can produce hallucinations. An *illusion,* on the other hand, *is just a perverted sensation;* there is a corresponding external object but it is *falsely interpreted.* For instance, when a person, suffering from alcoholic psychosis, declares that there are snakes crawling over a carpet, he is simply misinterpreting the figures and designs there; he calls them snakes because of certain poisons in the nerves of the visual centers. Thus, too, an individual who hears someone talk and insists that the latter is talking about him, whereas he really is not, is suffering from an illusion. A *delusion is a false idea which is absolutely fixed and from which you cannot reason the patient away.* When a man informs you that he is the emperor of China and you know that he is an ordinary New York tailor, then he has a delusion of grandeur; or if he tells you he is the real pope and his enemies have substituted a sham pope in his place, when you know that he is perhaps a hod carrier, he has delusions of grandeur and persecution.

Because the psychosis, then, is a form of abnormal adjustment in itself, an abnormal attempt at a solution of some inner problem, the expressions of the psychotic patient cannot be meaningless; they must have significance and value in terms of his essential psychic conflicts. Before Freud came on the scene, no attention was paid to the utterances of the psychotics. We know now that their hallucinations and delusions are not at all meaningless or irrational, that they have their *raison d'être*. In no light sense may we say that there is method in madness. Take, for instance, the psychotic woman who apparently falls in love with every doctor. Upon examination you will find that she had an unhappy love affair and that she now identifies some other man with her lover who has forsaken her. In other words, in order to checkmate nature, as one might say, she tears herself away from reality. It is in itself an abnormal adjustment. When people are overtaken by misfortune they seek refuge in different ways; some throw themselves into scientific or literary work, others into social activity or business. Thus, in time, sorrow loses its keen edge. Some, however, cannot do this; they represent a special type of sensitive material. More than 50 per cent of all the patients in mental hospitals are of this type. They are men and women who could not learn to accept the facts, who could not "forget." Instead, they tore themselves away from reality altogether and realized their wishes in their own way, thus solving the problem.

If we now review the origin and development of neurotic symptoms as elucidated by Breuer and Freud we wish to repeat that Breuer, who was not a psychiatrist, discovered the so-called Cathartic Method in his treatment of his patient Anna O.[2] as early as 1881. The technique consisted in his hypnotizing and questioning the patient about the origin of the symptom. After collaborating for a number of years, they published a preliminary report in 1893 "On the Psychic Mechanisms of Hysterical Phenomena," and two years later their *Studies in Hysteria*. In this book the authors did not aim to delve into the nature of hysteria but strove to elucidate the origin of the symptoms. Their main conclusions were that hysteria was a disease based on some of the patient's painful or unacceptable experiences. Freud later compared the symptom to a monument of some past event in the life of the patient which the latter did not, however, recognize as such. If we adhere to the analogy we would say that the patient knew no more about the meaning of this symptom than, say, an average American knows about Charing Cross or about any monument which one finds in some European or Asiatic

[2]Brill: *Freud's Contribution to Psychiatry*, Norton, N.Y., 1944, p. 53.

community. In other words, the patient is entirely unconscious of the meaning or origin of the pain which is so annoying to him.

Breuer and Freud thus distinguished between consciousness and unconsciousness in the psychic life by showing that the symptom was repressed and totally unknown to the patient. This concept was later amplified by Freud into the psychology of the unconscious. Breuer and Freud explained that the repression took place because the patient was unable to give expression to his feelings at the time of their occurrence, so that the whole episode, with all the emotional tension, was excluded from further conscious elaboration. But as the repressed material strove continually to come to consciousness, it finally worked its way to the surface on a wrong path to some bodily innervation and thus produced the symptom. The latter represented a *conversion* of psychic energy into a physical feeling. The patient then complained of some ache or some incapacity for which no organic or physical reason could be discovered. The cure, as we said, was effected by helping the patient to recall and verbally discharge the strangulated emotions.

When Breuer and Freud published these new theories in their first paper they were pleasantly received by the neurologists and psychiatrists. But when they published the above-mentioned book the picture changed. The rank and file of psychiatrists vociferously disagreed with them despite the fact that their theories were the same as those published in 1893. The reason for this extreme change was based on a statement which they gave in the introduction to the *Studies in Hysteria*. Briefly, they said that further experience convinced them "that sexuality plays the principal part in the pathogenesis of hysteria." This statement which touched upon the tabooed subject of sex raised such a resentment against them that Breuer finally withdrew from the field into which he accidentally (and, one might say, reluctantly) entered.

As we mentioned above, Freud gave up hypnosis and by resorting to "free associations" gradually acquired an increasing insight into the mainsprings of human emotions. The first problem he solved was why the patient who had forgotten all his experiences could nevertheless recall them by means of continuous association. He concluded that inasmuch as the forgotten material was always of a painful and disagreeable nature, something that was either terrifying or distressing or humiliating to the patient, he could not permit it to come to consciousness. The force which the physician had to expend in overcoming this impeding energy was apparently the measure of the patient's *resistance*. And having learned the psychic process of forgetting and resistance, Freud then reconstructed the pathogenic process in the following manner: If some craving arises in normal life which is strongly opposed by another force, a conflict results between the impulse and the resistance opposing it. The conflict then continues consciously until the impulse is rejected and its affectivity or its *cathexis*[3] is withdrawn from the craving. This represents the normal mode of adjustment. In the neurosis the conflict takes a different path. Here, as soon as the conflict starts, the *ego* retreats from the unpleasant impulse and thus shuts it off from any access to consciousness as well as to direct motor discharge; the impulse, however, holds onto its full cathexis or all the emotions that were generated by the conflict. Freud called this process *repression* and considered it as a new concept, the like of which was never before recognized in mental processes.

It should be emphasized that repression in the Freudian sense is an unconscious process, and should not be confused with suppression, which is a conscious process. We all have to suppress all sorts of cravings which constantly assail us but this process is perfectly natural and does us no harm. On the contrary, suppression or control is necessary in every civilized community and is beneficial to the individual. But when we speak of symptoms we mean abnormal manifestations which come into being as a result of repression—a process which originates unconsciously and always remains so.

The Symptom as Compromise

The basic meaning of the symptom, no matter what the symptom may be, whether paralysis, aphonia, delirium, phobia, or obsession, is absolutely unknown to the person; its mechanisms are entirely incomprehensible to the average observer. I can make this clear to you by giving you a complete example. A woman of about thirty-five is unhappily married. Her husband treats her most brutally

[3]Cathexis, from *Katexo,* I occupy. It is the amount of energy which invests an object or idea.

and she detests him; she would leave him but she loves her children deeply, and feels that such a move on her part would be quite detrimental to their good name and welfare. In her distress, she turns to a certain friend of her husband, who sympathizes with her and is very eager to do all he can to help her out of her difficulties. In the course of time they fall in love. He is a married man and that, of course, complicates the situation even more. He assures her that she is perfectly justified in behaving as she does, for her husband's brutal treatment is without doubt unjust and reprehensible. That, of course, carries much weight with her, because she met this man originally through her husband, who was a former classmate of his. They begin to think seriously of securing divorces and marrying, but here again the man cannot resign himself to the idea of leaving his children. This is quite characteristic of people of this type; they can never gather sufficient strength to carry out what they wish to do because they are so much under the influence of their early upbringing. Be that as it may, they played with the idea for years. She used to reproach herself for her conduct, for at bottom she was really quite religious and regarded matrimony with a deep sense of sacredness. In time the man suggested sexual relations, to which she objected quite strenuously.

One day he made an appointment with her to meet her at a certain place; she knew very definitely the nature of the rendezvous. However, she apparently decided to go, left her home, and walked over to the trolley which passed in front of her house. As she was waiting for it, she suddenly felt a pain in her heart, she became flushed, her heart began to palpitate, and she feared she would faint. An officer assisted her home and she was confined to bed. At first the doctor thought she had some heart trouble, but after a few days she was able to leave the bed and it was found that there was really nothing wrong with her heart. She presently went out to shop and the moment she found herself in the street she began to fear that she would have another such attack; she returned home and kept her little girl with her, so that she might not be alone in case something serious should happen to her. The family gradually began to realize that she was afraid to go out alone. Finally she came to see me, because she was told that she had a phobia.

What is the deeper significance of this situation? We see here two opposite psychic streams in conflict. From a biological view-point, the woman was entitled to her share of love and affection; there was the primitive instinct which a woman of this type, and for that matter every woman, would naturally experience when confronted with a situation of this character; here, on one side, was her husband who maltreated her, on the other, a man who sympathized with her, loved her, and was ready to help her in every way. But, on the other hand, there is the thought of religion, our early training and society; we are brought up to consider such a feeling as immoral, that only legitimate love is right. And so, as you see, there was a constant struggle; she felt that had she kept the rendezvous, she would have committed adultery, she would have sinned, and so, unconsciously, she decided not to go. When I inquired what she feared when she went out into the street, she replied that she was in terror of falling. You see what she really had in mind was a moral falling. Her fear of falling and perhaps of being run over and killed was a symbolic representation of her fear of committing adultery. Thus, in a sense, she solved the problem. There was a compromise effected by the two streams in the form of the symptom. We designate a nervous condition of this type as an "anxiety hysteria." It is a psychoneurotic disturbance which manifests itself predominantly through fear or anxiety.[4]

There are, of course, many forms of nervous disturbances into which we cannot enter here. There is one type about which I may say a few words right now, because it is so commonly referred to. It manifests itself in all kinds of *obsessions, doubts,* and *fears,* and is known as a "compulsion neurosis," that is, a neurosis which is characterized throughout by a marked compulsiveness in thought and act. A patient suffering from such a condition may go to bed, for instance, then pause and wonder whether she locked the door, get up, assure herself that she did, and return to bed. A minute later it occurs to her that in locking it she may have perhaps unlocked it, and so she cannot rest until she makes sure. She may continue to go through this little performance perhaps one or two dozen times through the night. We call it doubting mania, *folie du doute.* Some sufferers of this type have a tendency to reason perpetually, *ad nauseam.* A person will begin to reason about some problem that he himself knows is absolutely absurd, but he cannot refrain from

[4]This particular form of fear is known as "agoraphobia."

doing so. A man, for instance, who is not at all interested in social-
ism will suddenly begin to think of it; no matter where and when
he meets a person he will be wondering whether that person is a
socialist; he will bombard people with the most absurd questions on
the subject. Another man who is not a bit interested in hypnotism
will constantly ask questions about it; he consults all doctors who
have the reputation of being specialists on the subject and finds
out what they think on this or that phase of it. He feels that it is
absolutely important that he should know all about it. Such patients
suffer from *folie raisonnante,* or reasoning mania.

The case of the woman I have just described is, as you see, a
nervous disturbance essentially growing out of the conflict between
what she considered right and wrong, moral and immoral. It is a
neurosis, and we distinguish it from a psychosis in that the latter is
a mental disturbance in which the individual, unlike the neurotic,
detaches himself completely from reality and behaves as if he does
not belong there at all. To illustrate: A young lady of about twenty-
nine was brought to me by her brother, who is a physician. He
informed me that she had been acting strangely for the last four
weeks, and he feared that she was a little out of her mind. She
insisted that all the girls in the shop where she is employed talked
disparagingly about her; she cries, does not wish to leave the house,
and wants to move out of the neighborhood because all the neighbors are in a conspiracy against her. As a result, she is in a state of
marked agitation. Her brother is right: of course there is something wrong with an individual who deems himself so important
and popular as to have people everywhere talk about him. After
insisting upon her telling me what the world had to say about her,
she finally said: "Everybody keeps on saying that I am a bad girl,
that I have committed a lot of sex crimes." On further examination
I learned the following: A young man began to call on her recently;
he had been paying her quite a little attention. Some time passed;
she was feeling well apparently, when she got a toothache. (It is
significant that the young man was a dentist.) She had the tooth
extracted, and, as gas had been administered, she was a little
nervous and delirious after the operation. Since then she had
entertained those ideas. She went on to assure me that the condition
is entirely because of the fact that those girls were mean and
jealous; that they made these slanderous remarks about her because

they were anxious to estrange the young man from her. Her brother then told me that he felt quite convinced that the main cause for her nervousness was the fact that the young man upon whom she had built so many hopes had not shown himself attentive enough of late; that, in fine, he stopped calling on her.

The sexual import of the situation is quite patent. The girl was well brought up, quiet, and well-behaved, and respectable in every way. Why, then, should she have such hallucinations and delusions? you will ask; they would seem to be incompatible with her own nature. Now there is a mechanism which we call "projection," by virtue of which we throw out on the outside world feelings and ideas which we have repressed. We say other people are saying or doing what we have repressed, what, indeed, we ourselves once would have liked to say or do. Such delusions are called ideas or delusions of reference, *Beziehungswahn,* in German. We mean by this that a person interprets everything that is being said by people in his environment as referring to himself. The deeper meaning of the situation, then, lay just in this, that when the man stopped calling on the young lady, everybody in her home began to criticize and blame her. Her mother and brother declared that she was by no means bad-looking, that, on the contrary, she was quite attractive, intelligent, and sensible; that she had friends; but that her great drawback was that she was too "good." She had native gifts, but of what value are they if one does not put them to the best use? That was their mode of reasoning. In other words, they hardly troubled to disguise the fact that what she had to learn yet was to be a trifle bad. Apropos of this, I might say that this is one of those fanciful ideas that practically all moral women sometimes secretly desire to taste. We have named it the "being naughty motive," the "prostitution complex." So many respectable women have very often told me that they wish they could have the experience of being a prostitute for a while so that they might know just what it means. They are shocked by the very thought, but it is pleasing and thrilling none the less. This woman perhaps never thought of it, but when it was driven home to her that she lost this man simply because she kept him at such a distance, because she adhered too strictly to the little proprieties and conventions of social life, she fully realized its significance and straightway the repressed thoughts came to the surface and her unconscious wish was realized: she is really im-

moral, and for that reason the young man left her. Thus she who is
at bottom an ethical individual must perforce come to the conclusion that the young man repulsed her because she is bad, and
immoral, and not because she is too good and moral.

The underlying significance of such conditions, the nature of all
these mechanisms, had not been understood, as I have said, before
Freud; nowadays we can always find the reason for these phenomena and in this way we can cure many of the patients. By this,
of course, I do not mean to imply that psychoanalysis is the panacea
in all nervous and mental diseases, that every and any disease is
amenable to the psychoanalytic therapy. I wish to say, on the
contrary, that this treatment, like every other, has its marked
limitations. It is applicable to a limited number of diseases only;
and, furthermore, the person who is treated by this method must
be an individual of the higher type, mentally, morally, and in every
other way. Not everyone can be psychoanalyzed; analyzing and
curing a patient are parallel matters; and the wise physician will not
attempt to analyze one whom he does not think he can cure. There
is no doubt, however, that psychoanalysis can help us to understand
problems in various fields of vital human interest that were formerly altogether inscrutable. Furthermore, it enables us to see very
clearly the forces that tend to upset and unbalance the individual
and society, and thus is of invaluable service as prophylaxis.

3. The Psychology of Forgetting

Forgetting a Protective Mechanism

THE MAIN BASIS of Freud's psychology is that there is nothing accidental or arbitrary in the psychic life, that everything has reason and meaning. It matters not how complex or simple the condition may be, it has significance, and this significance may be discovered through analysis. Thus there is a tremendous number of mistakes in speech and thought manifestations that we commonly make, which reveal, in a surprising way, the individual's real thoughts and motives. They are, as we say, symbolic expressions or psychopathological actions, incorrect psychic activities which the individual daily performs and of which he is not aware at the time. They have not been hitherto investigated, I mean psychologically, because they were regarded as essentially organic disturbances. I am referring to such faulty actions as lapses of memory, lapses of talking, mistakes in writing, dreams, convulsions, deliriums, visions, and obsessive acts in neurotics and psychotics.

The psychologist has paid little attention to these phenomena because they presumably belonged to pathology and the physician, to whom they were baffling and recondite to the last degree, passed them by, as if they did not exist at all. Freud in working with his patients began to pay attention to them because he found, as I have already said, that they all had a certain import and genetic basis. He thus developed in time what we may call a symbolic language. If you understand this language, you will then realize how it manifests itself practically all the time in our daily lives. Understand this symbolism and how full of meaning will be your friend's forgetting to do or say something! Sometimes a patient will be startled by what seems to him nothing short of "psychic" powers on the part of the psychoanalyst. I asked a woman whether she has had a particular dream during her life, and she replied: "Oh, yes, I usually dream of mountains and water and waves and I delight in them greatly; but, then, I have the same dreams when I am half awake and I despise them." My next question was: "Tell me, up to what age did you wet the bed?" and quite embarrassed she answered: "Until I was quite old." This type of dream is quite characteristic of people who wet the bed; and there was really nothing remarkable in my arriving at the conclusion.

Everything that a person does, the way he dresses or walks, his bearing and demeanor, his manner of talking, all have a definite meaning. I do not know whether you are aware of the fact that we are taught in medicine to observe carefully these seemingly trivial things. Take a patient, for instance, who may have had some brain disturbance, let us say a slight cerebral hemorrhage, but whose history is so vague that we cannot tell whether he actually has had such a hemorrhage or not. In such a case we may very often make a diagnosis by examining the way his shoe is worn out and thus determine definitely whether or not he had some brain disturbance. The result of the slightest cerebral hemorrhage shows its effects in the gait; the patient wears off a little of the right or left of his shoe, and that is enough to give you a clue to his condition. If it has been a slight attack, it will evade the observation of the average observer, but the experienced physician can detect it in the way the patient drags one of his limbs.

We must have a sharp eye for these little things, particularly in the practice of psychoanalytic psychiatry. Very few mental patients tell us what we want them to tell, and it remains for the physician to make the diagnosis at once, for he has the patient's relatives forever on his heels, anxious to learn of what disease the patient suffers and how long it will be before he gets well and is able to come home. Sometimes, too, in their great eagerness and solicitude, they will ask you all that before you have even had the opportunity of speaking to the patient. And, then, a great many mental patients do not talk and yet the doctor must make the diagnosis and give an intelligent answer. "But," you ask, "how can a diagnosis be made, if the patient does not talk?" That is just the point: to an experienced psychiatrist his inability to speak may be owing to some physical cause, such as aphasia, or perhaps to some mental retardation. The patient may move his lips, taking perhaps a half-hour in his efforts to answer; you can see very clearly without knowing anything about lip reading that he is trying hard to talk but cannot; he is suffering from mental retardation. Then, too, other patients actually refuse to talk, in which case, of course, the diagnosis must necessarily be different. We can tell at once that the patient who suffers from this mental retardation and has nothing organically wrong with him will recover; we can discuss his case with the same degree of definiteness as we can some physical condition. If the disturbance is organic, the prognosis can be made accordingly. In short, we must learn to observe and understand the patient.

In thus inquiring into the significance of psychopathological actions Professor Freud made a study of forgetting. People generally regard forgetting as a common occurrence and I hear a good deal about it from patients, who very often inform me that they are very nervous and that they are forgetting all the time. When I ask the person to give me an example, he stops and thinks for a long time, and then declares that last week he had to do such and such a thing at such and such a place, but forgot. Now imagine a person who is forgetful remembering what happened last week! In the final analysis there is but one kind of forgetfulness, organic forgetfulness. If one forgets in any real sense of the word he has some organic brain trouble which can be diagnosed by a psychiatrist in about ten minutes. If there is no organic condition, his so-called forgetting may be ultimately reduced to two causes: first, that he really did not wish to remember what he claims he "forgot"; second, that he either never knew it or that he never considered it important enough to know. Eliminating the second factor, we find when we ask ourselves why we have forgotten to do something, that we do not wish to do it, that there was something in that particular act that was unpleasant or disagreeable.

Think for a moment about the letter you forgot to mail; it is probably a letter someone has asked you to mail and you did not have enough courage to refuse; or perhaps it may contain a check with which, though perfectly honest, you hated to part. May I assure you that in nine cases out of ten it does not contain a bill? We never forget anything that we feel is important. I dare say you will not carry a love letter in your pocket for days and forget to mail it. Some of you, I am sure, will hasten to remind me that when you were in college you knew one hundred trigonometrical formulas and that now, strange to say, you do not know one. But did you ever really wish to know them? You had to know them, and just as soon as the examination was over you did not care to know them any longer. There is an important point here for pedagogues, it seems to me. What we really like, we do not have to memorize. If you desire a child to remember some subject matter make it so vitally interesting that he will be very glad and anxious to remember it.

It is a platitude to say that anatomy is a dry subject, and yet I once had an instructor who taught it in such an absorbing, fascinating way that students came to his courses quite voluntarily. When one likes and enjoys the subject he teaches, one can transfer his interest in it to others. In psychic studies the axiom is: like emotions beget like emotions. When you "forget" anything, then, it is either because you have never known it, and so there is really no reason why you should know it; or, if you had known it well and now find that you cannot recall it, it is because it is essentially connected, directly or indirectly, with something disagreeable and painful. The mind is always protecting us from pain by pushing whatever is disagreeable and unpleasant away from consciousness.

Psychoanalysis reveals that the various psychopathological actions are readily explainable on a psychological basis. Whatever we say or do must have a reason and can usually be explained without resorting to such superficial considerations as "absent-mindedness" or the like. The Scottish professor, who, on a momentous occasion, removed his everyday clothes and instead of dressing for dinner went to bed, cannot be excused on the ground of "absent-mindedness." We must assume that he really preferred to go to bed than to the dinner, for anyone who looks forward to a dinner of some importance will not forget and go to bed. It is such "little" things that disclose the individual's real motives and give us the key to the more complicated mental activities. There is a physical reason for a person who has an organic brain disturbance to forget what he has once well known, but if he shows no such disturbance there can be no other than a psychological reason for his lapse of memory.

A Typical Case of Forgetting

When I was an interne in the Clinic of Psychiatry at Zurich I had an interesting experience in forgetting a name which I may say finally converted me to Freud's teachings. At that time I was not fully convinced of his theories, and my attitude was skeptical though by no means unsympathetic. I approached the whole subject in the spirit of an investigator and student who made every effort to discover and understand all the data before passing final judgment on his psychology. Spurred on by Professor Bleuler, all the physicians in the hospital were firm and ardent workers with the new theories. In fact, we were in the only hospital or clinic where the Freudian principles were applied in the study and treatment of patients. Those were the pioneer days of Freud among psychiatrists, and we observed and studied and noted whatever was done or said about us with unfailing patience and untiring interest and zeal. We had no scruples, for instance, about asking a man at table why he did not use his spoon in the proper way, or why he did such and such a thing in such and such a manner. It was impossible for one to show any degree of hesitation or make some abrupt pause in speaking without being at once called to account. We had to keep ourselves well in hand, ever ready and alert, for there was no telling when and where there would be a new attack. We had to explain why we whistled or hummed some particular tune or why we made some slip in talking or some mistake in writing. But we were glad to do this if for no other reason than to learn to face the truth.

One afternoon when I was off duty I was reading about a certain case which recalled to my mind a similar one I had when I was in a hospital here in New York. I am in the habit of making marginal notes, so I took up my pencil to write down the case, but when I came to note the name of the patient whom I had known for a number of months and in whom I had taken an unusual amount of interest, I found that I could not recall it. I tried very hard to bring it back to my mind, but without success. It was strange and puzzling; but as I knew definitely whom I meant I finished the note. Now according to Freud, I thought at once to myself, the name must be connected with something painful and unpleasant. I decided right there and then to find it by the Freudian method. As I have already said, this consists essentially of freely or spontaneously associating until finally the disagreeable element is brought to the surface. It was my Sunday afternoon off and I had been looking forward to it with no little eagerness. The weather was clear and bracing and I was very anxious to be out in the open; besides, I had an appointment in the town which I did not like to break. But I was so eager to utilize every opportunity to test the Freudian theory that I at once took down one of those long yellow pads we used and began to write down my associations.

Now the patient whose name I could not recall was the same man who some years ago attempted to set fire to St. Patrick's Cathedral in New York; he gathered together some odds and ends before the entrance of the church and set fire to them. He was, of course, arrested, brought to the psychopathic pavilion in Bellevue, and later to the State Hospital, where he became my patient. I diagnosed him as a psychic epileptic. I decided that he suffered from a form of epilepsy which does not manifest itself in fits, as the typical cases do, but rather in peculiar psychic actions which may last for a few minutes or hours or perhaps for weeks, months, or years. Nobody agreed with me in the diagnosis; my senior doctor held that the patient suffered from dementia praecox. I was firmly convinced, however, that my patient was what I designated him, for there are a great many epileptics who, instead of having the physical paroxysms which are usually associated with epilepsy, have what we call psychic equivalents, by virtue of which they go through all manner of complicated psychic experiences. They become dazed and unconscious and lose track of their old self; they are then virtually different personalities and may commit all sorts of crimes in their new person. I have actually known of murders committed and houses burned by people of this type. One man was reported to have killed his entire family, father, mother, and six brothers, in a fit of this kind; and when he came to himself again he was not at all aware of the horrors that he had perpetrated.

Within a week or so the patient recovered and was entirely normal, thus corroborating my diagnosis in every respect. The patient told us that this was his fifth attack and that in some of his previous ones he had burned a railroad station, a church, and several barns. He would run away from home, his wife and children, and wander off, scotfree, when one of these fits came upon him. He was an editor of a journal and newspaper in Canada, a man of considerable intelligence and refinement. In one of his attacks during the Boer War he ran away from Canada and went to London, where, seeing calls for volunteers, he enlisted and was sent to South Africa. He fought bravely and was promoted to sergeant in a few weeks. When he came to himself, he was quite surprised to find he was a soldier. He did not have the least idea how he got to South Africa. Previous experience told him, however, what his condition meant, and upon reporting it to the physicians, he was honorably discharged. He sent a cable to his wife and returned home. He gave us various details about himself, the hospital where he found himself last, his former doctor, all of which we were soon able to corroborate. He had what we called a "fugue" or "poriomania." Cases like this have been reported where the person disappeared for as many as three years. Indeed they are not so rare as may be supposed.

Everybody congratulated me on my diagnosis, and I myself was greatly elated. The superintendent assured me that I had reason to be proud of myself, and he went on to state, to my profound disappointment and displeasure, that he would report the case to a medical society. I had spent a tremendous amount of time and effort on it and desired to publish it as my first contribution to psychiatric literature. But he was the superintendent of the hospital, I was merely a junior doctor, so there was nothing else to do but face the situation with a stout heart. "Very well, sir," I said, but I felt quite differently, of course. When I told my colleagues about it they thought it was a huge joke; some of them even ventured to assure me that I had good reason to be happy, for was I not saved the trouble of reading the paper before the medical society?

A few days before the meeting the superintendent asked me to bring him my prepared paper, but when I read it to him, he found himself face to face with an embarrassing situation. He asked me where I had gotten my numerous references, for I quoted from Italian, German, and French sources, and when I told him that they were from the original and not mere translations, he felt reticent and faint about reading the paper as his own, for he could neither read nor translate these languages. "Now, I'll tell you, Brill,

you had better go there and read it yourself," he said. I was very
much pleased at this and felt quite relieved. But I soon learned that
the programs were already printed and that the superintendent was
down for reading the case. I went before the society, and everybody thought it was the superintendent's paper and that he had
sent me merely to read it for him. You may realize how deeply I
felt about the whole affair. Finally, to cap the climax, after I had
read the paper, an editor of an obscure medical journal asked me
for it for publication in his journal. I refused, telling him that I
would have it sent to a journal of neurology or psychiatry. But he
lost no time in speaking about it to the superintendent, with whom
he had considerable influence, and I was compelled to give him the
paper with as much grace as I could then command. Now I am
dwelling quite at length on this phase of the situation because I
would like you to note carefully that there was enough of the disagreeable and unpleasant associated with the whole experience to
account for my forgetting the name of the patient.

For hours on end I sat there writing down the free associations,
but I was not a whit nearer to knowing the name than when I
began. Various details and incidents came swarming into my mind
and I had to write very rapidly to keep pace with them. I could
see clearly how this patient looked, the color of his hair, the peculiar expression on his face. I became discouraged, and thought to
myself, "If that is the way to find a thing through the Freudian
method, I shall never be a Freudian." It was now evening, and
one of my colleagues, surprised to find me indoors, asked me to
make his rounds for him inasmuch as I was not going out. I consented gladly, for I was tired of these Freudian labors. But when
I was done, I felt refreshed, and returned to the associations with
renewed interest.

At eleven o'clock I was still in as much darkness about the name
as before. I went to bed disheartened and thoroughly disgusted with
the whole affair. At about four o'clock in the morning I awoke and
made a supreme effort to dismiss it from my mind, but in vain.
Nolens volens, I soon began to associate in bed, and finally, at about
a little after five, the long-sought name suddenly came to me. My
joy and elation were not at all free from a sense of relief; it was as
if I had solved a long-vexing problem. I have no doubt now that
had I not been able to find it, I probably would never have con-

tinued to take the slightest interest in Freud. I spent so much time and effort in trying to ferret it out that I felt quite out of humor with myself; but I was well compensated as much by the sense of pleasure and satisfaction that went with the discovery, as by the fresh conviction it gave me in Freudian psychology.

Now what was the situation? Let me say first that when you begin to associate freely, you will soon be surprised to find that thousands of associations begin pouring in upon consciousness. Sometimes three or four of these associations come at the same moment, and you pause and wonder which to write down first. You soon make some selection and continue. In my own case I observed that a very few definite associations kept on recurring continually. Every time I asked myself the name of this New York patient there would invariably come to my mind the case of a real epileptic I then had in the Zurich hospital. His name was *Appenzeller,* he was just a Swiss peasant, and I explained the association on the ground that they were both epileptics, the New York patient, as you remember, being a psychic epileptic.

Another continually recurring association was this: When I thought of the hospital in Long Island and all that happened there during the five years I was connected with it, one particular scene would stand out very clearly and prominently; my mind would revert to it all the time. Very often there were forest fires near the hospital, and on many occasions we had to go out and check them lest they reach our buildings. This particular scene was on a Friday; there was a big fire raging near the hospital and we had to send out as many doctors and nurses as we could possibly spare to help control it. I was there to see that there was no confusion, that things were carried out properly. I was chatting with a physician who was with me in the same capacity. The fire was consuming a good deal of scrub pine, and now and then an attendant would succeed in shooting one of the rabbits that was fleeing from the brushwood. While I was standing there, the superintendent came up to us, passed some remark or other, and then, spying a rabbit some distance away, asked one of the attendants for his shotgun to try his skill, saying: "Let's see if I can get that rabbit." We all looked on knowingly, for we never had very much faith in the superintendent's marksmanship. We were not mistaken. He missed and the rabbit escaped. He turned to me and declared somewhat uneasily, and by way of explanation, that his fingers had slipped, for it was beginning to rain. I seemingly concurred in the observation, but in my heart I smiled at his discomfiture. I could see him very plainly as he stood there, saying, "Let's see if I can get that rabbit," and he would then aim, shoot, and miss it. Finally I saw the scene again in the morning, and with the words, "Let's see if I can get that rabbit," the name came to me. It was *Lapin,* the French word for rabbit. Later on, when I actually counted my associations, I found that this particular association came up twenty-eight times more than any of the others.

This may seem strange, but that is exactly the way the mind works unconsciously. The name was symbolically represented by the scene; the whole situation was under repression, and that is the manner in which the unconscious elaborated it. The repressed emotion attached itself to an actual occurrence: the superintendent fails to shoot the rabbit; i.e., he fails to deprive me of the case. At the time of this incident I had recently come from Paris and I tried not merely to talk French, but to think in French; and though I was in that part of Switzerland in which Swiss-German is spoken, there were a great many people in my service from the French part of the country who spoke French. And so it was quite natural for the name thus to have presented itself in French guise. You can easily see also why I thought of *Appenzeller.* There was the sound association of the first part of Appenzeller, *Appen, lapin;* and, what is just as important, both patients were epileptics. You may thus see, first, that there was something distinctly disagreeable and painful associated with the name; second, that there was a definite symbolic expression of it in the form of a repressed emotion.

Symbols and the Unconscious

That the image of the superintendent's shooting at the rabbit should thus symbolically express the whole situation will not sound so strange to you when you understand what we mean by symbols. We may define a symbol as an imperfect comparison between two objects which in reality may have very little resemblance; it is nothing but a form of comparison. If you observe children as they grow up and learn to talk, you will find that they are always thinking in pictures or symbols. There can be no doubt that they do not think in the sense that we generally suppose, that is, in the sense of reasoning, but that they merely associate and compare. Numerous examples may be cited to substantiate this.

A little girl once pointed to her knee which was bruised by a fall and exclaimed to her father: "Papa, here is a 'babble.' " He was at first hard put to understand how she could think of calling the wound on her knee a "babble" because he knew that she called an apple a "babble." But upon a little reflection he soon saw what she meant. The little girl was fourteen months old when she first began to see apples in an orchard in the country; she would try to pick up those that had fallen from the trees and would call them "babbles." Now you have all observed that an apple in falling from a tree receives what appears to be a wound, a sort of round dark yellowish mark. To the little child the contusion on her knee looked exactly like this mark, and so, by association, she called that, too, a "babble," but there was really no more real resemblance between the two than between Lapin, the name of the patient, and a real rabbit. We see this same phenomenon among grownups; when one invents a new piece of machinery he always names it in terms of what he knows, or he may select its most important attribute or attributes and name it accordingly. Automobile means self-moving, "auto" and "mobile," but not everything that moves by itself is an automobile, so that the name by itself will tell very little indeed to a person who has never seen this horseless machine. This applies also to such names as hydroplane, airplane, and the like. The new invention was defined in terms of our previous experience.

I recall now a little boy whom I knew very well; he was only two and a half years old and he would come to my room and I would give him a pad of paper and a pencil to play with. One day he drew what appeared to be a little circle and came up to me and said, "Here's an autobile." He did, in fact, the very thing that the inventor or any intelligent grown-up person does: to him the wheel was the predominant and characteristic element in the automobile. Thus we see here a form of comparison, which is, in the final analysis, the sum and substance of all our thinking. When you declare, for instance, that you will think over some problem, you know very well from experience that if you wait a little while you will be able to reach some sort of solution. In the final analysis, we are empiricists. Meanwhile, it continues to revolve in your mind; the particular situation is juxtaposed to similar situations, the particular condition is contrasted with similar conditions. Finally you decide the problem; it is really decided for you. Of course the nature of the decision depends entirely upon the type and character of the individual. As a physician, if I defer stating a diagnosis of which I am not sure, I am merely taking a little more time to compare the particular patient in question with many others whom, it seems to me, he resembles. Finally I reach a conclusion: the case is either of this type or is allied to it, because it is absolutely characteristic of it. So, too, a tried and astute general can decide and act quickly, for his accumulated past experiences afford him an immediate basis for quick and sound judgment.

When my little boy was about three years old he was playing one day with a box of geometrical figures used in a Montessori school. As you may know, these figures are all of jet black pasted on a white background. Pointing to one, he said, "What is this, Daddy?" I told him it was a triangle, to which he replied, "Then I'll sing a triangle," and he motioned with his arms in accompaniment. He then put it aside and inquired about another figure, and when I told him it was a square, he said, "Then I'll sing a square." "And what's this, Daddy?" "An octagon"; and so he continued repeating in each case that he would sing that particular figure. I was wondering how he came to this strange idea when I noticed that among the figures he took out of the box was the circle; in fact, judging by its position it must have been the first figure to be removed from the box. Now the jet-black circle on the white background showed a close resemblance to phonograph records of which he was very fond, indeed so fond that he would even cry for them on many occasions.

When he looked at the figure of the circle he undoubtedly took it for a phonograph record and after going through the movements of playing it, he took the next figure from the box. This, being the triangle, looked strange to him and caused him to ask what it was, but it did not interfere with the association already established in his mind. In his infantile mind he saw a resemblance between two things and straightway he transferred the significant attribute of the one to the other. He at once realized what seemed to him the essential similitude in a concrete case; he carried it, so to say, to its logical conclusion. We see the same mode of association in modern art; the artist may say he has painted a nude lady walking down the stairs, but what we may really perceive is but a conglomeration of geometrical figures. We have here an infantile expression on the part of the artist. The same process of thought can be observed in some modern music. I know a man to whom every song is a color and every color a song; like my little boy who sang a triangle he is thinking in pictures or symbols. We see this same form of expression also in the dream.

Here is another incident relating to my little boy that I feel is characteristic of the mode in which children associate ideas. When he was about three years old he was attending school; he was accustomed to being taken there in the morning either by the maid or by my wife. One day it stormed so hard that we could not get a taxi or take him to school under an umbrella. My wife was worried and wondered what to do, and I told her that I would carry him to school myself. I had him put his head on my shoulder and quickly we made our way in the heavy storm to the school building, which, by the way, was only a few blocks from our home. He seemed to enjoy the experience immensely. About six months or so later it so happened that I had a little time and I said: "Shall I take you to school?" At once he answered: "Is it raining, Daddy?" I did not know at first what he meant, but I soon saw its significance. In other words, to him at that time the act of my taking him to school became associated with rain. Behaviorists have pointed out that animals think in the same way; it is indeed stupid to maintain that they do not reason; they merely have less developed brains than the human being, therefore not so many associations. The same holds true in defectives: they have not so much wealth of association at their disposal as the average individual.

Observe children who have not yet realized the nature of abstract ideas and you will find that they invariably express themselves concretely, by means of comparison. A little girl three years old was once taken to the aquarium where she saw a seal with whose characteristic alacrity of movement she was greatly impressed. A few days later she talked enthusiastically about all that she had seen there, and said, among other things, that she had seen a thing that went this way, and she motioned with her hands the quick movements of the seal. She had forgotten its name but she remembered its important attribute. You have observed children very often say "by-by" when they finish drinking their milk; it is usually the first word they learn. The idea is suggested to them by the analogy to departure. One can always find a definite reason for the apparent incongruous expressions evinced by children. It is simply a question of tracing their mode of association or comparison of things. The same mechanisms are constantly seen in the bizarre behavior of the insane.

There was a patient in the psychiatric clinic at Zurich who would place folded rose petals against her forehead and hit them, thus producing a crackling sound. Nobody could fathom the meaning of this action until Professor Bleuler began to study her case thoroughly and found that she became insane after her lover committed suicide by shooting himself in the head. Thus her behavior in this particular instance was a symbolic representation of the shooting; she was reliving an old episode.

The infantile form of thinking through simple comparison which Bleuler calls *dereism,* from *de* and *reor,* becomes less apparent as age advances. The child gradually enriches his vocabulary to enable him to express in words the constant acquisition of new knowledge. He is compelled to accept new terms for abstract ideas without resorting to conscious elaboration as he was wont to do in childhood. In his unconscious, however, the same process of imperfect comparisons prevails. That is why later in life such imperfect comparisons or symbols strike us as strange and foolish. When a grownup hears her mother reminisce that as a little girl she said "la" when she meant "color," she not only experiences a feeling of strangeness but is also somewhat abashed at her former childishness; but the situation becomes clear when she consults her father's diary. She then finds that when she was ten months old her father gave her a pad of paper with a pencil and encouraged her to scribble by drawing for her crude pictures of the house dog King. She soon learned her lesson, and whenever she saw her father with the pad she would point to it and say "la," which meant "draw." La was one of the few syllables she could utter at that age. Later, when she would call King "Thim," she would often say to her father "La Thim," which meant "draw a picture of King." Still later "la" not only meant to write or draw but also became identified with color, undoubtedly because some of the pencils she used were colored, so that when a multicolored ball was given to her for the first time she immediately designated it as "la-ball," in contrast to the plain white ball with which she played for some time. Such symbols constantly recur in dreams and in other productions of unconscious mentation, but as we are usually ignorant of their origin they strike us as mysterious and foreign.

So words uttered or written are nothing but symbols of actual activities. The alphabet originally consisted of symbols; the addition of vowels and consonants was a much later development. In the Hebrew alphabet, for instance, which is a direct descendant of the Phoenician or first known alphabet, the *alef* represents graphically an ox and the *beth* a house. So, too, the Chinese ideographs and the hieroglyphics of the ancient Egyptians are also symbolic representations of definite objects.

We find certain characteristic symbols among all nations. We, for instance, have the eagle as an emblem; the Romans had the wolf; the English the lion, et cetera. It is also interesting to note that the guilds the world over had special symbols for the various trades, some of which still survive, the barber's pole and the pawnbroker's sign, for instance. The barber's pole was originally white spotted with red that signified blood, for in the old days the barber was a sort of half-doctor, performing such operations as bloodletting and cupping, for instance; indeed he is still regarded as such in rural Russia and some other European countries. I am sure you are all also aware of the symbolic significance of colors; green signifies hope; red, love; yellow, jealousy or cowardice. In the same way, too, there is not a word but what has a definite symbol, and it is instructive to note how the original symbol is in time distorted. Examples of this are legion. You all know, I am sure, that the word "person" is derived from the Latin *per sonna,* which means through a mask; originally an actor performing before a large audience used a megaphone to make his voice carry, but as it was somewhat ludicrous and unaesthetic to have him strut about the stage with a megaphone, it was found best to conceal it under a mask. Likewise, "imbecile" at present denotes a person who is mentally weak. Originally it signified merely physical debility or, more particularly, a person walking on a cane, *in baculo,* the Latin for on a cane.

Now there are some symbols that are ethnic;[1] they resemble certain things to such an extent that you find them wherever there is an unconscious mentation. Mythology and primitive religions particularly abound with them, for in this sphere of mental activity we find the human being in yet an infantile state; the difference between reality and fiction is not yet clearly marked. We note here, as in the dream, the preponderance of sex symbols. Indeed when one delves into the mainsprings of primitive religion one finds that it is centered entirely around sex; it may be said that all our religions are intrinsically precipitates or extracts from the original phallic worship.[2] In every Hindu temple even today, for instance, the altar is made up of the *yoni lingam* which is only a union of the male and female genitals on a pedestal surrounded by a snake, which euphemistically is a symbol of eternity. Those students who have delved deeply into the subject have pointed out, however, that the snake is really a symbol of the male genitals. Primitive man, before he knew enough about the principles of biology, could think of only one thing, that the genitals, because they produce life, were symbols of life; and that is why they were carried in procession and worshiped. What is unusually interesting is that you find this same symbolic expression even today. When we examine the language that we find in dreams, deliriums, hallucinations, and delusions, we are at once impressed with that fact; our unconscious mentation is still swathed in the mystery of this age-old symbolism, and it is altogether inscrutable to one who does not understand the language of the unconscious.

There are many symbols that have lost their original meaning for us today, though they are still commonly used under different forms. It is noteworthy that the cross was originally a phallic symbol and, like so many other symbols, was absorbed into Christianity from paganism. St. Paul and other leaders of the Christian Church apparently deemed it best to allow these pagan symbols, gradually giving them, however, different connotations. As has been well pointed out, "the church has played a double part, a

[1]Brill: "The Universality of Symbols." The *Psychoanalytic Review,* Vol. 30, January 1943.

[2]Richard Payne Knight, *Two Essays on the Worship of Priapus.* Privately printed, London, 1865.

part of sheer antagonism, forcing heathen customs into the shade, into a more or less surreptitious and unprogressive life, and a part of adaptation, baptizing them into Christ, giving them a Christian name and interpretation, and often modifying their form. Thus Christmas, which was originally a pagan holiday full of many primitive symbols, was transferred to Christianity, and gradually acquired an altogether different significance; that is why we may still see traces of the old celebration of the Roman kalends and saturnalia in a great many of the ceremonies that go with Christmas, particularly in Greek churches in the Orient.

The same is true of Easter, which also antedates Christianity. Originally it was a holiday dedicated to Venus-Ostera, the goddess of spring. As the egg was sacred to this goddess because *omne vivum ex ovo,* and the rabbit because of its fertility, the Church fathers have not yet been able to stop rabbits from laying colored eggs on Easter and our children from searching for them. Nor have they stopped our girls from dancing around the Maypole which was originally a phallic effigy around which danced and frolicked grown-up, mature girls instead of little girls. Some even claim that the Resurrection in itself is nothing but a continuation of the ancient spring holiday when everything in nature is resurrected. Still, it makes little difference in what name people obtain outlets. The celebrants of today care little about the origin of pleasurable outlets. The fact remains that pleasures once experienced are difficult to renounce. The old pagans were quite willing to accept Christianity but refused to abrogate their holidays. What we said above about Christmas can be equally applied to Easter.

It may perhaps have occurred to you to inquire why the snake should be a symbol of the male genital. In the light of what I have already told you about the nature of thought processes, the reason is not far to seek. Though there is no resemblance between the snake and the male genital to the conscious eye, there is, nevertheless, a hidden, suggested similarity between them sufficient, at any rate, for the unconscious to draw the analogy.[a] The story of Adam and Eve now takes on its real allegorical significance. Adam and Eve represent the infancy of humanity, when it was untroubled, naked, and free; when it was in spiritual paradise. Then comes the

[a]Dreams about snakes are very common, and we must guard against the conclusion that the snake necessarily signifies the male genital in every case.

snake, the symbol of sex, and the situation takes on an altogether different aspect. In other words, the child in its infancy is in paradise, but as soon as it grows to the age of puberty it is driven out of paradise and must now "live by the sweat of its brow." The story becomes perfectly comprehensible to us in this light.

Thus far, then, I have tried to make clear how the unconscious mental activity consists essentially of comparison, and how the results of this comparison, by reason of their peculiar symbolic character, are naturally not quite clear to the conscious mind. Consciously, for instance, you can tell a potato or an apple just at a glance, but in the unconscious or in mental confusion you may associate a host of other things with their more or less characteristic qualities of roundness, smoothness, or color, before you will know that it is the one or the other. We find a similar state in clouding owing to some organic brain disturbances, such as aphasia, in which certain fibers of the brain tissues are destroyed through a hemorrhage, for instance, and the brain, as a result, cannot function normally.

In brief, a symbol is simply an analogy between impressions of the present and past, and, depending upon the individual, it is either simple or complex.

Concealing Memories

Besides the form of forgetting, already considered, there is another form which we find in what we call "concealing memories." The latter are really not lapses but distortions of memory. We encounter them when we begin to investigate how far back into life the memory can go. Ask people what they remember of their childhood and it is remarkable how little they can tell you; indeed, some will say that they can recall nothing. You will be furthermore impressed with the comparative insignificance of the reproduced material, which is surprisingly trivial in character and seems to have little or nothing to do with the individual's life. The earliest recollections seem to preserve the unimportant and trivial, whereas, usually, though not universally, not a trace is found in the adult memory of the weighty and affective impressions of this early period. An individual recalled, for instance, that his father lifted him up to a bird cage; one man told me some time ago that he remembers that his mother found a cent—and nothing more. Examination shows that these indifferent childhood memories owe their existence to a process of *displacement,* by which we mean a deflection of a certain amount of feeling to some extraneous material, to an idea or object to which it really does not belong. We observe the phenomenon daily. A man may have quarreled with his wife, for instance, and now relieves himself of his ire by finding fault with his stenographer's spelling and discharging her. These memories represent in the reproduction the substitute for other really significant impressions whose direct reproduction is hindered by some resistance. They owe their existence not to their own content, but to an associative relation of their content to another repressed thought and are therefore justly called "concealing memories." They themselves are not important, but they conceal something. The individual whose father lifted him up to a bird cage did not remember the experience because of its importance, but because there was back of it something that was repressed and was now concealed under that memory.

The content of the concealing memory seems to belong to the first years of childhood, but the thoughts it represents belong to a later period of the individual in question. Freud calls this form of displacement *retroactive* (acting backward) or regressive. The reverse relationship is more often found, that is, an indifferent impression of the most remote period becomes the concealing memory in consciousness which simply owes its existence to an association with an earlier experience against whose direct reproduction there are resistances. These are called encroaching or interposing concealing memories. What most concerns the memory lies here, in point of time, beyond the concealing memory. They all show a remarkable resemblance to the forgetting of proper names and faulty recollections, as, for instance, in the case of "Lapin," where I thought of "Appenzeller." These new names or memories that encroach upon our consciousness when we try to recollect the original one are always, in some way, related to the real memories that are behind them.

The question as to how far back into childhood our memories go has been investigated by many writers. They found that there is a wide individual variation, inasmuch as some trace their first reminiscences to the sixth month of life, while others can recall nothing before the sixth or even eighth year. Simple questioning is not enough, as everyday experience in psychoanalytic work demonstrates. The results should later be subjected to a study in which the person furnishing the information must participate, that is, the memories should be analyzed. For the infantile amnesia, that is, the failure of memory for the first years of our lives, should not be accepted as a matter of course. We should remember that a child of four years is capable of great intellectual accomplishments and complex emotional feelings. I have seen children of that age fall in love. Dr. Sanford Bell of Clarke University has found this amorous disposition to exist even at the age of two. It is really remarkable how little of these psychic processes have, as a rule, been retained in later years, and yet we have every reason to believe that these forgotten childhood activities have not glided off without leaving a trace in the development of the person. We must remember that a person is always the product of the sum of his impressions and that it is absolutely impossible for him to cut out a period, or segment, as it were, of his life and go ahead. There is no break in the continuity of the psychic life.

I have found that many individuals, who declared they had not the faintest memory of their childhood experiences, had really accomplished in that early period many significant things which were gradually revealed in dreams or casual associations and which were later corroborated by the diary kept by the parent. Perhaps the most interesting case of this kind was that of a man whom I analyzed for six months, during which time he brought to the surface many things which we felt were probably true. After five months he received a letter from his father in which the latter stated that he was sending him under separate cover a diary that the parent had kept from the day of the patient's birth until the age of about thirty. We were very glad to receive it, and it has given me much pleasure, because it has confirmed practically everything concerning which we entertained any doubts.

In some cases it is remarkable how special incidents are corroborated. A man whom I have been treating visited the nurse whom he had from the age of one and a half to eight. She related experiences of his early childhood that he never knew anything about, and here, too, her information corroborated everything that I assumed on a theoretical basis.

As I pointed out, children take up impressions from the very beginning of their existence. As time goes on, Locke's *tabula rasa* becomes more and more filled with them, and, like a book, the older the individual, the more voluminous it is. These traces of early life always remain, and because they are subjected to repression, they come to the surface more or less disguised and incomplete; they are falsified or displaced in point of time and place. Motives may be discovered, however, which explain these disfigurements, and we find that these memory lapses are not the result of a mere unreliable memory. Powerful forces from a later period have molded the memory capacity of our infantile experiences, and it is probably because of these same forces that the understanding of our childhood is generally so very strange to us.

A case of "concealing memories" reported by Professor Freud is that of a young man who declared that he remembered seeing himself standing by the side of his aunt and asking her the difference between the letter *m* and the letter *n*. There was no reason why he should remember this particular experience, except that it concealed something else vastly more significant and important. The thought represented by the memory concerned itself with his wish later in life to know the difference between a boy and a girl; he wanted his aunt to tell him the difference, but he dared not broach the subject. Later on, however, he found that the difference was very similar to that between the letters *m* and *n*—one has one stroke more than the other.

One of my patients informed me once that his memory went back to the time of his baptism, when he was about a week old. He maintained that he distinctly remembered the house and the stairway leading up to the first floor where he was supposed to have been baptized. He particularly recalled a lamp standing at the foot of the stairs, and the minister who performed the baptism, a tall man in a black frock coat. He remembered vividly how his head was totally submerged in a basin of water. I was naturally skeptical and explained to him that I thought it was a concealing memory which probably hid something else of a much later date. He then informed me that he had entertained this memory for many years, but that when he imparted it to his mother a few years before she laughed, declaring that there was no truth in it, that, in the first place, he was not born in this particular house, but that he had merely lived there from the age of four to six, that she could not recall this particular lamp, that the minister who really baptized him was not tall, and, what is more, that the baby's head is not submerged in a basin of water during baptism. Notwithstanding his mother's absolute denial, the patient continued to entertain this memory; he strongly felt that it was true despite all facts to the contrary. I called his attention to the fact that his mother had no motive for denying it, and that, so far as I know, it would be impossible to retain anything from so early an age. We then proceeded to analyze it. He stated that the most vivid element in the memory was the lamp, so I asked him to concentrate his attention on it and give me his associations. He could see the lamp at the foot of the stairs, the stairway, and the room on the first floor.

He then recalled that at the age of about five years he was standing one afternoon in that room watching a Swedish servant who was either on a high chair or a stepladder cleaning the chandelier. He became very inquisitive sexually and made a great effort to look under her clothes. She noticed it, and gave him a very strong rebuke. He next recalled that a few years later he watched through a keyhole to see his mother dress, and somehow she caught him and punished him very severely for it. He was very much humiliated, for she took him downstairs to the dining room and told his father and brother what he had done. At about the same age, probably a little before this episode with his mother, he was on the roof one evening and spied a woman undressing in a house across the street. In his great excitement he ran down to call his brother, but when he returned the woman had already slipped on a nightgown and was now pulling down the shades. He told me that for years he regretted that he went to call his brother. He kept on reproducing more scenes, all of which dealt with frustrated sexual looking.

We must remember that sexual curiosity is a very common, indeed, I may say a universal impulse in all children who are brought up as many parents bring them up today, without answering their questions, imparting nothing of the vital knowledge for which they crave. Children perpetually ask questions, and if these are not answered, they develop a strong inquisitiveness for looking, particularly in homes where the mother is prudish and takes every opportunity to conceal and thus impress upon the child's sensitive mind that there is something to be hidden. If it is for nothing other than the exercising of the faculties of intellect, the child already possesses here sufficient grounds for becoming inquisitive. But consider also the presence of the biological factor; nature has endowed every human being with the desire to know about sex because the latter is a tremendously important aspect of life. The lamp, therefore, represented in the psychic life of this patient a contrast association of darkness which stood in the way of his sexual inquisitiveness. That is why the lamp element was so accentuated in his memory.

The question now presents itself, "Why did he remember the fact of his baptism?" This young man is a good Christian, his parents are Christians, but his paternal grandfather was a Jew. He himself shows no traces of Semitism; the only thing he retains from his grandfather is the name. It is a German name which is often taken for a Jewish one, and for this reason it has given him considerable trouble. He was refused, for instance, admission to a certain school because of his name. At college it was suspected that he was Jewish and on that account he failed to be elected to a fraternity which admitted only Gentiles. The concealing memory of his baptism is thus a compensation for his suspected Judaism, and that is why it retained its vividness, his mother's denial to the contrary. He had to be assured that he was baptized and therefore was a Christian.

On the whole, the memory represents a religious scene in order to hide an immoral scene of marked affective content. At the age of puberty there was a complete repression of all sexual elements, and he became a model boy in every way. He is now more than thirty-six years old and has never had any kind of relations with the opposite sex. He is a shy, seclusive, reserved personality, and is remarkably ignorant of everything sexual. This is only a reaction to his early immorality, and was effected by the various shocks or setbacks he sustained in his effort to adjust himself to his adult sexuality. Had his mother realized at the time she caught him peeping that his curiosity was only an expression of his budding sexuality, and had she explained to him in a frank, sympathetic way that it was not nice for a little boy to do this or that, he would probably have been able, like his brother, to adjust himself

normally, to find a mate, and marry. But, as it was, his parents regretted to the day of their death that they could not see him
married.

Thus, what we generally look upon as forgetting is not that at
all; certain things are merely pushed out of consciousness because
of something unpleasant associated with them; we are not aware
of them consciously and so we naturally presume we have forgotten them. We may crowd out something from consciousness,
but we never forget it; it always remains in the unconscious. What
profound truth there is in the observation of an old Greek phi-
losopher who, when called upon to teach one the art of remembering, replied: "Rather teach me the art of forgetting!"

4. Psychopathology of Everyday Life

WE DO NOT have to go far to be convinced how significant a role the unconscious plays in life. The proof is at our door. All the "little" mistakes that we all are constantly making, lapses in talking, writing, et cetera, our so-called forgetting and absent-mindedness, show very definitely to what a surprising extent our thoughts and actions are influenced by the unconscious. If we have our eyes open, examples of such unconscious manifestations may be found on all sides. I shall cite some of a vast number that have come to my attention from time to time, and I hope they will prove sufficiently interesting to stimulate you to observation in your own daily lives.

Forgetting Names

Mr. L., a newspaperman, once assured me that he could disprove Freud's theory of forgetting with very little effort. He proceeded at once to tell me that he had occasion to write to a friend living in Boston, and upon addressing the letter he found he forgot his last name, and that it was only after a considerable amount of thought that he could recall that it was Murphy. He continued to declare quite warmly that it was strange and surprising that he should thus forget the name of a friend, formerly his schoolmate and chum, whom he could not associate with absolutely any disagreeable or painful experience. We proceeded to analyze the case. I asked him to tell me something about his friend whom he designated as Jack. He associated his name with Murphy of Tammany

Hall and though his friend was a Republican he felt that that was no reason why he should dislike the name of Murphy. After associating for a little while he ended by saying: "You see, then, Doctor, there is absolutely nothing disagreeable connected with the name." Upon being urged to continue his associations, there finally came to his mind another Murphy who played an altogether different part in his life from that of his friend. The moment he uttered his name, I could see a marked change in his facial expression and voice: he became flushed with anger. This man deceived him and owed him money, and L. hated him. That was sufficient to explain his temporary forgetting. He never had occasion to write to his own friend before, he always knew and thought of him as Jack and never associated him with Murphy; besides, his friend had no parents, so that he had no opportunity to use the name Murphy even under other circumstances. We must remember that we think of a person in terms of the name that we call him by. On the other hand, there was the name Murphy, which was associated in his mind with something distinctly painful, and it was therefore natural that when he came to write to his friend for the first time he could not associate the disagreeable element in his repression with his name. That was why he was compelled to stop and recall it; he simply refused to identify his friend with a name that was connected in his mind with something painful and disagreeable.

We find the same mechanism in such episodes as this: A woman meets a friend of hers who married recently and instead of addressing her as Mrs. Smith, calls her by her maiden name. When you investigate the mistake you discover that she has absolutely no respect for Mrs. Smith's husband, and, what is more, she did not want her to marry him from the very beginning. We see this same thing when a woman refuses to use her husband's name. There is no other reason than that of expediency why a woman should drop her own name; the practice of adopting the husband's name was inaugurated originally mostly for the sake of convenience; it eliminated various unnecessary complications. As a matter of fact, there are still primitive tribes that continue the surname of the mother right through the family line. But if it is customary for a married woman to take her husband's name, we may safely say that it augurs little good if she persists in holding on to her own maiden one; it is particularly significant if she reverts to her own name after having been accustomed to use that of her husband with whom she has lived for quite some time.

A case was reported to me a few years ago in which a woman wrote a letter and instead of her married name signed her maiden one. I remarked then that it was a bad omen, and I know now that she is separated from her husband. It is a different matter when a married woman retains her maiden name because of some distinction or accomplishment to which she properly can lay claim. Here the purpose is to maintain whatever significance her special position may have, distinct and separate from her relations as wife. Among professional women, accordingly, it is common to retain the maiden name, and as far as I know the husband does not seem to have any objection to it at all. We are always laying emphasis on the importance of individual cases; but we may safely say that, as a rule, when a married woman uses her maiden name, it means that in the unconscious she does not wish to consider herself married.

It is interesting to observe a further illustration of this principle in the substitution of another person's name for one's own. A few years ago I received a letter from a minister in Oklahoma asking me to send him a list of books along Freudian lines. The letter was typewritten and there was at the bottom his name in handwriting, "C. A. Brill." His real name was Beard, and there was the irresistible conclusion that he signed my name because he considered me an authority on the subject, and unconsciously identified himself with me; he wished, one might say, to know as much about psychoanalysis as I did. When I related this incident to my class it was suggested that the letter might have been signed by the minister's stenographer, whereupon one of the students assured me that if I showed her the letter she would be able to verify the minister's signature, for she knew his handwriting very well. She came from the same city and knew him personally; what is more, it was upon her suggestion that he wrote the letter to me. When she glanced at the letter she immediately recognized his signature. And so my conclusion was completely corroborated.

Now it was essentially no pleasant or agreeable motive that prompted him to make that error; there was the unconscious wish to eliminate what seemed to him a shortcoming, a condition of ignorance in relation to a subject which he consciously desired to know and understand. We find this same condition among neurotics. In treating them we often learn that they cannot pronounce certain words, particularly certain names. This whole motive of names plays a most fascinating part in mythology; discover the name in some fairy stories and there is the greatest misfortune. You may very often find among neurotics that the only reason why they have difficulty in pronouncing and therefore stammer over some particular word or name is because there is something painful and disagreeable connected with it. I am going to illustrate this presently by a definite case of stammering.

By way of digression, perhaps, let me say at this point that it has been recognized by most students and observers that most cases of stammering are not due to organic conditions, that indeed very few cases may be traced to any disturbance in the throat or vocal organs. It is essentially a neurotic disturbance that usually comes on at an early period in a nervous type of individual and then gradually assumes the character of a habit, in which form it continues. In studying an abnormal condition, it is highly instructive to examine its normal counterpart. When do you stammer yourself? It is a common observation that upon being asked your age you will never answer immediately. Some among us will even anticipate the next question and hasten to answer it. I have heard of a woman who was asked how old she was and after stammering for a while replied quite blandly, "In Boston." She did not wish to reply, and at once turned her attention to the expected question as to her place of birth. But we show no degree of hesitation when we are called upon to respond to a question to which we have no resistance. When you ask a friend for a loan of ten dollars and he at once says, "All right, take it," then he really wishes to give it to you; but if he pauses and says, "Now, let me think," you may be certain that he does not want to lend it. Invite a friend to dinner, and if he stammers and stutters a reply, he is not anxious to go; there is a psychic impediment somewhere.

When we study speech disturbances we find that they have the same origin. They may be ultimately reduced to some very simple inhibition begun at a very early age. The child, for instance, may have done something that it knows it will be punished for; let us say it has stolen jam or candy. When questioned it will hesitate to speak, but on being compelled to confess it will stammer on the significant word. In time this particular word or expression connected with the unpleasant episode gradually becomes generalized and the resulting condition remains more or less fixed. Now I do not wish you to get the impression that stammering is a simple condition that may be remedied by merely probing its beginnings in the individual's psychic life; it is one of the hardest neuroses to cure, and only a few of those who receive treatment are ultimately in any real sense cured. But to get more or less successful results at all one should combine psychoanalysis with vocal training, and continue the treatment for a long time. All my successful cases have been under my care at least a year, sometimes longer. This, of course, applies to those who began to stammer early in life, to the so-called congenital cases, though there are very few cases that I have seen in which the history reveals the condition from the very beginning. Patients of this type are difficult to cure, and every so-called remedy can be of only temporary benefit to them.

A very intelligent stammerer, for instance, came to me for treatment. He was a man of means and he had tried all sorts of methods; some of them were indeed very ludicrous. One man sold him some sort of appliance that the former maintained was sure to cure him, but it was merely a belt which the patient had to wear so tight around the waist that every time he uttered a word he was made conscious of the belt by its pressure on his sides. That distracted him, of course, and he talked fairly well for a while. But the remedy soon lost its magic potency; it is hard to say whether the belt stretched or his waist became thinner, but he soon began to stammer again. The sum and substance of the usual treatment that patients of this kind get at the various schools, such as stamping with the foot or speaking in a certain fluctuating way, consists entirely of this distraction principle; there is no doubt but what it helps them a little, but that of and by itself will not make for permanent results; the psychic factors in the case must always be dealt with.

Of course there are some patients who never stutter at all until they merge into a neurosis; these can be cured through analysis; but they can derive no permanent help from mere training or distraction. The case of a man of this type came to my attention some years ago. He stuttered in different ways, with the arms, body, and mouth. He could not touch a glass of beer or a plate of soup without a fatal result: his hand would turn down and the contents would be spilled. Of ice cream he could have as much as his heart desired, but for some mysterious reason beer and soup were absolutely tabooed. He also stammered badly, and as his position demanded much telephone conversation, he was compelled to give it up. I treated him, and he did very well; in the course of time he was able to drink all the soup and beer he wished, much to his great delight. But I could not make any headway with his stuttering, and it finally occurred to me that there must be something unconscious connected with it. This was his history: He lived a sort of common-law life with a woman for whom he maintained an apartment, while he stayed with his mother, who was a religious Catholic. He introduced the woman to a friend with whom she presently fell in love and who offered to marry her. She consented and left him. It was a terrible blow to the patient, for he had really intended to marry her himself; and it was following this misfortune that he suffered his nervous breakdown.

It occurred to me that his condition might perhaps be connected directly or indirectly with this experience. When I began to investigate the matter, I learned that he began to stutter with the sound of *k* or in other words with the sound of *ck;* but as *c* has two sounds, his condition soon spread to *s* and then to all words beginning with *k,* regardless of whether it was pronounced or not, as for instance in such a word as "knife"; and so finally he seemed to stammer on almost every letter. I had noticed that he always referred to the particular woman in question as "that woman," and I decided to investigate the matter. But the moment I asked him what her name was he grew visibly affected, and declared excitedly that he could not tell me. I assured him that I asked the question out of no mere curiosity, but for a very definite and important reason. When he refused to give me the name, I closed the matter by stating that I could then do nothing for him under the circumstances, for there is a tacit understanding between me and my patients that they are to hold nothing back from me, that they are to be an open book to me, as it were. He was quite willing to leave me, particularly since he felt he was much better anyway. But in a few weeks he grew worse and returned to me. He then explained that in his anger he actually had vowed never to utter the woman's name again. I quieted him, and assured him that I would take the sin upon myself. He finally was willing to tell her name if I promised I would not write it down. I readily consented, and pointed out to him that, in my notes, I designated her as Miss W.

Thus I finally succeeded in persuading him to disclose her name to me. It was Keith. I was now quite convinced why he stuttered; it was the sound of *k* which was under repression that was the significant factor in the origin of his condition. I concluded at once that if my theory was correct, he would now necessarily stutter on every word beginning with *w*, for, as I said, I substituted that letter for the *k* in the woman's name, and impressed it upon his mind when I showed him the substitution in my notes. About a week later he told me that he was otherwise appreciably better but that his speech impediment was growing worse; he proceeded to state that now he was not able to pronounce even his brother's name; and upon my inquiring what it was, he stammered out the name "W-W-W-William." To be sure the moment it became intimately connected in his mind with the name of Keith in the substitutive relation noted, the letter *w* was at once tabooed and repressed. After I explained to him the deeper meaning of these psychic processes he gradually began to improve in his speech and finally recovered.[1]

To return to the psychopathology of forgetting names. Here is an interesting lapse of memory that was brought to my attention by one of my patients. She told me she was trying to think of a name of a small town near White Plains and that the first name that came to her mind was "Prudence." She knew that was not the name of the place, but after thinking for a long time she finally found it; it was "Purchase." Analysis revealed that she was a woman who always had differences with her husband over her expenses. One of her great interests in life was to purchase things, and she had to try very hard to live within her means, for her husband was often unable to pay all the bills she ran up. Thus the moment she wanted to think of the name "Purchase" there at once came to her consciousness a repressed and painful element fol-

---

[1] No one should think that all cases of stuttering are as simple as this one. The average case begins in early life and is most difficult to cure.

lowed directly by the word "Prudence," denoting, to be sure, a good New England virtue which teaches one to live frugally.

Here is another case related to me by a friend of mine. He recently met in a café a young lady with whom he was evidently very much impressed; she was the type of woman that he liked. He engaged in conversation with her and when she left, they exchanged names. To her query whether he would remember her name, he answered pleasantly and positively: "Why, of course I will!" Her name happened to be "Raub." In speaking of her the next day to his intimate friend, he referred to her quite unconsciously as Miss Braun. When his friend betrayed utter ignorance as to whom he meant, he paused, thought awhile, and saw his mistake. As you see, "Braun" closely resembles "Raub," and when I asked him who this "Braun" was, he immediately told me of an important and interesting character in the third volume of *Jean Christophe* who made a powerful emotional appeal to him and was more or less his ideal type of woman physically. Thus he unconsciously identified Miss "Raub" with this fictitious woman. But why should he change her name? In the first place, it did not appeal to him; Raub suggests in German the thought of stealing or plunder. But what is of greater significance, he was a literary man and at the time identified himself with Romain Rolland as he had done on previous occasions with other authors. Like Jean Christophe, who had that powerful love affair with Mrs. Braun, he, too, would have an amour with this Miss "Raub" and straightway the latter's name was changed. The whole mentation was absolutely unconscious. The significant element to observe here is the strong identification which also played so interesting a part in the case of the minister who identified himself with "Brill."

People very often take exception to this psychology and I have had many interesting experiences with skeptics. I once read a paper at the New York Academy of Medicine and there was a well-known professor of academic psychology present who took the opportunity to call me to account for the theory of forgetting of names. He declared that while reading a paper of mine on this subject it occurred to him that there was a stenographer in his college whose name he could never remember, and this, despite the fact that she has been there for a number of years and that he has occasion to talk with her very often. And then he went on to state

that it was not at all a peculiar name, that it was—— Here he
stopped, utterly unable to recall it. The audience smiled, and then
he said: "You see I have the bad habit of forgetting proper names.
But I now have a mnemonic for this name; it is 'Watertown.' " He
then stated that to test our theory he resorted to the continuous association method à la Freud and there came to his mind first
Waddling, which he at once recognized as incorrect; the next associations were: "You are making a pun—she is indeed far from
Waddling." Here he interpolated the little remark that he always
had the bad habit of making puns of persons' names, but, he continued, he was glad to say that he was gradually growing out of
it. Then he thought of "Waddington," and after giving about ten
associations, he said: "You see from my associations that there is
nothing painful or disagreeable connected with this name."

When my turn came to answer, I first made it clear that he did
not associate long enough, for it often takes us hours to analyze a
name. Then I asked his permission to take advantage of some
remarks that he had made and to make some impromptu analyses.
In the first place, he informed us that he had the bad habit of forgetting all proper names. Though it is well known that we do not,
as a rule, remember all names heard, nevertheless, when we meet
some striking or important personality with whom we are impressed we almost invariably remember his name. Hence when a
person asserts that he forgets all names, the only conclusion is
that he finds no one in the world of sufficient importance to play a
role in his life. This, I continued, was confirmed by the professor's
remark that he had the bad habit of making puns of proper names,
for here again we do this only with names of people for whom we
have little regard. It is commonly observed among young boys
and very intimate adults. Nevertheless he showed good psychological insight, as he made an effort to overcome it, realizing that
it was wrong. I am glad to say that the professor did not take my
explanation amiss.

We find also the element of the unpleasant and disagreeable at
the root of all deliberate changing of names. Note some instances.
There was a business firm in New York that was called "Yvel
Jewelry Co." After a little thought I realized that as its place of
business was on Broadway, "Yvel" was preferable to "Levy." And
so, too, when you see the name Honce and are quite sure that it

is not Irish or Scandinavian, reflect a little and you will find that it is Cohen. There once was a club in New York that went under the peculiar denomination of the "Sesrun"; it used to baffle me before I became a Freudian; now I read it backward and know that it is the "Nurses' " club. It is said that the Damrosch family in New York was originally "Rothkopf," redhead, but as the latter was not quite euphonious, it was translated into original classical Hebrew. During World War I particularly it was quite a common thing to change foreign names (especially German names), and I consider such a practice advisable and justified. It is undoubtedly highly desirable that we identify ourselves with the country we call our own, that we enter as far as possible into complete harmony with our environment; and I heartily disagree with the famous judge who did not approve of changing the name Beneditsky to Benedict, for instance. It seems to me that he showed a distinct lack of psychological insight. It is quite remarkable to observe that after going through this Americanization process the new name still shows its old origin. We have Hearst for Hirsch, Redstone for Rothstein, et cetera. The motive in changing the name is undoubtedly to eradicate the painful or disagreeable element that has become attached to it. Let us not forget the countless nicknames for the devil which superstitious people have coined for "self-protection."

It is interesting to note that among primitive people names are often changed on religious grounds. In one of Ibáñez's short stories the author refers to the practice, common among Jews, of changing a sick child's name; the little girl's name in the story is changed from *Bona Hora* to *Luna;* the thought is that the angel of death will thus be unable to find her. As you see, it is the same mechanism; there is fundamentally something painful and disagreeable connected with the name.

I have recently learned from a work by Captain Baudesson that the same practice is found also among some tribes in Indo-China. When a child is born among some of the savages in Indo-China that appears to be weak and sickly, they call it by some such name as "Bat," "Distress," or "Agony"; if it is fair and pudgy, they may call it "Peace" or "Gold" or "Flower." Whenever a child outlived one or the other attribute they changed the name accordingly. That is why historians sometimes find in documentary evidence names such as Typhus I, Scarlet II, Cholera I, and the like. In brief, primitive people in history confirm our views by evincing the same mechanism underlying the giving and changing of names which we find today in the examples we have already noted.

I have given you some illustrations of how unconscious mental activity manifests itself in the forgetting of names. There are also other mistakes that we commonly make in reading, writing, and talking which are no less interesting, and it may perhaps be advisable to dwell on them for a little while so that you may thus get a little more insight into the deeper significance of these unconscious psychic manifestations.

Lapses in Reading and Writing

One of my patients related to me the following experience: He knew a young lady from his earliest childhood and was deeply in love with her. He never failed to invite her, together with her mother, to all his college affairs. When he graduated, he took up engineering at Cornell and upon completing his course of studies, he naturally invited them to the commencement exercises. He wrote a very warm letter in which he stated that he was very sorry that his fraternity had no chapter house in Cornell and that he was therefore compelled to provide outside quarters for them. He meant to continue as follows: "I am sorry that I cannot offer you the luxurious surroundings of a fraternity home, but I have engaged rooms at a hotel for you." But instead of that he wrote: "I am sorry that I cannot offer you the luxurious surroundings of a *maternity* home." Without being aware of the error, he mailed the letter. The girl's mother was highly indignant over this seemingly brazen directness, and at once returned it. He could not understand what occurred, but with the help of his roommate, to whom he showed the letter, the mistake was quickly discovered. He then simply addressed a little note to the girl in which he expressed his hope that she did not take the matter in any ill spirit, but that she would regard it as merely a slip on his part. At any rate, mother and daughter came to the commencement.

He asked me to tell him why he made the mistake and why the mother was so wrought up over it. What was uppermost on his mind at the time of the incident was the fact that he was nearing the goal of his ambition, i.e., that he would soon be independent as an engineer and thus be in a position to marry. When he wrote "maternity," he unconsciously expressed his deep regret that he was, as yet, not able to enter into matrimony. The question of why the mother reacted toward the letter in the manner she did was, of course, a little more difficult to explain. Though she realized very well that it was essentially an error on his part, she nevertheless could not ignore it for the simple reason that her mind was in a state of what we may designate "complex readiness," or, as it is called by Bleuler, *"Komplex-Bereitschaft."* It was incumbent on her to appear innocent and deeply touched, though she knew only too well what the young man meant. But in this way she only betrayed herself the more. That is how some apparently well-meaning people betray their real state of feeling: they disclose their vulnerable point in their eagerness to conceal it.

Perhaps I may make this a little clearer by an illustration: One of my patients was having an affair with a woman of questionable character and I urged him to drop it; I maintained, with good reason, that she was not faithful to him. He was loath, however, to do so, but intimated that he thought I was right and that if he himself had proof of it, he would have nothing more to do with her. One evening while they were both passing a certain hotel in New York she paused and asked him to tell her what sort of place it was. He felt embarrassed, for it was difficult for him to answer the question, as it was known as a place of ill repute. When he asked me to tell him the significance of the event, I stated that, in all probability, she knew all about the hotel and frequented it herself, and that in order to throw him off his guard she was constrained to inquire about it so that she might thus appear entirely ignorant of the matter. He was skeptical and replied dryly: "That's all theory." A few weeks later he had an appointment with her in the lobby of a New York hotel; after waiting for her awhile he was paged and informed that she could not meet him, as she had company at home whom she could not leave under any circumstances. He was disappointed. It was raining and dreary and, feeling depressed, he drifted into that same hotel about which she questioned him. He took a few drinks, and as he was standing there at the bar, chatting with the bartender, he presently saw the elevator descending and who, to his great surprise, should step out of it but his young lady and another man. That, of course, closed the whole affair. So, as you see, she had a complex readiness, and though there was not the faintest possibility of his suspecting her when they passed the hotel, she nevertheless suspected herself, and perforce, indirectly and unwittingly, expressed the suspicion that was on her mind.

Here is a mistake in talking, related to me by one of my patients: She was present at an evening dance that continued until about 11 P.M., when everybody, of course, expected a more or less substantial repast. Instead, just sandwiches and lemonade were served, and the disappointment was as keen as it was general. It was at the time that Theodore Roosevelt was running for president; the guests were discussing politics with the host, when one of them, an ardent admirer of the colonel, wished to say: "There is one fine thing about Teddy, he always gives you a square *deal*." Instead of that, he said: "There is one fine thing about Teddy, he always gives you a square *meal*." All were embarrassed but understood each other quite well.

Slips of this nature occur all the time. I was speaking once to a French patient, who had the annoying habit of wandering from the subject, meandering, then stopping, and wasting a considerable amount of time. On one occasion I wanted to tell her to "go on," *"avant,"* but instead I said, "good-by," *"au revoir."*

I have found myself making similar mistakes at various times. One of my patients who was very paranoid, really psychotic, consulted me about her condition, and I advised her to go voluntarily into a hospital. She was quite willing to do so, but claimed that she had some complication that made such a step rather difficult. She had an apartment with some friends who would not let her go. I became impatient and said to her: "You are perfectly *incompetent* to take care of your own affairs." I wanted to say *"competent."*

Another one of my patients, a young lady, had an annoying habit of repeatedly using her powder puff in my office. I got tired of it in time and remarked that it must be some sort of symbolic action on her part. One day when she came I noticed that she did not have her powder puff with her; she seemed to be rather dull and listless, and I remarked: "You don't seem to have brought along your mental *powder*." I meant to say, "your mental *power*." I really thought she could do so very much better with the aid of her powder puff.

Another young lady whom I treated was unusually liberal and lavish in the use of cosmetics. I had advised her to drop a certain young man; following her meeting with him she came for a consultation. I was naturally very much interested to know what had occurred, and I asked at once: "How did you make *up?*" I meant to ask: "How did you make *out?*"

I advised a woman against an amour she carried on with a certain man who lived in Baltimore. She promised me that she would never see him again. One day she told me that she was planning a little trip to Washington, and in the course of the conversation remarked, "I am going to do this, if my *pleasant* plan is successful." She wanted to say *"present"* plan. "You are anticipating very great pleasure in seeing Mr. S. again," I added. "Oh, well, Doctor, you know I am sick and tired of not seeing him," she replied.

I once wrote a prescription for an elderly lady. My remarks were: "I am giving you thirty pills; I want you to take one three times a day after meals." Upon which she said, "Doctor, don't give me big *bills,* because I can't swallow them." Thereupon I asked her in a matter-of-fact way whether she thought that my fees were too high for her. "Oh yes, Doctor, I really meant to talk to you about it; I can't afford to come to you," she replied. Of course she had no idea why I put the question, and had I not taken her mistake as an indication of her dissatisfaction with my fees, she probably would have left me.

A woman was given a telephone number by her friend who suggested that she write it down lest she forget it. "Oh no, I do not have to write it down, it is simple, number 1740; I can easily remember it by saying seventeen which I am sorry I'm not and forty which I regret very much I am." She nevertheless made sure and jotted it down. The next time she had occasion to call up her friend, she asked her maid to get the number for her, but when she was connected she found that she did not have the right person. She was cross and fretful, but it was soon discovered that instead of 1740 she had given the number 1704. Here, as you see, her mistake revealed her aversion for the number forty; she would have preferred to be much younger.

I was asked to explain President Truman's *lapsus linguae* which he made in his Jefferson-Jackson dinner speech in Washington on

February 19, 1948. Mr. Truman referred to the Democratic party as "a parcel labeled progressive liberalism" headed by Jefferson, Jackson, Woodrow Wilson, and Franklin Roosevelt, and to the Republican party as "a parcel labeled reactionary conservatism" headed by Alexander Hamilton. But in finishing his speech he said: "If anyone chooses to call this politics then it is the politics of Jefferson and Jackson, Woodrow Wilson, and *Theodore Roosevelt* —and it is good enough for me."

He surely wished to say Franklin Roosevelt, whom he mentioned before in the same sequence of great Democrats but said instead Theodore Roosevelt, who was a Republican. The press featured this slip in their next editions and Mr. Truman was asked to explain it. He glossed over it by saying that Theodore Roosevelt, too, was a liberal. But he did not explain the real reason for his *lapsus linguae*. For it is immaterial whether Theodore Roosevelt was a liberal or not, he did not belong in Mr. Truman's speech. The latter meant to say Franklin D. Roosevelt. There were surely unconscious reasons for the slip, some of which are as follows: The President's chief opponent was Senator Robert Taft. At that time he was being discussed as the most probable Republican choice who would run against Truman in the next presidential election just as Teddy Roosevelt ran against his old friend William H. Taft in 1912. If we substitute Wallace for Teddy Roosevelt, the Democratic party is in about the same situation now as the Republican party was in 1912. An old friend bolts and forms a new party. Whether Wallace will do for the Democratic party what Teddy did for the Republicans is questionable. But many predict just that for the Democratic party in the election of 1948. Last but not least, Mr. Truman's slip also shows a lack of distinction or a vagueness in his own mind about the differences between both parties. Southerners are still influenced by the past, they are still chafing under the defeat of the Civil War. They know they were wrong but hate to admit it. Mr. Truman is now assailed by his Southern confreres simply because he wants to bring the South into the fold of liberalism by abrogating some of their old outlawed prerogatives. But he is undoubtedly affected by this revolt sufficiently to make him doubtful of the position he is assuming.

This recalls a similar slip for similar reasons made by a Southern lady (New York *Times,* October 7, 1937). Mrs. Walter D. Lamar, eulogizing Jefferson Davis at a delegates' convention of the United Daughters of the Confederacy, ended her speech as follows: "Let the world know the wisdom, the kindness, the justice of the great and only President of the Confederate States of America—*Abraham Lincoln.*" Mrs. Lamar was very embarrassed. But her slip was based on the fact that in her unconscious she was in doubt whether the praise she was heaping on the President of the Confederacy was really justified. The image of the Great Emancipator obtruded itself, and she unwittingly said what she did not wish to say consciously. Her slip was based on what we call the "narcissism of small differences" or the desire to feel important and better than one's neighbors. This feeling is particularly strong when one must espouse a cause of which one is not convinced.

A friend of mine, a writer, in speaking about a certain book he was reading, observed: "This is the best book I have ever written." He wished to say: "This is the best book I have ever read." The inference is that it was such an excellent book that he wished to be the author of it.

A woman who reproached herself for various sexual transgressions asked me once whether I had seen a play called the *Everlasting Madonna.* I told her that as far as I knew there was no such play on the stage at that time. "You mean, perhaps, *The Eternal Magdalene,*" I said. She saw her mistake at once.

A pregnant woman came into a department store and wished to ask for a material called "fruit of the loom." Instead, she asked for "fruit of the womb."

Here is an interesting lapse of memory related to me by a friend: "During the trouble in the reorganization of a certain railroad, the bonds of the company fell in value, and as I had a few of them I was very much disturbed. When I expressed my fears to an acquaintance, he explained to me that I had no reason to worry about the 4 per cent bonds but that the 5 per cent ones were now hardly worth half their value. As I did not know which I had, I immediately hastened to the safe-deposit vault to find out. I requested the clerk to open the outer locker of box 170 in which I kept my bonds and other valuable papers. When he unlocked it, I inserted my own key into the box, but try as I would, I could not open it; the key did not seem to fit. I called the clerk, and after a number of unsuccessful attempts he asked me whether I was sure that my box number was 170. I was very positive that the number was correct and was even angry with him for questioning me, for I had had the box for the last ten years. I suggested that the key was perhaps bent; he tried it with the duplicate key, but with no success. He finally decided to verify the number in the records of the bank, and imagine my surprise when he came back and told me that it was 175 and not 170!" As you see, the narrator was afraid that his bonds were the 5 per cent issue; and as he now had good reason to dislike the number five, he immediately dropped it from consciousness.

The following is a striking example of lapse in talking that came to my attention: A very methodical gentleman who was wont to make many Sunday-afternoon calls was quite assiduously attending to this pleasant function one Sunday, when, as he was about to go home, he suddenly recalled a lady friend, living not far from his own house, and in his accustomed punctiliousness, he decided to pay her his last visit. He expected to stay a few minutes, when to his great dismay the young lady, knowing quite well that he was of a musical temperament, declared very enthusiastically: "I must play something for you." Without remonstrance she at once made for the piano and began to play. She played and played to the great despair of the gentleman, who was very anxious to get home to dress for dinner, for one thing, and then, too, because he suffered from extreme discomfort of a tense bladder. Finally, to his great relief, the young lady stopped playing, remarking quite proudly: "You know it took me a couple of weeks to memorize this." In his wonted urbanity he wished to say, "Yes, you played it excellently and I can see that it is a very difficult piece to play," but instead of that he said: "Yes, you played it excellently, and I can see that it is a very difficult place to . . ." Here the gentleman's state of mind, the discomfort of a full bladder, the desire to get home betrayed itself in his *lapsus linguae*.

In the first edition of my book *Psychoanalysis* there was a mistake in spelling about which I knew nothing until the second edition was published, when I received two letters from different people asking me to account for the misspelled word "omission." It was written with double *m,* thus: "ommission." When I looked into the matter I found that the mistake was also present in the first edition, which appeared in 1912, and for which I was absolutely entirely responsible. The second edition, however, that came out a few years later, was read by a professional proofreader who, as you know, is just an objective reading agent, and so the responsibility for the error lay entirely with him. Now I thought to myself: "The stenographer, the compositor, the proofreaders, and myself have made the same mistake. Why?" To understand the reason for it you must know in what connection the word occurred. I quoted in the book a mistake that was made in the so-called *Wicked Bible,* printed in 1631, where instead of "Thou shalt not commit adultery" it stated, "Thou shalt commit adultery." The printer was fined and the Bible was confiscated; I added that the publisher had to pay a large sum of money for this "ommission." The explanation is that as there was a fine in this case for an omission, my publisher gave me unconsciously an additional *m* for good measure, so to say. It was a purposeful, unconscious oversight on the part of everyone who read the account.

A Hartford, Connecticut, paper a few years ago made the error which gave rise to a great deal of animosity. It wished to say about a certain congressman that "it is unfortunate that Mr. H. G. is no longer a member of Congress." Instead, it stated that "it is fortunate that Mr. H. G. is no longer a member of Congress." I have no doubt that the person who made the mistake really thought that it was fortunate that Mr. H. G. was no longer in Congress.

I reported a case of a newly married woman who, much to her displeasure, was compelled to typewrite her husband's manuscripts. Instead of going to church one Sunday morning she had to sit there at the typewriter, and her work was full of errors like these —parson for person, bridle for bridal. You see what was on her mind. She simply gave vent to her real thoughts: "I am a bride and instead of taking it easy and going to church on Sunday morning, I am harnessed and have to work here."

A doctor once asked me to render him a favor and introduce a certain Mr. K. to him. I wrote him, saying: "I am very glad to do so, as Mr. K. had considerable experience *inn* this matter." He returned the letter with the request that I explain to him why I wrote "inn" and not "in." Mr. K. was very much addicted to alcohol and was always to be found in a certain inn which I knew very well and which I associated in my mind with a particular experience that occurred there in connection with him.

Some years ago I received the following: "Dear Doctor: After reading your valuable book *Psychoanalysis* I beg to enclose a cutting from the New York *Times* dated 30 April 1916, containing the following passage which might interest you: 'Declaring that international law is international *mortality*, Judge Gray of Delaware expressed belief, et cetera.' Undoubtedly Judge Gray said *morality,* meaning that international law is intended for international welfare and happiness; however, the *Times's* reporter or printer unconsciously manifested by his mistake that international law as it stands today does not bring happiness and welfare to mankind (morality) but destruction and misery (mortality). This nicely bears out your contention that no mistake is utterly unintentional."

Note the following little slip: A woman writing to an acquaintance asking her for a loan of $300 said, among other things: "I am *rolling* on you as a friend," instead of "I am *relying* on you as a friend."

There are also numerous lapses in reading that we frequently make. Let me give you an example. Once on board a ship I met a gentleman who was bitterly incensed at doctors. We managed to get along very well together, but every time he had the opportunity to knock the profession, he took full advantage of it. One day he imparted to me this bit of information with no little gusto: "I just read a name of a doctor and it is the most appropriate name I have ever met; it is Dr. Slayer." The name strongly appealed to him. I asked him to show me the magazine where he read it and I discovered that it was "Salyer." In his complex readiness he unconsciously distorted the name to suit his own feelings.

Other Symbolic Actions

Besides the lapses we have discussed there are also symbolic actions which a person performs unconsciously and automatically and which he considers entirely accidental. Depending upon their mechanism they are either simple or complex and manifest themselves in such unconscious mannerisms as playing with one's mustache, jingling of coins in one's pocket, disarranging or arranging of one's clothes. These acts always conceal a definite meaning, though it is a common observation that when people are questioned about them, they usually shrug their shoulders more or less indifferently and assure you that they were just playing. They are instructive to the physician, who often gathers from them many valuable hints for the interpretation of symptoms; to the student of human nature they are replete with interest, and writers such as Dickens and Thackeray have described them quite at length and with considerable insight. The common observation that "actions speak louder than words" contains a deeper meaning than we generally suppose. An individual has two languages in which he expresses himself, one of which consists of these little actions of which he is entirely unaware. I recall a woman, for instance, who would invariably rub her hands on her lap in a characteristic fashion whenever she came to some matter that she did not wish to dwell on. In time I learned in that way just what she wished to disclose, and when I finished for her what she had begun to say, she would add, "Of course you know it, that's why I did not want to talk about it." As Freud has so aptly put it, "When the lips are mute, the fingers talk."

Some of these symbolic actions are, of course, very much more complex. A young lady, for instance, whom I have known was unfortunate enough not to have good looks. It was one of the reasons why she was nervous. I tried hard to console her, and reminded her of Dostoevski's contention that there is no woman who is ugly. She had no friends and was morose and depressed. It was at the time of World War I and one day she informed me that she had decided to go to France. When I asked her what she was going to do there, I learned that she was going to nurse blind soldiers. You observe here the force of the unconscious, though she had no idea, of course, of the deeper significance of her decision.

One of my patients, a suburban commuter, came to me one morning and I noticed that he was very irritable. When I inquired what had occurred, he at first declined to talk, but finally told me that he had just quarreled with his best friend because of the manner which the latter used in talking to him. Instead of "Please hang up my coat, John," his friend, he went on to say, just said, "Hang up my coat," and he felt that he should have been more polite. Now we must remember that whenever we find too much emotivity associated with an idea there must of necessity be a good reason for it. To discover it we must track the emotion to its hidden sources. Analysis revealed that the patient happened to read in his morning paper about a man who committed suicide by hanging himself; that brought back to his mind the skeleton of a similar experience in his own family, which I may say in passing he did not disclose to me in spite of the fact that he had been consulting me for a few months. He was altogether unconscious of the family misfortune when he was bidden to hang up his friend's coat, but the word "hang" soon touched a sensitive spot in his psychic life, it struck a complex, and there at once followed a flow of repressed emotion. As you may see, the emotion attached itself to altogether exogenous psychic material, it was related to his friend's innocent remark only in respect to the mere association of the word "hang."

Losing is another interesting symbolic action. I know I will surprise many people when I make the broad statement that we lose nothing that we really want. It is nevertheless true. No one likes to carry an umbrella or wear rubbers, and that is why such things are so often lost. Sometimes you leave or forget an article in a certain place; this may mean one of two things: either that you would like to come back to the place, in which case the article will serve as an excuse for your return, or that you know that it is quite safe there. A young girl told me recently that a young man asked her to keep his diploma for him. I remarked that she would have to be careful, and no mistake. The inevitable happened: the young man showed symbolically exactly where he wished to be.

A man consulted me once, and brought along a big, heavy overcoat. When he left my office, he forgot to take it and I called him back. Upon returning it occurred to him to inquire about something else he was anxious to know. When he was done, he left, again forgetting to take his coat, and when I called him back for the second time, he exclaimed: "Damn my father-in-law, I have to carry this coat to his office." I have often quite a collection of these forgotten articles in my office; just at present I have among other things a half-dozen gloves, a number of pairs of rubbers, and the lining from a man's hat.

Mr. M., a landscape gardener, lost some valuable photographs while I was with him on a train. Some time later I met the man who originally introduced me to him and I commented on the loss. "Oh, isn't that funny," he immediately interposed, "he also lost them when he was with me." I had good reason to suspect that the photographs were not his own. The next time I met Mr. M. I asked him whether the pictures he exhibited were really his own genuine work, and he answered, "No, not exactly my work, because the people don't allow me to take a photograph of the work I have done on their estate, but they are almost the same as mine." He was a conscientious man and hence continued to lose the photos; he suffered from qualms of conscience.

Many times we lose things because we wish to make some sort of sacrifice, we wish to atone for some guilt. I have reported the case of a young woman, who, while shopping one day, threw away a ten-dollar bill and only upon reaching the department store did she realize what she had done. She was a very ardent church member before she married, and was accustomed to donate liberally to the church. When she married, her husband, who was a bit stingy, explained that inasmuch as times were rather hard, she had better not make any further contributions for the present. The ten dollars was the sum she was wont to give to the church in the past. When she threw it away, she unconsciously expressed the thought: "He does not permit me to donate it to the church, so I'll just let someone find it and keep it."

Losing keys also has a definite symbolic import. I recall the case of a woman at a Western hotel who had the reputation of perpetually losing the key to her room; it seemed that every time she took the key out of the door, she lost it. On the other hand, she had the habit of not only locking her room, but also of barring the door with a trunk or a chiffonier so that it was thus barred even more securely. How are we to explain this peculiar condition? Analysis reveals that her losing the keys expressed her unconscious desire to have her room open all the time. But if that is so, why did she bar the door? Consciously, no doubt, she desired to have the door closed, but unconsciously there was a different set of forces operating. The motive that induced her to lose the keys is of such a nature as to repel her in conscious life. She was a young woman who had been separated from her husband, and there is no doubt that she was unconsciously disturbed by sex impulses which she could not fully repress.

We often observe this same mechanism in the morbid fear of burglars. You perhaps know that a great many women are in mortal dread of burglars; particularly does this hold true of old maids. One of my patients of this type was a woman who resided in one of the finest apartment houses in New York. Though her room was right between her father's and brother's, she was nevertheless always afraid; it was a common practice for her, upon retiring, to look very carefully under the bed to make sure that no unwelcome stranger had perchance surreptitiously entered. As I have already said previously, whenever we see so much affectivity, we must pause and ask ourselves what is its source. This woman herself realized how absurd was her fear. Indeed, when she came to me she said: "Doctor, you don't have to tell me that it is impossible for a burglar to get into my room, because I know that too well myself, but despite all that I am afraid." We know that repressed desire is always at the root of a disproportionate amount of fear; there is repressed libido at the basis of a strong emotivity. Language has recognized this condition, when it associates the word "panic" with the sensual god Pan. You can well imagine how a woman of her age, who has been brought up very prudishly, will repress a sexual thought or fancy the moment it enters her consciousness. But the "cosmic" sex energy is there and it is forever striving to come to the surface, much as her whole being revolts against it. The mind, under the circumstances, makes an interesting detour; the hidden wish to have a man illicitly in the bedchamber expresses itself in the fear of an intruding burglar.

Collecting Manias

In "collecting manias" we see other interesting symbolic actions. I am not referring to the collections of books, paintings, and the like, engaged in by so-called professional collectors. I am interested at present only in those collections that people generally regard as more or less peculiar. I have known a man, for instance, who collected stickpins. One woman collected pictures of pigs; another candlesticks. One lady had a few hundred of all kinds of pocketbooks which she guarded most jealously; her daughter, who was a patient of mine, informed me that when she wanted one, she had to fight with her mother for weeks before she could have it.

A man came to my attention who collected those collar buttons that one finds in newly laundered shirts; he requested all his friends to save them for him; he would most industriously assort them in boxes. One lady collected stones, not from the walls of Jerusalem or Rome, to be sure, but promiscuously, wherever she happened to stray; she would assort and name them. When I saw the collection for the first time I thought she was engaged in some definite scientific pursuit, that perhaps the various stones represented different fossils. A German writer who investigated the subject found that some people collected the most peculiar things. The Countess Chavan Narischkin, for instance, paid enormous sums for bedpans from Marie Antoinette and Mme. Pompadour and other celebrities. A naval officer collected uniform buttons; a man collected corkscrews for thirty years; the famous obstetrician Braun collected pubic hair, which he skillfully acquired while examining his patients.

The question naturally arises: "Why do people engage in such things?" I may perhaps best answer this by giving one or two illustrations. At a meeting of a psychoanalytic society in Zurich, one of the members, an old bachelor, took occasion to reveal this interesting bit of information: "Gentlemen, I want to tell you something quite strange. I take my vacation every year when a certain fly is swarming; I want to say that I have absolutely no interest in its scientific aspects. But I love to catch the insect, and for about two weeks or so I gather it in great numbers and then throw it away. It is my most pleasing pastime." On inquiry it was found that the fly was of the order Ephemerida, designated in the Swiss dialect as the "maiden." This innocent little pastime was thus a highly interesting symbolic action, which revealed his unconscious thoughts and tendencies; how natural for this old bachelor to be thinking of catching the "maiden" while he was on his vacation! He was a little astonished at this bit of analysis, but he confessed that he could see no other explanation for his hobby. He was quite frank. There surely was a reason why this man did not marry; and whatever were the inhibitions in his case, he showed his real motives by occupying himself in this way. When single men go on vacation, consciously or unconsciously, somewhere deep down in their hearts they think of "catching" maidens. It has been observed, and very aptly, that many engagements take place at summer resorts, on steamers, and similar places.

Miss T., a woman of considerable education and refinement, was greatly interested in collecting works on mushrooms; knowing that I read foreign languages, she asked me on one occasion to recommend to her some books on the subject, particularly those with illustrated cuts from German, French, or Italian sources. I brought her some, and on inquiring whether she had a reading knowledge of those languages, I learned that she was not at all acquainted with them, but that her whole interest was centered in the illustrations. I knew very little at the time about matters of this nature, and her behavior in this regard seemed strange to me. I learned, for instance, that on one occasion she paid as much as six dollars for one German work. Some years after I had become interested in psychoanalysis I had the opportunity to meet Miss T. and I took occasion to find out what was back of her interest in works on mushrooms. On inquiring whether she still collected cuts on the subject, she replied: "Oh yes, I have quite a collection." I asked her to tell me how she happened to begin her hobby, and she merely replied: "Well, I really don't know how it came about. I was on my vacation in the mountains. One night I could not fall asleep, hard as I tried. I arose very early the next morning, and walking out on the lawn, I found some mushrooms; I took them to the cook, who fried them for me. Since then I have been interested in pictures of mushrooms."

What is the significance of Miss T.'s hobby? In the first place, we know that when a person suffers from insomnia it can be attributed to only one of two causes, either to some organic disturbance, such as lung or heart, or to something psychic. Most of the nervous insomnias are always due to a lack of emotional outlet; and people suffering from them usually go to bed and fancy and daydream, and thus are unable to fall asleep. As Miss T. appeared perfectly healthy, I concluded that she must have experienced some emotional disturbance that night. When I had explained to her the motive that prompted me to inquire into the situation, she gave me the following information: During her vacation there was a middle-aged man who met her quite frequently and with whom she would take long walks. He apparently paid her a great deal of attention. One evening he was a bit intoxicated, and his behavior toward her was rude and suggestive; she left him and returned to her room. It was following that night that she began to take an interest in the mushroom. It is not hard to surmise what transpired. His suggestive remarks, disquieting and repelling as they were, aroused sex fancies which she could not shake from her mind. Thoughts of this nature are instinctive and persist always, no matter how hard we try to banish them. Now if we remember that certain types of mushrooms are scientifically designated as "phallus," which means penis, we may readily see what it was that unconsciously attracted her attention to the mushroom; indeed, the very object that so shocked her the evening before now unconsciously acquired a tremendous significance and interest for her. That is why she continued to collect the mushroom plates; there was absolutely no reason why she should take a scientific interest in the work.

From the above considerations it is clearly seen that such collections serve as emotional outlets. This is borne out also in the collections of stamps, birds' eggs, or nests, that we find at the pubescent age. It is then that the emotions of sex and love become manifest and the young man finds it difficult to control them. It is the age when the boy undergoes marked psychological changes; powerful latent forces begin to manifest themselves in the psychic life. Youth, as we all know, is then dissatisfied, it often revolts, leaving home and kindred. Some children may become very religious; according to statistics from evangelists, most conversions take place at this age. The boy becomes critical; he seems to lose his old regard for his parents; and it is perhaps with no little degree of disappointment or even pain that he begins to realize that after all Mother and Father are not so omniscient and omnipotent as he supposed. What he really craves is expression of the sexual emotions in the form of mating. The mating season begins at this time; but as this gross manifestation of sex must be deferred in the human being to a later period, and as we are taught to suppress it from the very beginning, this emotional unrest and sexual craving merely express themselves in a vague groping for something not altogether tangible or concrete.

Owing to cultural forces, the real aim is gradually distorted; we have crying spells among girls, and boys often take an interest in the manifest part of sex. In the main, however, sex is repressed; the child may, of course, occasionally consult the dictionary about the meaning of certain significant words, or read suggestive stories, or write little things that are lewd. The desire for outward expression nevertheless remains; and unconsciously the collection offers in some cases the necessary emotional outlet. Collecting among children, therefore, is to be encouraged, particularly if it furnishes knowledge at the same time.

That the collecting mania is a reaction to an unconscious need, to an inner feeling of voidness concerning some particular craving, is best seen in the collections made by psychotics. It is common to see an insane patient strutting about with all sorts of things bulging from his pockets. The patient has to be searched from day to day lest he accumulate enormous heaps of rubbish. When in the mental hospital I would sometimes secure a big bundle belonging to one of the patients and begin to unravel it; it would be wrapped in about a hundred papers, and when I reached the nucleus, I would find but a few pieces of glass or stone; in other words, nothing but trash. Patients consider this refuse extremely valuable, and it is impossible to take it away from them in the waking state, for they will resist tooth and nail. I found, very soon, that such patients usually have delusions of poverty; they feel that they have lost everything. It may surprise you to know that many such patients are well-to-do; you see that borne out particularly in private practice. I knew a wealthy old woman whose children asked me to examine her because she would store away a lot of old newspapers and rubbish in a safe; indeed she would fill an extra safe with them. On inquiring why she did that, she said, "Well, every little thing counts nowadays." The mental deterioration in such patients blurs their sense of value, and, like children who experience a vague craving for something, they blindly follow the impulse.

I have found a good many people who collected on a large scale until some marked change occurred in their existence. I knew a man, a bachelor, for instance, who had a room filled with long, narrow vases which he collected for years. He felt that there was something very artistic in that particular form of vase, and formulated various theories about the origin, et cetera. He had more than thirty such vases and every one of them had a name. Most of them were labeled in his own very small script as Miss Essie, Miss Gwendolyn, and similar fancy maiden names. When he showed them to me he remarked: "You see I'm not so lonesome as you imagine. I have plenty of girls with me." To my question he answered that the name of one of the vases was Mrs. Gamma.

As this man was not analyzed by me I could not obtain direct information about the origin of this collection and can only surmise the meaning of it. He told me that he began his collection hobby with violins and that he changed to vases because, although violins are also elongated and graceful, they did not lend themselves to his hobby so well as vases. For one thing, he did not care to buy cheap violins and he could not afford expensive ones. The naming of his vases came to him as an inspiration. He once bought one and the idea occurred to him that "she recalled Gwendolyn" and henceforth he called it by that name, and gradually christened all the others. I could not obtain any reason for his naming one Mrs. Gamma except that this particular vase looked to him something like the Greek letter Gamma. As I said, this man was a bachelor of about forty-five, who had nothing whatever to do with the fair sex. He lived with his maiden aunt after his mother died, and when the former was gathered to her ancestors he kept a bachelor's apartment with a Japanese valet. Years later I was informed by the same man who first introduced me to him that the vase collector suddenly married a young widow with two children. It was following some operation during which he was nursed by this widow that he decided to make her his wife. "Does he still collect vases?" I inquired. The answer which was sent to me a few weeks later read as follows: "I paid a visit to Mr. Vase Collector and saw little of his former hobby. He lives quite contentedly with his family in a six-room apartment. He told me that his family claims all his spare time, that for the present at least he has no interest in his former hobby."

I have had occasion to analyze some people of this type, and I have concluded that such feverish collecting activities represent what we call "fetishism," a condition in which an inanimate object is endowed with certain marked emotional feelings. It was essentially a form of fetishism for the valiant knight, wandering forth in quest of adventure, to take along with him a handkerchief from the fair lady which he guarded most religiously.

Get me a handkerchief from her bosom, a garter of my love.

The cases I have in mind have, however, a much greater emotional endowment than that of the valiant knight. These fetishisms always have a symbolic signficance. After the first edition of my book *Psychoanalysis* appeared, I received a letter from a gentleman who informed me that when his old grandfather died it was found that he left thousands of horseshoes which he collected, and that it was quite a problem for his children to know what to do with them. He stated that the man was one of the pioneers in the state of Indiana where he was born, an individual absolutely typical of that pioneer type; he had three wives, and when his last one died, he began to make overtures to the hired girls. The writer closed his letter by remarking that he thought that every horseshoe represented a certain amorous thought in the old man's mind. When you learn the origin of the horseshoe symbolism,[2] that it was originally nothing but the genitals of cows or camels which were stuck up over the doors to avoid evil spirits, you will see that there is good reason for believing that the correspondent's interpretation is correct. We may posit, then, the general rule that no person who is emotionally satisfied, whose work sufficiently absorbs him and satisfies his emotional demands, really collects to any marked degree, except, of course, if he is a professional collector.

It is very difficult to convince people who are not acquainted with the work we have done of the deeper psychological meaning of these collecting manias. There is nothing arbitrary or fortuitous about these occupations; they have a definite significance in each individual's life, and if you once gain the person's confidence you will find that they are symbolic of some latent erotic striving or wish, which, by reason of certain inhibitions, he was unable to realize.

Das Ewig-Weibliche
Zieht uns hinan.

They are unconscious symbolic actions of which the average person is altogether unaware.

We have thus far dwelt on the psychopathology of everyday life, and I have attempted to show you how such simple or complex indicators are present in everyday conversation and actions. Our fundamental principle is that nothing can be hidden; repressed thoughts forever strive to come to the surface, and our real motives and wishes become manifest in the "little unconscious ways" of everyday life. As Van Dyke has so happily put it: "Men's little ways are usually more interesting and often more instructive than their

[2] A. A. Brill: *Psychoanalysis, Its Theories and Practical Application.* 3d edit. W. B. Saunders, Philadelphia, 1922.

grand manners. When they are off guard they frequently show to better advantage than when they are on parade."

It may be asked, "What value is there in knowing these psychic mechanisms?" I may perhaps best answer this question by relating a story told to me by one of my patients. An admirer of Freud, she brought up her children to understand these unconscious psychic manifestations. One summer her daughter, a girl of nineteen, invited a young man to spend a few weeks at their country home. Everything went well and everybody was happy; the young man thought highly of his young friend, and Renée confided in her mother. He was invited to come again the following summer, but this time the daughter had also her classmate with her and the young man was sufficiently indiscreet to show attention to this new arrival. Very soon the mother began to learn how much Renée hated him and how she wished that he would leave, but nothing could be done, because the invitation was for a certain number of weeks. Meanwhile he was fed on psychopathology of everyday life, its nature and meaning, and he was soon well up in the new study. One day he broke this news to Renée: "I just received a message from the city and I have to go home." He left, and when he reached the city, he addressed her a little note, saying: "I didn't tell you the truth. I really didn't have to go, but I noticed for a few days that you called me Jack, and knowing that you hate Jack, and as your mistake shows that you identified me with him, I thought you hated me too. So it was better for me to leave." When the girl had finished reading the little missive, it was as if lightning had struck her from a clear sky. Running up to her mother, she exclaimed: "There you are with your Freud!" The mother could not understand at first what had happened, but upon learning the situation she began to calm the girl. "Now look here," she explained, "after all, you were very anxious that he leave, for you said you hated him; and now that he is gone you have no reason to be angry."

Thus the daughter was deeply hurt merely because her real state of feeling was discovered. The young man did exactly what she wished him to do, and she had no reason to take offense. It seems to me that if we all regard matters of this sort in their proper light we would be relieved of a great many distressing problems. It was good for the young man to take the hint; they were really both benefited; he felt more comfortable, and she was freed of an unnecessary burden. We should learn to regard our unconscious motives as much a part of our true selves as our conscious acts; there is no reason why we should be ashamed or alarmed when they are discovered. There is nothing shameful in the fact that an ardent worker for the prevention of cruelty to animals had tortured chickens when she was a child, or that a prison reformer had indulged in primitive acts in early boyhood. Our civilization is a resultant of these contrary forces in the individual. The good in us is only a reaction to what was once bad and had to be repressed. The saint is a former sinner. We are all human and have our shortcomings. *"Homo sum, et humani a me nil alienum puto."*[3] And so I feel that we would all be happier if we would only be truthful at all times. But the point is that we are for the most part *not* truthful to ourselves, and hence these slips or mistakes which, in their own small way, have the same relation to the unconscious as the symptom itself. After all, it was best for everybody concerned that the young man understood the meaning of this identification and terminated the unbearable situation by his departure.

[3]"I am a man, and I think nothing relating to man is foreign to me."

5. Wit: Its Technique and Tendencies

The Technique of Wit

SOME OF the examples that I have given you of the psycho-pathology of everyday life were distinctly mirth-provoking and could easily pass as witticisms. As a matter of fact the slip made at the evening dance when one of the guests remarked: "There is one fine thing about Teddy, he always gives you a square *m*eal," when he wished to say a "square *d*eal," called forth no little laughter from the guests, who caught at once the significance of the slip, for it expressed just what they were thinking about. Here the unconscious not only showed the disappointed state of mind, but the technique employed in expressing it rendered the error witty. In other words, besides being a mere *lapsus linguae,* it was also a witticism. The question now suggests itself: "How was the wit produced in this case?" At first sight one might say that it was accomplished in a very simple way—by changing just one letter in the word "deal" and thus giving an entirely different meaning to the whole phrase. If the guests had been regaled with the appropriate meal, the slip would not have been made, or if perchance it had been made, it would have passed unnoticed. We may say, therefore, that the wit was technically produced by the slight changing in the word which, in turn, reproached the host for serving sandwiches and lemonade when something more substantial was expected. If one should ask what actually produced the pleasure in the witticism, we would have to say that the guests were fascinated and amused because through the slip the speaker could openly voice their sentiment by telling the host what everybody thought of him but could not otherwise say because of social proprieties. In other words, one may say that every guest thought: "What a stingy host," but no one could say it aloud. Through the *lapsus linguae,* however, the host was actually told: "You are stingy; you can afford to give us a generous meal, instead you serve merely sandwiches and lemonade." But such an open expression was impossible in that social gathering. We may say, in brief, that a change of the letter *d* to *m* allowed the guests to *draw pleasure from otherwise forbidden sources.* Because the truth was told where one usually lies, everyone was happy, except the one to whom the truth was told—the host. The particular example shows that there is some connection between faulty actions and wit in both technique and psychology. In order to understand this connection better, it may be wise to go a bit deeper into the nature and mechanism of wit.

In a paper that I wrote some years ago on "Wit" I mentioned the fact that in a short story I had read one of the characters, a "sport," speaks of the Christmas season as the "Alcoholidays." Here two words are fused together because of a certain intimate connection between them, and the resultant new word expresses a certain sense to the hearer which he conceives as witty. We know that on holidays one allows oneself a greater degree of freedom than on ordinary days, and that this is conducive to alcoholic indulgence. And so when one hears the word "alcoholidays," one smiles and knows what the sport meant to convey. The word represents a fusion, a *condensation* of ideas as well as words. Instead of saying "On holidays one gets drunk and feels well," the speaker fused the whole thought into one word—"alcoholidays."

Let us take another example of condensation as it is seen in wit. In his work *Lothair* Disraeli said, "When a man falls into *anec-dotage,* it is time for him to retire." We may readily see that the fused word is made up of "anecdote" and "dotage." We know that in old age people resort to anecdotes. This is borne out among normal and abnormal alike. In senile dementia one of the most important diagnostic points is a lack of impressibility for recent impressions and a continual return to the past. The patient does not remember what he had for breakfast a half-hour after; he goes out to do an errand and forgets what it is. But he remembers things of the remote past. He usually begins, "When I was in the Civil War . . ." or, "You should have seen the girls of fifty years ago

. . ." et cetera. Normal aged people show the same mechanism, but of course not to so marked a degree. When an individual resorts to anecdotes it means that he no longer feels himself a part of the present, that he is in dotage, and hence may as well retire. As a matter of fact he has retired, psychiatrically speaking. The word "anecdotage" is therefore a condensation of a number of thoughts as well as of words.

Someone said: "All men are homeless, but some men are home less than others." Here the word "homeless" is not a new word, but if you break it up into two parts you get two distinct words expressing an entirely different idea. The wit here is altogether due to the technique.

Another illustration is the following: "The man who says the present styles are shocking, is always willing to be a shock-absorber."

Once I ran on to this remark: "Some lawyers earn their bread by the sweat of their browbeating." Here again we see the condensation. The misquoted biblical phrase, "To earn thy bread by the sweat of the brow" is modified here, the fusion of the two words giving an altogether different meaning to the expression, for one at once recalls a well-known characteristic of many lawyers.

In the category of condensation of words we may place also the following: "Not being favored by Dame Luck, he became a Lame Duck." This form of wit is what the Germans call *Schüttel-rheim*—shuffling rhyme. Here is another example of it: It was Mr. Smith's first Sunday as usher in church. He was all flustered, and turning to a lady who entered he said: "This way, lady, I will sew you into a sheet." A very fine example of this technique is seen in the case of that punctilious gentleman who made the indelicate slip to the musical young lady.

Just as we have condensation of words, so we have condensation of thoughts. For example, an army joke that I have cited in one of my papers: "A corporal, during drill, shouts to the recruits: 'Keep it up, boys, courage and perseverance bring everything. The egg of Columbus was not laid in a day.' Here you see there were two thoughts, two sayings fused together: 'Rome was not built in a day' and the anecdote of the egg of Columbus. What the corporal meant to say was, all that you boys need is practice; it is as simple as it was for Columbus to stand the egg on end; don't be discouraged, Rome was not built in a day. He fused these two ideas, however, and thus produced the substitutive formation, 'The egg of Columbus was not laid in a day,' which on account of its absurdity and incongruity carries the wit of the jest."

We may also produce condensation of thought by using the same expression or the same words in different meanings. For example. The question is asked: "Why was Goliath surprised when David struck him with a stone?" The answer being: "Because such a thing never entered his head before!" Here the humor is solely due to the fact that the expression "entering one's head" is used in an entirely different sense from the idea of a "stone entering one's head." If the answer had been, "Because such a thing never *pierced* his head before," there would have been no wit. It is because the word "enter" was used in the figurative sense, as denoting cognizance or awareness, that the joke was produced.

The mechanism of condensation noted above plays an extremely important part not only in wit but also in dreams. In the dream, words, pictures, ideas, and situations are all subject to the process of condensation. Let me give you an example. Miss R. dreamed "that she saw a woman, whom she later identified as her sister-in-law, standing on a sort of platform, surrounded by a multitude of people who were apparently applauding her. She was brushing her clothes, but instead of brushing them down, she brushed them up." The dream was a condensation of the following thoughts: "My sister-in-law always likes to be in the limelight; she always wants an audience. She is very coarse, and doesn't know how to act delicately in polite society." Brushing one's clothes with a brush upward is sometimes extremely impolite and coarse, and describes well what the dreamer wished to convey.

Let us now turn to another form of the technique of wit. By way of illustration, take this witticism:

Contributor: "You sit down on every joke I write."
Editor: "Well, I wouldn't if there was any point to them."

The technique lies here seemingly in the double meaning of the phrase "to sit down," which is used first, metaphorically, meaning to reject; second, it is used in the actual sense of "sitting down." If, instead of "to sit down" one would say, "to reject," just as in the preceding witticism, if it were said "to pierce" instead of "to enter," there would be no wit. When one examines the witticism more closely, however, one finds that the reduction has not been applied to the right place. The jest does not lie in the contributor's statement, but rather in the editor's rejoinder, that is, in the answer, "Well, I wouldn't if there was any point to them." The editor takes advantage of the double meaning of "to sit down" and produces wit by ignoring the empty sense and using it literally. His own use of the word in the idiomatic sense furnishes the wit. For if his answer had been, "Well, I wouldn't if there was any wit to them," there would have been no joke.

Displacement Wit

In order to understand better the mechanism illustrated by the above jokes, let us take another example:

The Mendicant: "Could you help a poor homeless guy that ain't got a dollar nor a friend?"

Old Multirox: "Not a friend? No one to tell you disagreeable things for your own good? No one to touch you for a dollar? Man, you don't know your luck."

How is the wit produced here? You see Old Multirox displaces the accent from the mendicant's request for material help to something entirely different when he says, "not a friend," et cetera. He deliberately ignores the first part of the mendicant's recital asking for money, and dwells on the last part of the sentence which the beggar gave as a secondary reason for asking him for help. He thus tries to give the beggar the impression that far from being badly off because he has not a friend, he is to be congratulated for being so fortunate. Whatever he said about a friend may be generally true of some friends, but that was beside the question here. The beggar asked for money and cared little about a lecture on the badness of having friends. In other words, the supposed benefactor *displaced the accent* from the main issue, the request for money, to the explanatory though unimportant part of the whole thing.

In both of the above examples the technique lies in the *displacement of the psychic accent;* this is especially marked in the last joke: "Not a friend?" The supposed benefactor answers as if the request were for a friend, and the element of charity does not appear at all.

Take another example: A man loses his gold-headed cane. The next morning he recalls that he must have left it in a café, but it occurs to him that he visited four cafés during that evening. He inquires in one of them: *"Waiter, did I leave a cane here?" "No cane was found," was the answer. He then calls at the next restaurant, asks the same question, but receives the same answer. He visits the third place, and again asks: "Alphonse, did I leave my cane here yesterday?" "No, monsieur, nothing was found." When he reaches the fourth restaurant, he is pretty well discouraged. He asks the same question, but this time the waiter replies: "Yes, we have it." He was very pleased and said: "I shall never go to the other cafés again: this is the only place I will visit hereafter."* Where does the wit lie? Here again the man displaces the whole emotional accent from the important point to something very trivial. He is keenly disappointed in those cafés where the cane was not found, forgetting that it was no fault of theirs that he did not leave it there. He behaves as if the cane had been in all the four places and all but the last refused to return it to him. In other words, he assumes that there are four canes and that he lost three.

Automatism Wit

The above joke illustrates also another mechanism which we call "automatism." A person falls into a certain trend of thought, gets accustomed to it, and follows it automatically, regardless of whether it has logic or not. The following examples will serve as illustration:

A dentist had to crawl under his auto in order to make some adjustment in the machinery. Applying the monkey wrench to it, he said soothingly: "Now this is going to hurt just a little."

The father of the bride, an undertaker, was busily engaged in getting everything ready for the departure of the newlyweds for their honeymoon. At last all the baggage was in the car and after taking affectionate leave of his son-in-law and daughter he slammed the door and cried to the driver, "Cypress Hills" (one of our great cemeteries).

In both examples one observes the automatism of thought. The dentist could not forget his profession whenever he applied any instrument to something. His assuring formula became so automatic that he used it even on inanimate objects, while the undertaker could think only of the removal of a corpse when he slammed the door of the vehicle.

This leads us to another form of wit which is well illustrated in the following example:

"Why were they married?"
"Because they fell in love."
"And why were they divorced?"
"Because they fell in love."

The witticism may recall "the manifold application of the same material," but in this case the double meaning plays no part. The important factor in this example depends on the formation of a new and unexpected identity and on the production of ideas and definitions related to each other and to a common third. "And why were they divorced?" It is a form of *unification*. Unification is also the basis of the quick repartee in wit, for ready repartee consists in using the defense for aggression and in "turning the tables" or in "paying with the same coin"; that is, the repartee establishes an unexpected identity between attack and counterattack. It is also well illustrated in the following examples:

A lawyer of small stature came into a court to look after his client's interests. His opponent, not knowing him, asked him what he wanted, and on being told who he was, jokingly remarked: *"What? Such a little lawyer? Why, I could put you in my pocket!"* *"You could,"* tranquilly responded the former, *"but then you would have more brains in your pocket than in your head."* Here the repartee consists in forming an unexpected identity between pocket, smallness of stature, and head brains.

Unification or Repartee Wit

Likewise there is a story told about Augustus Caesar who, traveling in the province, met a man who resembled him very much. He turned to him and said: *"Tell me, was your mother ever in the service of the emperor at Rome?"* The man replied: *"Not my mother, but my father!"* This is as clever a retort as one could give to a person whom one cannot possibly insult, by using defense for attack.

Other examples of unification wit or repartee are as follows:

After a poor recitation in English, a student suffering from the stigma of obesity is rebuked thus by the professor: *"You are better fed than learned."* To which the student retorts: *"Yes, you teach me, and I feed myself."*

He: "Yes, a married man lives a dog's life."
She: "Yes, barks all day and growls all night."

Nonsense Wit

There is another form of the technique of wit that we do not meet with very often, which illustrates a mechanism often observed in unconscious mentation. Here is an example:

The first cinder speaking to the second: "Why so angry?"
The second answers: "I have been wasting time in a glass eye."

The witticism is a fine example of animism, by which is meant, attributing an animate quality or condition to an inanimate object.[1] It is a mechanism which is found also in dreams. The wit arises here from the naïveté of the conception; everyone knows what it means to have a cinder in the eye, but when one hears that it is a glass eye, one immediately sees the comedy instead of the tragedy of the situation. No one would laugh if the word "glass" were omitted; in fact the answer would have been *mal à propos,* because when a cinder gets in the eye it is not a question of wasting time. The wit is produced altogether by the fact that a situation has been created which belongs to the naïve, to what we may regard as non-sensical.

Ellipsis Wit

Another form of wit we may designate as elliptical; the figure "ellipsis" is used in rhetoric, denoting omission. The question is asked: *"Do you think ignorance is bliss?"* And the answer is: *"Well, you seem to be happy!"* As is seen, at least one thought is left out between the question and the answer.

[1]The conception of talking trees in Greek mythology, for example.

We find this same form of wit in the following example:

Husband to his wife: *"If one of us should die I'll live in New York."* The wit is produced by ignoring the possibility of the first part of the statement and acting as if there was no question that his wife will die first, thus revealing what was omitted in conscious thought.

Representation Through the Opposite

There are also witticisms which express other mechanisms than those thus far considered. Take, for instance, the following:

Dyer: "How do you like your new car?"
Ryer: "Fine! It won't do a thing the salesman claimed it would."

Here the wit is produced by uttering the exact opposite of what might be expected. One would expect such an answer as this: "Very well indeed. It does everything that the salesman assured us it would do," but the average automobile owner's faith in the auto salesman is rudely bumped when he finds that the car does not run at least twenty miles on a gallon of gas, that this or that part does get out of order or broken, et cetera, et cetera. The wit-provoking element is the universal knowledge of the very exaggerating proclivities of salesmen which customers always take into consideration. The technique is *representation through the opposite*.

Sense in Nonsense

The following example represents another technique of wit which we designate as sense in nonsense:

Sometime after losing her grandfather little Ethel asked her mother if she could play the piano.

"No, dear; don't you know that we are in mourning?" her mother replied.

"Well," insisted the child, *"I don't think it would be wicked if I only played on the black keys."*

The child's answer is witty because it is so senseless and naïve, but as a matter of fact it is made nonsensical only to express a senseful reproach to the mother for her way of following this conventional hypocrisy of modern life, the absurd idea of wearing black to express one's sorrow over the death of near relatives. What a child usually observes is that in reality there is very little mortification over the death of a grandparent, indeed in most cases there is a sigh of relief when dear Grandpa is gone, because one needs the money and one has been terribly annoyed by his protracted illness, et cetera. A child always observes much more than parents realize and soon notices that mourning does not deprive the mourner of anything that he really wants, but is used as an excuse for refusing invitations from people one dislikes, et cetera. In brief, the child's thoughts could be reduced as follows: "As far as I see you haven't given up a single pleasure over the death of Grandpa, all you do is wear black. Why prohibit me from playing? I suppose I could play if the keys were black."

Outdoing Wit

From the mechanism of sense in nonsense we will proceed to "outdoing" wit, of which the following is an example:

Mrs. A to Mrs. B.: "Can you recommend your former servant, does she understand everything well?"
"Oh yes, she understands everything even better," *answered Mrs. B.*

What produces the wit here is that she recommends her servant so very highly that she expresses the very opposite! In other words, the servant does not understand anything. . . . It is the mechanism of representing by the opposite, or the mechanism of outdoing.

Take, for instance, this excellent joke: *A Jew and a Greek are in a café, enjoying their coffee and talking. Says the Greek: "You know, Jacob, the old Greeks were the most wonderful people that ever lived. They knew everything. Just recently they were digging around the Acropolis in Athens and they found wires, which shows that the old Greeks used telegraphy." Then the Jew: "That's all right, but I tell you the Jews were the most wonderful people. They recently dug around the walls of Jerusalem and did not find anything, which shows that the old Jews used wireless telegraphy!"* This is a very fine example of outdoing wit; at the same time, as you see, it also tries to represent something by the very opposite— because nothing was found, therefore the supposed condition!

Wit Through Similarity

Very often wit is produced by the expression of something *similar* and *cognate,* as given in this example from Heinrich Heine: *"This woman resembles Venus de Milo in many points: Like Venus de Milo she is extraordinarily old. Like Venus she has no teeth; like Venus she has white spots on the yellow surface of her body."* In other words, Heine begins with the idea that she must be very beautiful, he compares her with Venus, but he selects certain points of similarity that show just the opposite. Yet all the points that the poet mentions are perfectly true. He thus depicts something very ugly by comparing it with something very beautiful.

I have described thus far, briefly, of course, the most common forms of the technique of wit. As it has been pointed out above, the process of *condensation* which was noted in the technique of wit appears also in the formation of dreams. So, too, *displacement, absurdity, indirect representation,* and *expression through the opposite*—all these are found in the technique of dreams as will be shown later. It is the process of *displacement* that renders the dream so incomprehensible to us and thus prevents us from seeing in the dream only a continuation of our waking thoughts. The existence of the naïve and absurd in the dream is the reason why people generally think that there is a deterioration of the psychic activities in the dream. We find also in the dream expression through the opposite, indirect expressions and other mechanisms found in wit. We thus see how much alike in technique are the two psychic phenomena.

The Tendencies of Wit

When we inquire into wit, as concerns its tendencies, we find that it falls into two classes: purposeful wit, or that which shows definite aims, and harmless wit, or that which shows no particular aim. As an example of harmless wit, take the following: Smith asks Brown: *"Have you seen the new Murillo?" "No, I have not gone to the Zoological Garden for a year."* This is only understood when we know that Murillo was a great Spanish painter. The name, however, sounds like that of some sort of animal. It is only purposeful wit that is apt to be met with resistance from hearers or persons concerned. A harmless joke may be produced by witty words or witty thoughts, and any of the techniques described may serve to produce a purposeful witticism. Whenever wit is not harmless, that is, when it is purposeful and shows a definite aim, it has two tendencies: it is either hostile and aggressive, or it is obscene and sexual.

Take, for instance, the smutty joke. We may define it as a joke which brings into prominence some sexual facts or relations through speech. Such jokes are constantly read and heard in theaters and at the finest social gatherings. A typical example is the following:

> *Mrs. Chatterton:* "There's D'Auber's shocking picture, *Love in Arcady*. They say it's a portrait of you. You don't mean to tell me you posed for it?"
>
> *Mrs. Proudfit:* "Certainly not! He must have painted it from memory."

Of course rendering prominent something sexual does not necessarily produce wit. A lecture on the anatomy of the sexual organs or on the physiology of reproduction need not necessarily provoke laughter. The smutty joke must fulfill certain conditions. In the first place, it must be directed toward a certain person who stimulates one sexually, and who becomes aware of the speaker's excitement by listening to the smutty joke, and who in turn becomes sexually excited. Very often, instead of becoming sexually excited, he reacts with embarrassment or shame, which only shows a reaction against the excitement and thus signifies an admission of the same. The smutty joke was originally directed against the woman, a fact amply borne out in the histories of smutty wit. That nowadays, however, smutty jokes are mostly told among men, is only because civilization and culture have rendered the original situation impossible of realization; this is counterbalanced, however, by the theaters and comic periodicals. The smutty joke is only a form of exhibition directed against a person to whom one is not sexually indifferent. Through the utterance of obscene words, the person so attacked is stimulated to picture the parts of the body of the person in question, and is made to feel that the aggressor thinks of the same thing. In other words, when a man seeks out a woman and tells her a sexual joke, it is because she stimulates him sexually, and he hopes by telling her the joke to stimulate her sexually in turn. She may either laugh at it, which shows that she enjoys the situation, or become embarrassed, which to the person who makes the joke means the same thing. The following is a good example of this kind of wit:

Rub: "A woman has just been arrested for carrying concealed weapons."
Dub: "Where?"

There is no doubt that originally the motive of the suggestive risqué joke was *exhibitionism*—the pleasure of seeing the sexual displayed. As Freud has pointed out, one of the primitive components of our libido is the desire to see the sexual exposed. All animals exhibit during the mating season. And among human beings it is a common observation that the greatest amount of showing off on the part of men is done in the presence of women. There probably would be no football games or other college exhibitions were it not for the fact that the participator expects to see at the event his best girl, or perhaps his sister or mother. This form of showing off is nothing but a sublimated activity of the infantile exhibitionism. The desire to see the sexual is probably only a substitute for the desire to touch the sexual, which may be considered the primary pleasure. The libido for looking and touching is found in every person. We all know that touching the skin of the sexual object causes pleasure and excitement. The same holds true of looking, which is analogous to touching.

Sexual excitement is frequently awakened by optical impressions, and selection taking account of this fact makes the sexual object a thing of beauty. The fact that one animal is preferred to another is undoubtedly owing to only one thing—that the one looks better to the mate than the other. Of course originally everything was done very frankly, and touching and looking were perfectly normal mechanisms. The introduction of clothing to cover the body has served to arouse much greater sexual curiosity, and the individual constantly strives to supplement the loss by uncovering the hidden parts through his imagination. Looking and touching are intermediary sexual aims, that is, they are not ends in themselves, they merely lead to mating; they conduce to the selection of the person who pleases the individual more than any other person. If one lingers very much at one of the intermediary stages, that is, if one is not using the partial impulses and compoent of sex for the selection of a mate, but makes it his primary aim, he suffers from an abnormal sexual tendency which we regard as a *perversion*. That is to say, such a person is fixed on looking as the main sexual pleasure instead of directing it toward the normal sexual aim. He is what is designated as a *voyeur* or a "peeper." The desire to exhibit is normally seen in children and if not subjected to the normal sexual repression, it may develop into a desire for exhibitionism, a common perversion in some grown-up men.

It is such partial impulses and components as exhibitionism, looking and touching, which, when repressed, still leave a certain amount of libido ungratified that men try to supplement through speech. By arousing a picture of this type in the woman the man leads her into a corresponding excitement and the reaction of laughter or embarrassment thus produced in her gives him a certain amount of pleasure. We know from everyday experience that though the joke may have nothing in common with smut, the fact that it provokes laughter in others gives the person who made it a marked degree of pleasure. That is why we always seek an audience to tell a joke. The speech of courtship is certainly not regularly the smutty joke, but may very often pass over into one. We may say, then, that sexual aggression when inhibited often expresses itself in speech.

Another factor that favors smutty wit is the unyieldingness of the woman. Nature has purposely designed the woman to be passive in that regard, for it was intended that only the fittest and strongest should mate and survive. It is necessary for the woman not to yield too readily, for only in this way is she able to attract many men. Thus only the most persistent and strongest men are finally chosen. If the female of the species should yield immediately she would mate with any weakling, and a rather poor progeny would be the outcome. So among human beings, as among animals, the female, though she may crave the man, always holds back; she does not do this deliberately, as one might think; it is quite an unconscious reaction. The only point is that sometimes women, particularly of a neurotic type, hold back too long and the man gets tired and finds another woman. I have many cases of women who suffered nervous breakdowns when the man left them sometimes after years of courtship. The typical case of such resistance on the part of the woman usually results from the presence of another man which precludes the immediate yielding of the woman.

We may say then that tendency wit requires three persons: first, the person who makes the witticism; second, the person who is taken as the object of the hostile or sexual attack; third, the person in whom the purpose of the wit to produce pleasure is fulfilled. The way it is done may be described somewhat as follows: Just as soon as the first person meets with resistance on the part of the woman to the gratification of his libidinal impulse, he at once assumes a hostile attitude toward her and turns to the third person as to a sort of confederate. Through the obscene wit the first person is able to expose the woman before the third person, who, as a passive hearer, obtains pleasure from the easy gratification of his own libido. The wit enables, therefore, the first person to gratify his original lewd or hostile craving, despite the hindrance which stands in the way; it enables him to draw pleasure from an otherwise forbidden source. It is not hard to see what the hindrance is. It is nothing less that the higher degree of social propriety which makes it difficult for the woman, and, to a less degree, for the man, to countenance the bare sexual. With the advance of civilization, the force of repression became correspondingly stronger and what was once conceived as pleasurable now appears as inacceptable, and is rejected by all the psychic forces. But the human psyche finds absolute renunciation difficult, and it is through the medium of tendency wit that we are still able to enjoy many of those primary pleasures that civilization and higher culture have found inacceptable. We may say, accordingly, that the obscene delicate witticism heard among people of culture and refinement and the coarse obscene joke of the ill-bred both have the same source of pleasure. The only difference is that owing to cultural development, the coarse, obscene joke causes shame or disgust; the obscene, delicate witticism incites us to laughter because wit has come to its aid. At a gathering of ladies and gentlemen of the highest culture it is not at all uncommon for one of the company to make a joke so risqué that were we to examine the actual thought behind it, we would in all probability be terribly shocked and order the person out of the house; but because it is given in the form of wit, everyone is fascinated and laughs.

It also frequently happens that such wit is produced by the most cultured persons in an involuntary and unconscious way. A gentleman whose words I have no reason to doubt vouched for the truth of the following story: A well-known clergyman addressed a women's club and was very profuse in his praise of the ladies of the club and the fair sex in general. Among other things he said: "As one who knows the frailties of mankind I am repeatedly astounded at the strength of women. In the face of terrible temptations to which women are constantly subjected it is wonderful what force they display, yes, *it is wonderful that you don't fall, but it is also wonderful when you do fall."* The last sentence was uttered unwittingly. The ladies were highly amused, but the clergyman assured my friend that he was never more embarrassed in his life. It was an echo from his unconscious, or, as he himself put it, it was the devil in him who spoke. For the devil is only a personification of our own primitive impulses. Praising the women for not falling was only a reaction to his repressed wishes.

When we examine the part wit plays in the service of the hostile tendency, we at once meet with similar conditions. Here, too, we have been taught from time immemorial to repress our anger; not only are we not allowed to use violence against our enemy, but we are taught that it is bad form even to use insulting language. With the advance of civilization our hostile feelings, like our sexual cravings, have had to be repressed more and more. And though we have not yet reached the point where we are ready to turn our left cheek when we are smitten on the right, we have, on the whole, made considerable progress in controlling our hostile disposition. To be sure aggression in conventional form is still the *vis a tergo* of life, and although the early Christian reaction to the then-existing pagan sadism was a masochistic exaltation of humility and suffering, the Christian nations have only formally subscribed to it, they have never practiced it. Indeed those races who actually practice the virtues of humility and non-resistance have been treated with contempt by the leading Christian nations. As the Yonkers *Statesmen* put it: "It's all right to sympathize with the underdog in a fight, but a fellow would be a fool to bet on him." But as society forbids us to express most of our feelings in action, we have developed, however, as in the case of the sexual aggression, a new mode of invective, by means of which we are able to enlist the third person as a confederate. Through wit we can humble and ridicule our enemy and thus obtain the pleasure of his defeat through the laughter of the third person, the passive hearer.

The wit of hostile aggression, then, gives us the means to make our enemy ridiculous, and wins over to our side the third person, even though he may not at all be convinced of our position. The anecdote of the two lawyers mentioned above illustrates the process admirably. By way of another illustration, take the following example which I have cited in a book.[2]

Wendell Phillips, according to the biography by Dr. Lorenzo Sears, was, on one occasion, lecturing in Ohio, and while on a railroad journey going to keep one of his appointments, he met in the car a number of Southern clergymen returning from some sort of convention. One of the ministers felt called upon to approach Mr. Phillips, and asked him, "Are you Mr. Phillips?" "I am, sir." "Are you trying to free the niggers?" "Yes, sir, I am an abolitionist." "Well, why do you preach your doctrines up here? Why don't you go over into Kentucky?" "Excuse me," said Wendell Phillips, "are you a preacher?" "I am, sir." "Are you trying to save souls from hell?" "Yes, sir, that's my business." "Well, then why don't you go there?" You can see how a witticism like this serves to do more than disarm a man. The average individual approached in this fashion would have in all likelihood retaliated with some such invective as, "Go to hell," but Wendell Phillips used tendency wit, and expressed in this way exactly, though in an indirect, brilliant way, just what he wished to say. The minister's behavior was offensive, yet Wendell Phillips, as a man of culture, could not defend himself in the manner of an ill-bred person. The only alternative that was left him was to take the affront in silence, but wit came to his aid and enabled him to turn the tables on his assailant. By its means he not only disarmed his opponent but fascinated the other clergymen to such an extent that they were won over to his side.

In summing up, it may be said that the main function of wit is to produce pleasure from sources that are otherwise inaccessible to us. Perhaps the clearest demonstration of this is seen in the fact that smutty wit is so often enjoyed by elderly respectable men whose position in society prevents them from giving vent to their

---

[2] W. B. Saunders, *Psychoanalysis, Its Theories and Practical Application.* 3d edit. Philadelphia, 1922.

love outlets, and by persons who as a result of physical or mental factors are incapable of leading a normal love life. The greatest purveyors of smutty jokes belong to this class. This is clearly the case in tendency wit and is also true of harmless wit. When we laugh over Johnny's answer to his teacher when he names the "jailbird" as the most common bird in captivity, we obtain pleasure through our feeling of superiority.

When an audience bursts out laughing when a lady in the cast shouts "Go to hell!" it shows its resentment of the conventional repression constantly forced upon it by society. Just because a woman is supposed to be more delicate in expression than a gentleman one is sure to be happy when she uses a profane expletive on the stage. It represents the height of social violations. So, also, one is terribly jarred to hear that no less a personage than Abraham Lincoln was very fond of vulgar wit, a fact which gave his biographers no little amount of worry. They seem to be puzzled at this crass incompatibility and find it extremely difficult to explain. Thus Mr. Leonard Swett, Lincoln's political associate and later a United States attorney general, states: "Almost any man who will tell a vulgar story has in a degree a vulgar mind. But it was not so with him; with all his purity of character and exalted morality and sensibility, which no man can doubt, when hunting for wit he had no ability to discriminate between the vulgar and refined substances from which he extracted it. It was the wit he was after, the pure jewel; and he would pick it up out of the mud or dirt just as readily as from the parlor table."

Lord Charnwood, from whose work on Abraham Lincoln the above is taken, states: "In any case his best-remembered utterances of this order were least fit for print, were both wise and incomparably witty, and in any case they did not prevent grave gentlemen who marveled at them rather uncomfortably from receiving the deep impression of what they called his pure-mindedness." The trouble with most biographers is that they always leave out what they consider the un-nice parts of their ideals, forgetting that no matter how exalted a human being may become he is still very human in all his thoughts and actions. Abraham Lincoln was essentially a very aggressive man, he was a fighter and known as such; anyone reading his life can readily see how this "naughty," aggressive boy brought up in wild pioneer days had to overcome enormous primitive forces to become sublimated into the ideal being we know him to be. Strong and aggressive he remained all his lifetime, and we know that aggression in life also means sexual aggression. This is just what one fails to find in Abraham Lincoln. Unlike so many other great personages, there was no sex gossip about him. On the other hand, those who understand the psychic forces of human reactions cannot fail to see many things in his life which point to strong psychosexual repression. Perhaps by way of contrast one is forcibly reminded of another ideal character. I am referring to King David, who is not only so regarded by the Jews but also by Christians and Mohammedans. The great psalmist was also a very aggressive and pious man, but at the height of his glory he did not hesitate to commit the sexual crime with Mrs. Uriah, the lawful wife of one of his active generals whom he ordered to be killed in order to escape the wrath of this outraged husband. Well, the Lord sent his prophet Nathan, who gave him a good calling down for it. David wrote a psalm which has been repeated ever since by devout sinners, and then married the lady in question. Nowadays not even a successful king could get away so lightly with such an affair. Psalms or no psalms, all modern men must renounce much of their sex aggression.

Lincoln wrote the famous address at the dedication of the Gettysburg National Cemetery; he could not write any psalms because he was not conscious of committing adultery. Yet he was a very repressed being and one of his outlets was coprophilic wit of aggression. Perhaps if the biographers had kept a record of those pithy but indelicate Lincoln jokes it might have helped some equally-minded but repressed individuals to leave behind great names instead of repeating King David's psalm and remaining disgraced forever. For in order to be happy one must nowadays get some substitute for reality. The substitute may in itself be a bit shocking, but it is much better for the individual and society than to follow reality. Which recalls the following joke:

> *A missionary was shipwrecked near what he imagined was a cannibal island. He was in mortal terror of the savages, so he remained in the thickest part of the forest. One day he suddenly heard voices, he became terrified, thinking that his end*

> *was near. He listened tensely and heard: "What in hell did*
> *you play this card for!" He got on his knees, raised his hands*
> *in prayer, and said: "Thank the Lord they are Christians."*

Now the missionary recognized the Christians by the fact that they cursed and gambled; the cannibals could do no such things. But then the cannibal needs no such substitutes. He lives his natural life without much repression. He kills or is killed as the case may be, so that he needs no cursing as substitute; he does not expect anything for nothing, so he needs no gambling. He is just like the child in this regard; when the child begins to develop a sense of humor and begins to curse it is already alive to the burdens of civilization; it is already repressing and compromises on substitutes. Smutty jokes are nothing but substitutes for natural sex. For years I have asked my patients to tell the best jokes they ever heard. I don't ask this question until I am sure that the patient will tell me exactly what comes to his mind. Most of the answers were obtained from ladies and gentlemen of the highest type. I have read some of the answers before a group of scientific men and they enjoyed hearing them, but they all agreed with me that, like most of the Lincoln witticisms, not one of these jokes was fit to print.

When one watches the trend of the times one observes that as soon as a new taboo comes into existence one is sure to hear all sorts of jokes cracked about it. It is for the same reason that government and marriage furnish so much material for wit. Both are artificial institutions which the average individual finds hard to bear, and as marriage, which is only a phase of sex, touches the individual more vitally than any other cultural institution, it is the principal theme in wit. Although long accepted as an absolutely necessary state in the life of every normal person, it is forever criticized and blamed. The following illustration sums up the situation:

> *Simpson* (greeting his old friend): "Why, Jones, it's ages since
> I saw you last. Married now, aren't you?"
> *Jones:* "No, no, old man, it's not that. Just business worry and
> nerves."

In describing some of the more important mechanisms of wit, my main purpose was to pave the way for the psychological mechanisms of the dream. There are many resemblances between the two psychic phenomena, both in technique and formation. Such mechanisms as condensation, displacement, et cetera, play no small part in the technique of wit, and as we shall see in the following chapters, they are found also in the technique of dreams. We regard them as quite natural processes in wit only because we are so much more accustomed to wit than to dreams. The formation of wit resembles also the formation of dreams: both are unconscious psychic activities. Wit, like the dream, is an involuntary mental occurrence. That is why one cannot tell, a moment before, what joke one is going to crack. The above-cited witticism made by the divine addressing the ladies' club nicely illustrates this mechanism.

But there are also some differences between the dream and wit. The most important of these is that wit is a social product; it often requires three persons, and in its tendency always requires the participation of at least one other person. The dream, on the other hand, is a perfect individual psychic function, it is of the most personal character, and has no interest whatever for the outside world; one likes to hear a good joke, but unless one knows the meaning of dreams, he is bored to distraction when they are recited by the fellow boarder at the breakfast table.

6. The Dream:
Its Function and Motive

*I believe it to be true
that dreams are the true interpreters
of our inclinations,
but there is art required
to sort and understand them.*

MONTAIGNE

HITHERTO we have dwelt on those mental processes which are
found in both the normal and abnormal spheres, the processes that
may be readily explained on a normal basis. We shall now enter
upon the subject of dreams, which, though they are observed in
every normal person, present nevertheless a departure from normal
conscious processes. The dream has always been a subject of great
interest and from time immemorial has received considerable
speculation. We find allusion to it in all the earliest writings, to say
nothing of the literature of modern times in which it receives an
ever-increasing amount of attention.

It is noteworthy what a variety of ideas one meets in the literature on the subject. Some of them, I am glad to say, show some
signs of logic; the recent literature is particularly useful and instructive in that definite problems have been investigated. Most
of the material, however, is woefully deficient of any clear or
definite conception of the nature or meaning of the dream. You
may all know that the ancients attributed it to some altogether
external force; it was either a demon or God himself that was responsible for it. The scriptures tell us that "What God is about to
do, He showeth unto Pharaoh." To the Greeks there were good
and evil deities that presided over it. These views have come
down to us traditionally, and we may say that the present popular
belief in dreams differs in no respect from that of the classical

Greeks and the ancient Egyptians.[1] It is also noteworthy that the laity still continues to believe in their importance. In Europe it is quite common for people gambling on lotteries to have a little dream book which gives both interpretations and corresponding numbers. They play the numbers corresponding to the dream, and if they win, it is the dream to which they attribute their success. I understand that the same practice also prevails here among many of our population.

External and Internal Stimuli and Dreams

Everybody dreams, and those who think they do not may be easily convinced of the contrary by a very simple experiment. Make up your mind on retiring that if you have a dream you will recall it, and you will undoubtedly be convinced the next morning that you are no exception to the rule. I have known many people who, at first, insisted that they do not dream but who soon had to admit that they were mistaken.

There are those who believe that dreams are caused by a disturbance of the stomach. How grossly untrue this conception is may readily be seen from a careful study and observation of one's dreams. The condition of the stomach has nothing to do with the psychic determinant of the dream, though it is true that the dream may be more easily recalled if the sleep is disturbed. For it is then that the dreamer is thrown into a state commonly designated as the dreamy or crepuscular state, which is most conducive to the remembering of the dream. This fact accounts for the popular misconception: people generally have observed that they dream when their sleep is disturbed and have, therefore, associated the origin of the phenomenon with the condition of the stomach.

There is no doubt, however, that internal and external stimuli give rise to dreams. Attend, for instance, to your alarm clock and you will usually find on awaking that you have dreamed. But these stimuli do not determine the psychic content of the dream, they merely serve as dream inciters. It is a well-known fact, borne out by the experiments of many investigators in this field, that the same stimulus may incite different dreams at different times and

[1]Those interested are referred to *The World of Dreams,* edited by Ralph L. Woods, Random House, New York, 1947.

in different individuals. Thus, with an alarm clock acting as a stimulus, one person may see himself going to church on an early Sunday morning and hear the church bells ringing, while another person may see a wagon full of tin cans and an automobile colliding with it. What is highly significant to note here is that a short stimulus may produce a dream which will often require a half-hour to describe.

There was an interesting discussion a number of years ago in the *Revue Philosophique* in Paris over a dream that the dreamer described as follows: It was during the French Revolution; he saw himself present at a session of the National Convention; many royal personages were brought before it, tried, and condemned to die. He could see how they were being led away on the cabriolets, placed on the guillotine, and beheaded. Suddenly he himself was arrested, having been accused of some crime. He appeared before the Convention, defended himself, remembering the speech that he made, how he argued with the public prosecutor, and how finally he was sentenced to death. He was hurried off on the tumbrel, then taken from the prison to the guillotine. His head was placed on the block, he felt the blade strike the back of his neck, and presently he awoke to find that a board of the bed had fallen and struck him on the back of the neck.

The question that naturally arises here is: "How is it that so short a stimulus produced so long a dream? How long did the dream take, how was it possible to crowd all that material which required so much time to write down into a space of apparently a few seconds?" The board struck him, he awoke, and remembered the dream. Many explanations were presented, but with the exception of Professor Freud, who has succeeded in unraveling the secret of the dream generally, none of the writers really explained the mechanism. Analysis reveals that the dreamer was a Frenchman. As a boy he read about the French Revolution, and, like all boys, lived right through this stirring and romantic period. I have already drawn your attention, I think, in another connection, to the psychic mechanism of identification, by virtue of which we read ourselves into a situation of marked affective content or live through the life of an individual whom we love or admire. In reading, we usually select the hero or heroine upon whom we fix this marked interest; sometimes, too, I am bold enough to say, we may even identify ourselves with the villain. We feel deeply with whatever individual we identify ourselves with; we are with him in his moments of profound sorrow and joy, we live his life, as it were. It is nothing unusual to see one weep in the theater at some serious turn of fortune in the story of a "favorite" character. This mode of projecting ourselves into the lives of others, this profound and powerful sense of sympathy with their deeper experiences is quite unconscious and continues throughout life.

A little boy reading about Indians may identify himself with the brave and virtuous Indian, or with the scout. Many women have come under my notice whose whole course of life was determined by a certain book or series of books by a particular author; unconsciously and sometimes even consciously they governed their lives according to the characters depicted in the story, particularly according to some special character that strongly appealed to them. Now the identification mechanism enables us to endow every scene, every situation that appeals to us, with a certain emotional warmth and tone. We may only seemingly forget a situation that had once profoundly stirred us, but it always remains in the unconscious; it has rooted itself in our inmost thoughts and feelings, it has become a part of us. Any conscious or unconscious association may bring it back to the mind with all its former vividness. That is what happened in the case of the dreamer. As a boy he read the story of the Revolution with breathless interest. The unfortunates who were guillotined particularly impressed him; he absorbed to the full the pathos, the horror, the terrible meaning of the situation. And now when the board fell on the back of his neck it recalled, by association, the whole situation, in all its vividness and with all its attending emotions. The thoughts and feelings associated with the execution were registered in the mind as he read them and were now brought to the surface by this external stimulus. The action was similar to what we find in the theater: the stage manager pushes the button and the scene shifter brings on the appropriate scene. The external stimulus, by an accidental association, served to bring into play a whole group of formerly accentuated ideas and emotions.

Internal stimuli act in the same way. If, for instance, you experience certain sensations in your stomach today that you had five years ago, the likelihood is that your dreams will have a resemblance in some way to those of the former period. When we bear this in mind, we do not have to resort to supernatural causes to account for the fact that some people can foretell by a certain dream that they are going to be sick. Long before one is conscious of his sickness, long before, for instance, the mucous membrane of the nose and throat becomes so swollen that it begins to run and ache, the congestion starts and arouses associations in the mind which recall some similar situation in the past. That is enough to cause the individual to dream of the sickness. One woman actually had the same type of dream every time before she got a cold in the head, as she called it. We observe this phenomenon under different forms in everyday life. Patients in speaking to me of certain ailments, let us say, periodic headaches, may often tell me how glad they are that they did not have the headache for the last three months. I am not at all pleased to hear this, for I know that the fact that they thought of it is already an indication that it is coming on, but that it has not as yet manifested itself to consciousness. To be sure I learn the next day that the headache has arrived.

A disease does not manifest itself suddenly; long before the person consciously knows that he is sick, he experiences, though vaguely, some feeling of depression or uneasiness that carries with it a sense of foreboding to those who are ignorant of the psychological significance of the condition. That undoubtedly accounts for the fact that among both primitive and modern people the sneeze was always greeted with some formula that signified the wish to avert evil. Undoubtedly primitive man learned empirically that whenever he began to sneeze some disease would follow, because a great many serious diseases begin with coryza. One has a right to believe that primitive man had less chance to overcome pneumonia and other infectious or contagious diseases than his modern brother, and as sneezing was invariably followed by disease which often ended fatally, primitive man naturally tried to stop it through incantations such as "God bless you!" or its equivalent in other languages. I feel that this really explains the sneezing ceremonial in a much simpler way and is nearer to the truth than the explanation offered by Dr. Wallace is his interesting dissertation, *The Romance and the Tragedy of Sneezing.*[2]

In physical as well as in mental life a certain stimulus is required

[2]*Scientific Monthly,* Vol. 9, No. 6, 1919.

before a certain reaction is produced. I am sure that those of you who have studied academic psychology will recall the old Weber-Fechner law of the relation of stimulus to intensity of sensation— the intensity of the one being approximately proportional to the intensity of the other. One of the experiments that we perform in the examination of patients, particularly when we wish to determine their degree of attention, is to expose pictures to them very rapidly, the exposure lasting only a few seconds. We then ask them to tell us what they observed. A great many will declare at first that they saw nothing, but upon urging them to tell you what comes to their mind, they invariably will mention something that has a more or less fundamental resemblance to the picture. I show a person a Japanese scene, and he declares at first that he saw nothing. I urge him to reflect, and he soon replies, "Well, I think of China." You see that he noted the resemblance, although he has not consciously seen the picture. In order to be heard, I do not have to speak to you in a room, for instance, as loudly as I would have to in the subway. But if I whisper to you in a room, you may not hear me even though the stimulus is present and the sound is there. In other words, one may say that before you see, you have already seen; before you hear, you have already heard, but the stimulus may not always be sufficiently strong to make you feel conscious of the sensation.

Incidentally, I may say that if you remember this important law in psychology, you will be able to understand many of the occurrences to which people generally attribute so much importance. You are often asked to explain, for example, how it is that when you talk of Mr. Brown he is sure to appear. The fact is that you either saw or heard Mr. Brown before you talked about him. Let us remember that our senses tell us much more than we generally suppose, and though we have little use for them in ordinary peaceful times, they still operate, and render us knowledge long before we are really conscious of it. You may be on the avenue speaking to your friend, when somebody passes who has aroused certain associations in your mind. You begin to talk about him, although you have not consciously seen him, and suddenly, to your great surprise, he stands there before you in his own flesh and blood. "Talk of the devil, and he is sure to appear." But he has been there in your field of vision long before you actually saw him.

But I may be reminded: "I talked about a man while staying in the house and to be sure he came in." Usually we can hear the person approaching, and I still have to find the person who knows somebody well but cannot recognize the latter's footsteps. At home we can always tell who is coming, whether mother, father, or some other intimate person. We may also explain on this basis such occurrences as find expression in the following characteristic remark: "How do you account for my receiving a letter from a woman whom I have not heard from for a long time, and, strange enough, I talked about her only yesterday?" When you investigate you find that there is a similar mechanism involved, that the situation presents nothing at all mysterious or "psychic." You have established a certain connection in your mind between that person and yourself. At about that period you think suddenly of that individual by virtue of a psychic process to which I have already drawn your attention under the term of "post-hypnotic suggestion"; that is to say, at the expiration of a certain time, a certain impression received in the past will recur, and revive an old association. In other words our senses, which are so active in animals, especially in the Mammalia, our nearest relatives, are still active, and although we have become accustomed to look for protection from without, they continually receive and impart to us information from the inner and outer worlds. It is because we have learned to neglect them consciously that we are sometimes mystified by the sensations they convey to us.

The Dream the Guardian of Sleep

The underlying nature and meaning of the dream were not known until Professor Freud propounded his theories.[3] All sorts of interpretations were presented but there was no general, fundamental conception. In analyzing his patients Freud found that they all dreamed, and the question presented itself, "Are dreams definite psychic mechanisms or do they represent sheer nonsense, having no relation to the individual's psychic life?" The answer involved a fundamental conception; everything both in physical and mental life has a reason; as in the physical, so in the psychic sphere, there

[3]"The Interpretation of Dreams," in *The Basic Writings of Sigmund Freud,* translated by A. A. Brill. The Modern Library, New York, 1938.

is nothing that has not some functional significance. We have tears, not merely to weep, but to keep the eyes constantly moist to wash them; otherwise they would be coated with dust that would make it impossible for us to see. We have sweat glands in order to equalize the temperature of the body, and saliva to assist in deglutition and digestion generally. In the same way every psychic function has its *raison d'être*. The question then was, "Why do we dream?" He thoroughly investigated the literature on the subject but it was not there that the answer was to be found. It was only as he delved deeper and deeper into the neurotic symptoms and saw their profound intimate connection with the dream, that he was approaching a solution of the problem. He began to see that the dream is a perfect psychic mechanism, that it is not at all arbitrary, but that it has a definite relation to the individual's psychic life. The deeper he probed the dream, the more did its wisdom and underlying sense of order grow upon him, until finally he formulated the thesis that *"a dream is the hidden fulfillment of a repressed wish."* In other words, a dream is a wish that the individual could not realize in the waking state.

Now before dilating on this conclusion let me go back to the function of the dream. During the day we all think of a host of things; I am sure I am not exaggerating when I say that hundreds and hundreds of thoughts run through the mind; they glide by and we are not even conscious of them. But there are always some problems coming up that absorb us. It is well known that if any question should continue to engage our attention to a marked degree, it would be impossible for us to fall asleep. We are all aware that any strong or poignant emotion, whether it be one of pleasure or pain, may keep one awake. An individual who is elated does not wish to sleep, and, for that matter, cannot sleep, because his senses are too alive and stimulated. To sleep it is necessary to exclude all sensations from all senses. We go to bed so that we may relax; the lights are turned out in order to exclude all sensory stimulations. Experiment has demonstrated that sleep is usually induced when sensations are thus excluded. When sensory impressions are shut out from animals sleep usually follows. Thus, when there is any problem engrossing the mind, the tendency is not to fall asleep. Now what are the things that would keep us awake? They are usually those that we have not been able to attain, or those we have not been able to solve. One works out a problem, thinking to himself: "If I can put that through, I will be fortunate: my future will be assured. If I cannot execute it, I do not know what I am to do: I will lose my position and will not be able to take care of my family." He goes to bed and dwells on the problem. He would probably continue with it throughout the whole night were it not for his wish to sleep. What actually happens then is that the mind takes the problem and weaves it into a dream. The dream then realizes the wish and thus makes sleep possible. We must not forget that the word "dream" means to deceive, that is to say, the mind, which is the central station of all our activities, strives to deceive us into feeling that whatever keeps us from sleeping no longer exists.

In everyday life we know that once a question is solved, there is no further need for preoccupation with it. It is merely a matter of how to solve an existing problem. A child goes to sleep, crying; it wants a doll. The mother quickly appeases it by granting the wish. So far so good; but this same child, grown older, wants something that the mother cannot so easily secure. It has to go without it, but as it wishes to sleep, the problem is solved in a different way. Nature assures our rest by seemingly granting us our wishes. The child now dreams that it has obtained what it was refused in reality. This does not always take place, that is, not every wish can be realized in dreams, but the mind makes a strong effort to do so. If the wish cannot be realized, the sleeper is awakened in a nightmare. This is, comparatively speaking, a rare occurrence. Likewise, if you should go to bed tonight after eating a very salty supper, you will undoubtely desire water at night, but instead of waking up, particularly if the room is cold, you will dream that you are slaking your thirst with some refreshing water, or if you are more fortunately constituted, with some stronger and more inviting beverage. This is a very common "convenience" dream. If you retire hungry, you will invariably dream that you are eating. I spoke to Professor Macmillan who went with Peary to the North Pole and he told me what great pleasure they had experienced in their dreams. The reason is quite clear. These men who had known the delicacies of New York restaurants were compelled to live on pemmican and a simple Arctic Zone diet. They dreamed of the things they were anxious to have. They smoked fine cigars and drank highballs in their sleep. Children invariably show that they dream of those things that they cannot have in the waking state. Children's dreams and the so-called convenience dreams of adults are thus open wishes. When the dreams, however, are not of this type, the situation is quite different, and it is here that we encounter serious difficulties in understanding them.

To appreciate how the dream acts as *the guardian of sleep,* consider with me the following case of a businessman who has been with his firm for a number of years, whose ability was recognized, but for whom there is manifestly no real place in the proposed reorganization of the business. In order to remain in the new organization he must show that he can be a factor in it, that there is a special department that he can manage; otherwise he realizes that he will have to lose his position. He evolves a scheme which he is to present the next morning before the board of trustees. He goes to bed, constantly thinking of the matter: he sees himself before the board, he anticipates the arguments of his two opponents, he wonders what best reply to make. The clock strikes, one, two, and three, and he is still awake. Finally, exhausted, he falls asleep and has the following dream: *He is swimming in New York Bay on a board which he is able to manipulate just as if it were an excellent motorboat. The steamers are going and coming, but he is by no means disconcerted: every time a big boat approaches, he very deftly steers out of its course, or rides over the waves with ease and pleasure. He is enjoying the swim immensely.* He awoke with a feeling of satisfaction.

When he came to me the next day, he wondered what sort of wish his dream could represent. I reminded him at once that the dream is not always an open wish but a hidden realization of a repressed wish. The interpretation is simple enough. He was to appear the next day, as I said, before the board of trustees to lay before it his plans for the reorganization of the business; he knew that unless he could convince them to accept his scheme, he would lose his position. He knew, furthermore, that some members of the board were antagonistic to him and would raise objections regardless of whatever plans he proposed; on the other hand, he was aware that most of the members were favorably disposed toward him. It was some time before he fell asleep, because his mind was constantly dwelling on the whole situation. He would

have remained awake throughout the night, but as he was tired
and wished to sleep, the disturbing problem had to be solved in
some way. This could be effected only by weaving his emotionally
accentuated ideas into a dream which represented his wish as
accomplished. When I asked him what his dream recalled he told
me he used to engage, as a boy, in swimming races on *boards* on
the Ohio River, in which he was highly proficient. And so you see,
because he was thinking of how to control the board, a situation
in the past presented itself to him in which he actually managed
boards skillfully and won. The mechanism of *double-entendre,*
double meaning of a word, reproduced in his mind a scene from
boyhood in which he had perfect control of a board. It was a different board, to be sure, but that made little difference in the unconscious; the important thing was that he was able to guide it
through all obstacles. The dream not only enabled him to sleep
but the pain of tomorrow's uncertainty was replaced by pleasant
feelings of his remote past. Thus the dream was the producer as
well as the guardian of sleep.

From the above dream we may see the first difficulty in dream
analysis, viz., that the language of the dream is visual: we see
images, we express ideas in symbols. Whereas in the waking state
"to see" is used in the literal as well as the more or less figurative
sense of "to understand," in the sleeping state we use it entirely in
its literal significance. We do not think in the dream in any logical
sense, we merely see a succession of images, which have been
stored in the mind in the past. It would have been otherwise impossible for the dreamer who dreamed about the French Revolution to condense, as he did, so much thought in a few seconds;
what the dream really did was to revive pictures in his mind that
he actually gleaned from history books or that his own imagination
may have created, while he was immersed in his reading.

Abstract ideas in dreams can only be represented graphically.
In this respect the dreamer acts like the child or the artist. I have
asked many people how they would represent, for instance, the
abstract idea of charity on canvas or in marble, and I have never
found two individuals who gave me exactly the same description.
It is noteworthy that they always describe the first thing that comes
to their mind. One person may see a haggard, decrepit woman, in
a shawl, holding out her hand, and a well-dressed lady giving her

coins; another may see a little girl, ragged and frozen, begging alms, and a man pausing to help her. And so the pictures vary with each individual. But the significant thing that analysis reveals is that all these people invariably reproduce something that they had formerly experienced. When I asked, for instance, the person who gave me the first representation above to tell me what it suggested to him, he recalled a trip in Italy where he actually witnessed many such scenes in which an American woman would pause to give alms to some Italian beggar. Everybody has his own memory images for abstract ideas, which, although unconscious, have their peculiar, special meaning to him, and are represented in dreams in their original form.

Thus one of my patients associated in his dream a certain woman whom he knew with grief, because he thought of her as a "funeral bird" in the waking state. Likewise one may utilize in the dream any situation representing in his mind some idea or emotion, as a symbol for a certain feeling—a certain *Stimmung*. That is why it is wrong to attempt to interpret a dream without a knowledge of what the particular image represents in the particular person's mind. There are, to be sure, some dreams that evince ethnic symbols to which definite meanings may be ascribed, but one has to be extremely careful even with those; they may have an altogether different significance in different individuals. In other words, the meaning of the dream cannot usually be known unless the dreamer is well known to the analyst.

The following dream is a fine example of how abstract thoughts are visualized concretely in dreams. Miss S. dreamed that she *"passed a very tall building from which smoke came out. Then some flames burst forth. I could feel the awful heat."*

Analysis: Miss S. is not very fortunate in love. She is well-educated, intelligent, and good-looking, but a little too reserved to suit the average young man. She had many admirers, but for some reason or other the eligible man either failed to appear or made little progress toward matrimony. The day before the dream she visited a friend, who jokingly teased her about T., one of her admirers. She heard that he was a "steady caller," as she put it, and wanted to know when the engagement would be announced, and so on. Miss S. was embarrassed, and protested that there was no truth in the rumor, that it was nothing but idle gossip. Secretly, however, she cherished the thought that T. might marry her. The conversation ended with the significant remark from her friend, "Where there's smoke there must be fire." The dream fulfills her wish. The very tall building is herself—she is quite tall. She sees the smoke, then the flames, and can feel the awful heat. The saying, where there is smoke there is fire, is simply visualized by the dream, and as the dreamer is the chief actor of the dream, she is the tall building. A building or house, as is well known, is an old symbol for the body. We often speak of the body as the house we live in. Fire and heat are symbols of love.

An interesting little example of this identification of love with fire is found in one of Maupassant's short stories, "Always Lock the Door," which many of you perhaps have read. An old bachelor relates how his first real adventure in love miscarried by his failure to lock the door. He invited his fair friend to his private room one day, but to his great distress found that he had no fire because the chimney smoked. "The very evening before," he goes on to tell us, "I had spoken to my landlord, a retired shopkeeper, about it, and he had promised that he would send for the chimney sweep in a day or two to put it in order. As soon as she came in I said, 'There is no fire because my chimney smokes.' She did not even appear to hear me but stammered, 'That does not matter, I have . . .' "

Apart from the fact that the language of the dream is visual, another difficulty in dream analysis is that when the dream wishes to represent something hidden, it resorts to the same mechanisms that we use in the waking state when we wish to express something indirectly; that is to say, it has recourse to the double-entendre, distortions, and similar mechanisms. I need not give you examples; all you have to do is to think of the theater, of the different witticisms you hear and read; you will then realize that in a sense nobody expresses himself truthfully. Writers frequently resort to all sorts of detours, euphemisms, and symbolisms when they wish to express something which would sound either blunt or objectionable to polite society. Thus we find that the words thigh and staff are often used in the Bible to express that part which represents the male. No one is ashamed of taking nourishment, if he is hungry, or of quenching thirst, if he is thirsty, and that is why convenience dreams are quite open. But it is quite different with the other necessities of nature and with the functions appertaining to sex. Most people are trained to conceal all manifestations of the sex instinct, and, as a result, all expression in this sphere is indirect and distorted even in the waking state. It is instructive to note, for instance, some of the indirect expressions, such as the "curse" or the "old woman" that women use in referring to menstruation, a physiological function of which no one indeed need be ashamed. It is not at all surprising, then, that this secret language in which we speak about sex functions should so often baffle us.

A woman, for example, related to me the following dream: *"I was sleeping with a very disagreeable old lady and was quite disgusted."* She wished to know how such a dream could represent a wish. When I asked her for associations, she replied that nothing came to her mind; there was no one with whom she could identify this "old lady." Then I inquired what she had done the day previous to the dream, for we must remember to seek the determinant of the dream in that immediate past; the determinant is invariably an occurrence of the day previous to the dream. Some stimulus or impression through any one of the senses strikes, as it were, something similar in the mind with which the latter is engrossed, something that has emotional tone; and it is this that gives rise to the dream. I learned presently that the woman had been to a party the night before, at which one of the men proposed to take her horseback riding on Sunday. She went on to tell me that she feared that she could not accept the invitation; I inquired what reason she had for having to decline it and she informed me, after a little resistance, that she was afraid she might menstruate on that day.

It occurred to me then to ask her how she designates this function. "Why, we call it the 'disagreeable old woman,'" I learned. Here you have the analysis of the dream. When the young man invited her to go riding on Sunday, she wished to accept but expecting to menstruate on that day she had to give an indefinite answer. She turned to her sister, who understood her, and said: "I am afraid that the old woman might come." But as she was very anxious to go, she dreamed that she had already menstruated, that she had gone through with the disagreeable affair, that the "old lady" had already been with her. Upon superficial examination, then, it would have been nonsense to say that the dream represented a wish, but once one understands what is going on in the dreamer's mind, the deeper meaning becomes evident. I repeat, then, in order to analyze a dream it is absolutely necessary to know the dreamer well, not only as he is on parade, but also in those moments when he is most himself; you must know his intimate personality and his idiomatic expressions, as it were.

As an example of how dream analysis is made difficult by the "distortion" mechanisms, consider the following dream related to me by a patient. He dreamed he was translating Latin. *"I used the word 'whine' and the teacher said it should be 'when,' not 'whine.' "* Upon analysis it was found that the teacher in the dream represented myself, that the sessions with me reminded him of going to school again, of coming to me as to a teacher, and asking me questions. Associating further, he presently recalled that the week before he felt very much depressed; he came to me and complained bitterly. I told him not to "whine," that he would surely get well, but that it was only a question of time—i.e., "when." But why did he have to take up Latin? The first association that came to his mind apropos of that was that whenever he attended his Latin hour he was always nervous: he used an interlinear. I accordingly told him that he must be cheating with me, too, and he admitted that he was; he declared that there were certain things that he felt he could not reveal to me, that indeed it was rather foolish to think that one has to disclose everything to the physician. As you see, he was trying to use an interlinear again, but it did not work. I informed him that he would recover when he ceased whining; "when?" "When you begin to tell the truth; when you do not use an interlinear, when you will be willing to become independent of outside help."

Another example of distortion as found in dreams may be seen in the following case. One of my patients related to me how he was present at the usual New Year's Eve dinner that his father-in-law is accustomed to give to the whole family. At the appropriate moment the head of the family rose and made a speech in which he commented on every member of the family in his wonted good-natured way. In summing up the results of the past year, the old gentleman observed: "When I look upon the assets and the liabilities of the year, everyone of you is on the asset side." At this the patient smiled and thought to himself: "What about your son, the black sheep of the family, who is causing you so much trouble?" This son was quite a serious problem to his father; he was a ne'er-do-well, because he was absolutely unable to tell the truth; he was a pathological liar of the first order. Following this incident the patient dreamed that he saw a balance sheet. Under the assets were the names of the various members of the family, under the liabilities there was just the name of the son. But instead of "liabilities" the word was spelt thus: lie-abilities." The distortion in this dream is exactly of the same character as that found in wit. When a New York critic, for instance, in reviewing a play, the first two acts of which he evidently considered very good, the third rather poor, remarked: "The first two acts are capital, the third is labor," he was merely resorting to a technique which is by no means uncommon in dreams.

7. The Dream:
Its Function and Motive (*Continued*)

FREUD POSITED the fundamental principle that the motive of the dream is the wish. The individual craves for something, but as he cannot attain it in reality, by virtue of its unattainable or disagreeable nature, he realizes it in the dream. When someone assures you that he does not dream it simply means that he does not remember his dreams because he is little interested in the problem of dreams. Moreover, as dream function ceases on awakening, the repression reasserts itself. To be sure, some dream more than others. Of the many writers who have investigated this subject, there was Professor de Sanctis of Rome, who held that criminals do not dream. You can readily see what the explanation would be in the light of our theories. A criminal does not, as a rule, suppress much; whenever he wants something, he immediately sets about attaining it. When the average normal person sees something he wants, but that he knows is absolutely beyond his reach, he has learned not even to desire it consciously, in any real sense. The criminal does not, however, react in this manner. What has caught his fancy he immediately sets out to gain; by virtue of his weakmindedness no fear of society and law stays him. Because he does not suppress, he inevitably has nothing to dream about. I have found from my own experience, however, that De Sanctis was not entirely right in his conclusions; that whereas most criminals I have questioned did not really dream as much as the average person, they all admitted, nevertheless, that they dream occasionally. After all, there is no human being who can attain all his wishes.

In order to understand why the dream should thus be motivated by the wish it is necessary to have some idea of the mental evolution of the child from the very beginning of life. The average child expresses no wishes, all its wants are gratified by its mother; it lies in the cradle, frolics when satisfied, cries when hungry or uncomfortable. The only object the child needs from the outer world is its mother, and we say that it is in an *anaclitic* relation to her.[1] It leans on her for everything, and she is so constituted that she is always ready to supply the child's needs. The child does not, however, consider its mother as an outside object. It conceives of her as a part of itself. Gradually, as it grows older, its demands multiply and become more marked; it is then that the situation becomes a problem. Observe a child who does not as yet know how to express itself in speech and you will find that it wants everything that it sees in its environment; it will pull you to the object of its fancy; it craves to grasp and hold it. The older it grows, the more imperious become its wants. When it has learned to talk, you can readily see how powerfully the wish predominates in life; the child demands all the time; nothing can satisfy it.

The child starts its life with what we call the *pleasure principle;* it craves for nothing but pleasure. It eats, sleeps, and plays. When it is satisfied, it finds pleasure in sucking its thumb; and the Germans very aptly call thumb-sucking *Wonnesaugen,* pleasure sucking. When it has once experienced a pleasure it will always seek to reproduce it. Specialists have accordingly advised mothers not to rock a child to sleep. For motion is the most elementary form of pleasure and manifests itself throughout our lives. It may interest you to know that it is at the basis of our love for dancing and many other enjoyments. In all popular amusement resorts that I have visited both here and on the continent 99 per cent of the pleasure is essentially based on this principle. We find here a reversion to an infantile mode of gratification. This may be based on the fact that the cosmos in which we live is in constant motion.

Gradually, however, society begins to curb the child; parents cannot give it everything, and it feels, for the first time, the force of repression. The older it grows, the more it has to cope with the *principle of reality;* education and all other cultural forces are based on the realization that the individual has to be prepared to face that stern fact. If it does not adjust itself to reality, it will

[1] Anaclitic; from the Greek *ana-klino,* "to lean on."

flounder about and finally fail, despite everything one may do to help it. I saw a man many years ago whose parents were multimillionaires; he was brought up in the most attractive environment. He was destined for the Army, sent to West Point, stayed there a year and a half, and was then expelled on demerits; he would not follow the rules of discipline, nor study. When he related to me some of his escapades I could not help but wonder how he ever succeeded in staying at the Academy as long as he did. But he explained to me that his father was very influential and had considerable weight with the authorities. Expelled from West Point, he matriculated in other schools, but could not get along in any one of them. He was hail fellow well met with the students, for he had plenty of money to spend, but could not study. "Why should I? What's the use?" he would say to himself.

When his father died, he came into his own rights, and within two or three years he spent not only every cent he had, but all that his mother could give him. When the war broke out he enlisted. A great many of his old classmates were now colonels in the regular army; one of them who liked him needed a sergeant major and so took him into his regiment. He did quite well for a time, but was presently compelled to leave the post. He was sent to the guardhouse, and it was there that he passed most of his time throughout the whole war. He would have made a good fighter, but he was absolutely unable to adapt himself to the demands of reality; he could not be disciplined. He could not bear to have "those idiots," as he called some of his superiors, tell him what to do. Eventually a major of the Medical Corps advised him to see me. He was ragged when he came to me. I learned that he was a dishwasher in one of the hotels in the city and had just been "fired." The man was quite normal intellectually; he was merely a spoiled child, emotionally untrained and wild. He was able to do as he wanted when he had money, but now, as he put it, he was "down and out."

So it is absolutely impossible for the individual to get along in the world unless he adjusts himself to the principle of reality, which means nothing more nor less than the principle of inhibitions and repressions. Education, in the final analysis, is nothing but a means of equipping the individual with those experiences that have already been gathered by others, in order that he may thus be fitted to face and overcome the difficulties and obstacles of life, to cope with the problems of reality.

The child's education, accordingly, begins at a very early period. Long before he actually enters school he has been receiving at home instruction of the most vital importance; he has been learning all the while to *repress* most of his primitive impulses. Mothers and fathers who have carefully observed the development of the child know but too well that the first word that it learns to speak is "no," it is not "Dada" or "Mama." It either moves its head to say "no," or actually says it. The reason is clear. There is nothing that you wish the child to do that it wants to do; it always insists on doing things in its own way. Immediately corrective forces begin to operate and the individual who was destined by nature to be free and lead a lawless existence is curbed finally to the demands of actual life.

Centuries of civilization have left their mark upon us, and we must now live accordingly. No one, I dare say, would wish to live after the manner of our primitive ancestors. There is, therefore, a constant struggle; no one likes to submit to the repression that the inhibitory aspects of civilization demand; no one finds it easy to repress the primitive impulses. Thus it may be said in truth that the individual begins with "no" from his very infancy, and continues to declare it more and more vociferously until his death. His life, one might say, is one long struggle, one bitter revolt. In the light of this principle the ideal of absolute independence and happiness takes on a rather somber aspect. For no matter what you may do for the individual, he cannot be in any final sense happy or independent, for what he really wants is something that goes back to his infantile life. In the very nature of things, then, we can never be satisfied; no individual can ever be absolutely contented with his environment; there is always room for improvement.

There is a story that runs through my mind which some of you may have heard. It is the story of a king whose only child, a little girl, became ill. He had the very best doctors attending her; the chief physician finally informed him that nothing could be done to save the child. The king waxed angry. "You mean to say that with all your knowledge and skill you cannot do anything for the child?" he demanded. "It suffers from a condition that is incurable," replied the physician. The king became furious and began

to threaten. At last one of the doctors declared that there was but
one thing that could cure the child, and that was for her to wear the
shirt of one who was perfectly happy. The king was glad, for he
thought that that was simple enough. Immediately he had the news
heralded through the town. But it was impossible to find such a
person. Meanwhile the child's condition was growing more serious
and the king was in great distress. Immersed in dark thoughts,
he took a walk to the outskirts of the city. Presently he met a young
ragamuffin, a shepherd boy, whistling and very joyful. "You seem
to be very happy," said the king. "Yes," answered the boy. "But
do tell me, what makes you so happy?" inquired the king. "Why
shouldn't I be? Everything is lovely. Jane loves me and I am going
to marry her soon. I just feel fine." "Did you hear that the king is
looking for someone who is perfectly happy?" the king continued.
"Yes, I heard of it, but I haven't a shirt," was the shepherd's reply.
You see, only a person who can be satisfied with having no shirt
can really be happy, but are there such persons outside the realm
of fancy?

Now the significant thing to note is that although society has
actually succeeded in training the individual to forego and renounce
and thus adjust himself to prevailing conditions, we nevertheless
find, when we examine his intimate psychic recesses, that he really
never foregoes his desires absolutely, that he has a way of realizing
them. In his dreams, symptoms, and in the manifold unconscious
activities of everyday life the individual is still able to realize his
wishes more or less.

Consider for a moment a child who is little acquainted with the
restraining force of reality and gratification in phantasy. I once
observed a little girl of about four years of age who took a fancy
to a little wagon that another child was playing with. She went
directly up to her, got hold of the string, and wanted to take away
the little cart, but at the owner's loud protests the nurse soon
hurried up and compelled her to leave. The little girl's mother rep-
rimanded her in these words, "You must not do that; that's not
yours; that's the other little girl's wagon." The little girl cried so
bitterly that her mother finally gave her some chalk to play with.
Presently she drew some figure on the sidewalk and pointing to it
cried: "Here's a little wagon." I can assure you there was hardly
any resemblance to the real object, but there was enough likeness

there to impress the child. In other words, the little girl actually realized or strove to realize her wish: she now had that toy that she wanted so badly.

A little girl continued to cry for candy until she finally fell asleep. She awoke the next morning crying, and when asked for the reason, said that someone took away her box of chocolate almonds; she insisted that she had them in bed. She was only a little more than two years old and was barely able to talk. Undoubtedly the child dreamed that she had a big box of chocolate almonds, thus actually realizing her wish, and unable to distinguish between dream and reality, cried on awaking.

As the child grows older, however, one may observe how the wish becomes more and more distorted in the dream. There are more and more complex mechanisms appearing which reveal that the child's nature is growing more and more comprehensive; so long as its mode of reaction was simple, the dreams were simple. There is no difficulty in analyzing a child's dream before the age of five; it is later that the force of repression begins to manifest itself. It is noteworthy that the child also develops at this time a sense of humor. As we have already seen, humor and wit are nothing but modes of obtaining pleasure through a distortion of words and ideas, and as long as the child is young, it has no need for them. When a child bursts out in laughter, it does so because someone else laughs, it is not a spontaneous activity. Gradually children develop more ideas and suppress considerably more; laughter is then the result of complicated stimuli. In my walks with my little girl in the park I used to take her to a place where horses were usually watered. For about a year, every time I passed it, I would remark: "Here we bring the 'autos' to be watered," to which she answered nothing. One day I made the same remark, and she looked at me quizzically, smiled, and said: "Autos don't have to be watered." When she came home she told her mother of the funny thing I had said. It is significant that her dreams at this period began to assume a distorted aspect; she already showed all the marks of a complex mind; the associations were no longer simple.

The dream assumes, then, a more and more complex and distorted character as the child grows older. Thus a little boy is in the zoological garden, and seeing a tiger for the first time in his life, is very much attracted by the animal and remarks to his father,

"Wouldn't it be nice if we had a tiger home?" The father tells him that such a thing would be altogether impossible in an apartment. The next morning the boy tells his father he dreamed that they had five little tigers in the bird cage. So you see, since, as it appeared to him, the difficulty lay merely in the size of the animal, he solved it in the dream by appreciably reducing it. When this boy was a year older he wanted a pony. He asked his grandfather to buy him one, and the old man said he would try to do so; but apparently he never meant it seriously, for when Christmas came, the boy had to go without one and his disappointment was keen. His father explained to him that the old man was only joking, for he could not afford the purchase. Then the little boy dreamed that he had a pony, and it was lame, and he did not want it. You see how he reconciled himself. So, as the child grows older, the dream becomes more and more complex, and, consequently, with it the wish expression.

The following dreams illustrate remarkably well the essential point I am trying to bring home to you, namely, that the dream, in the final analysis, is nothing but a concrete visualization of a hidden wish. The first of these was brought to me by a very active and intelligent woman, and runs as follows:

"I was in a train and had a baby wrapped up in a blanket, and a Negro nurse. The baby was sleeping at the foot of the bed. I was in bed. The nurse was sitting on a bench in front. There came people—a whole crowd of them—from a certain club, and I said I had to nurse the baby. I looked to see whether he was awake, because he had been so very quiet. I saw that the child had a man's face; he smiled at me and said, 'I can wait; I am not hungry!'"

Now the dream appeared strange and comical to the dreamer. When she had related it to me, she laughed and observed, "Isn't that funny? I wonder what you can make out of it?" Knowing the patient well, it was no difficult matter to interpret the dream. She informed me that the previous evening she gave a dinner to a gentleman who was lecturing at this club of which we hear in the dream. It is an association which she founded about twenty years before for the advancement of child study, and its demands upon her time and attention were very great. Most of the duties devolved upon her, and she was therefore kept constantly busy. She heaved a sigh of relief when the dinner was over, and bewailed her lot to her husband, who remarked: "It's about time they got someone else to do the work. The association is now grown up and I should think there would be a great many others who could take your place." That was what she really wished. We now see how ingeniously the idea is represented: the baby in the dream is this association devoted to child study which she has founded and which she now desires to be sufficiently grown up to take care of itself and relieve her of her many duties. She wonders whether the child was awake, "he was so quiet"; we see here her wish that the association would not tax so much of her time. And, further; when she looks at the child she finds that he is grown up; he says, "I can wait; I am not hungry." We see here the concrete visualization of what her husband said, "The association is grown up and could get along without you." The dream thus realizes her wish: the association is grown up and can get along without her constant attention; the baby can get along without her constant nursing and care. "I can wait; I am not hungry," he assures her.

Miss W., a college student of about twenty, related to me the following dream: *"I saw Apollo embracing Venus de Milo, and then Apollo stabbed her in the breast."* The dreamer awoke in a state of anxiety almost like a nightmare. As we look at the dream, it does not seem to represent a wish, and, what is more, it does not contain the dreamer. Before proceeding any further, then, permit me at once to impress upon your mind that whenever you cannot find the dreamer, look for him under the guise of the dream's central or predominant character. That is the only way to get at the heart of the situation. If the dreamer is a man, he is usually concealed in the hero of the dream; if a woman, in the heroine. Remember also that it makes no difference whether he is represented by human beings or by animals. A man, for example, told me recently how he dreamed that two cats were engaged in a boxing match, how, strange to say, they were all the while exchanging bitter words, and how, finally, the smaller cat succeeded in "knocking out" the bigger opponent. When we resorted to continuous association, the dreamer recalled a scene he witnessed on the day before the dream, in the college gymnasium, in which two men were boxing; one was heavy and tall, the other was light and "quick as a cat." The latter, because of his agility, "knocked out" his adversary. If I were to describe to you the dream in full, you would readily see that the dreamer identified himself with the successful boxer; he takes, therefore, a situation in which he overcomes an individual whom he would like to "knock out" in reality, and because of the peculiarly intimate relation in his mind between the agility of the boxer and a cat, he transforms it entirely into a fight between two cats.

In this intimate relation existing between the dreamer and the central character in the dream there is a marked analogy to the relation that we find between the author and his work. In the final analysis we may say that a book invariably describes its author, directly or indirectly. He is always the central figure in the story, and if, like Bernard Shaw, he can talk under five or ten characters it merely shows that he is by just that much the more gifted and versatile author. The dominant ideas expressed are his ideas; they may be traced back ultimately to the one source—his own personality. That is why the hero generally overcomes all vicissitudes, is never vanquished. For unless the author is masochistic,[2] he does not wish to die or be conquered. In this connection I cannot help but relate to you a case about which a lawyer consulted me some years ago. The story received quite a bit of notoriety in New York. A young woman entered suit against her elderly wealthy husband for separation and alimony. She was said to be of a shady reputation and merely desired to get rid of him so that she could live with another man. The respondent's lawyer was anxious to know whether I could do anything to help him. Among the things he had with him was a typewritten manuscript which was written by the young woman; it was a story that she intended for publication. When I read it, I noted quite a number of significant things from which one was able to draw many conclusions. For one thing, I felt quite convinced that the authoress was carrying on an affair with the head waiter in some New York restaurant, for it was nothing short of such stuff from which she fashioned her hero. What was just as significant, the restaurant that she described tallied remarkably with several on Broadway. When I expressed my mind in

[2]Masochism is passive pleasure in pain.

the matter to the lawyer, I learned that it was just such a "character" that was suspected as the paramour. Following this clue, detectives soon corroborated my conclusion completely.

According, then, to this rule as to the dreamer's place in the dream, I could at once see the character behind whose skin, so to say, Miss W. lay concealed. I knew that Venus must undoubtedly represent the dreamer. To my query as to what she knew of the ancient goddess she replied tersely: "Oh! I just love her!" She then continued to inform me that she had a picture of Venus both in her room at college and at home. I could now plainly see why she identified herself with her. Upon investigating further, I found that Miss W. would often argue quite warmly with her roommate at college when they both undressed on retiring as to which of the two resembled Venus more, and that the final decision was in the former's favor. We thus see how she actually identified herself with Venus.

By way of another digression, I may remark that I have always found it instructive to question people as to whom in history they consider the greatest personage, their ideal character. There is, of course, the underlying assumption here that the individual who represents this idea is the one with whom we consciously or unconsciously identify ourselves. In a little paper that I have written on the subject[3] I have pointed out that most of the persons whom I have questioned mentioned Napoleon as their ideal character; and though 60 per cent of them were Christians only two mentioned Jesus. More than 90 per cent of those whom I questioned took individuals like Napoleon as their ideal type; Lincoln took second place. But we must bear in mind that the latter was far from being a weakling, that, on the other hand, he was in more than one sense an unusually strong man. I have drawn some significant conclusions from the data thus collected and have designated the individual's particular answer as his "empathic index." The latter shows the character one identifies himself with, whom one tries to emulate unconsciously, you might say. There is no doubt that Napoleon represents the very acme of primitivity; and the secret of the profound fascination that he exerts over us lies undoubtedly in the fact that he is an embodiment of those very things that we unconsciously and even consciously admire. There are many other

[3] "The Empathic Index," *Medical Record*, February 1920.

interesting considerations about the empathic index that we might dwell on, but for our purpose now I merely wish to point out that when a person states that he most admires this or that character, then it is that character after whom he desires to be modeled or whom he desires to emulate—like master like man, as it is said.

It is quite evident, then, that Miss W. wished to look like Venus. Now it is natural that if Venus is going to have an *affaire de cœur,* it cannot be with a common mortal of today, it has to be with Apollo. When I asked her to tell me something of Apollo, she said: "Well, I can tell you the story about him from mythology." I asked her to describe how he looked in the dream and she replied: "Just like that lieutenant I told you about." The latter was a young man with whom she had danced the night before. When she had described Apollo I found that she had at least a half-dozen men in that one character. In other words, this Apollo of hers was indeed a very modern gentleman; he was a *condensation,* a fusion of a great many individuals whom she knew. This is nothing unusual. Ask a man, for instance, to describe his ideal woman and he will draw on ever so many women to describe her; she must be as tall as Miss So-and-so, have hair like Miss Brown's, et cetera.

One man to whom I put the question had no less than the attributes of fifteen women in his conception of his ideal wife. Miss W. met the lieutenant with whom she associated Apollo at a war-camp sociable where the men who were presently to leave for overseas were entertained. Flushed and stimulated by the dance, she came home, feeling a sense of "pity" for this aviator who, in his full manhood and strength, was going forth to the war perhaps never to return; and indeed did he not express that very sentiment to her himself? He had taken her home on the night of the dance and on parting asked her to kiss him good-by, but she had refused. Of course, later, on retiring to bed, she was sorry that she had denied him that request. We may thus see that the whole scene had a distinct erotic setting. Analysis reveals that the dream represented the realization of a wish which could just as well have been open. If the young woman had not been brought up in the manner that she was, she could have consciously thought to herself, "Yes, I am very pleased with the lieutenant, and how I do wish he were here to court me." But such was her moral training at home that she did not dare think of such a thing: she was trained to regard such a thought as immoral and ugly. And so in repressing this very thought she has this particular dream. I should add that she awoke markedly excited and with a feeling of palpitation of the heart. We may accordingly designate her dream as one of anxiety, and, like all dreams of this type, it denoted gross sex, physical sex. The young woman never consciously thought of that in the waking state, of course; all that she was aware of was the usual stimulation that any refined and modest girl would experience on a similar occasion.

The question now presents itself: What does the dream represent? To answer this, we must turn our attention for a moment to a brief consideration of a highly interesting psychological mechanism often encountered in the unconscious mentation of dreams and myths. Whenever we wish to speak in the waking state about any delicate situation that refers to the lower part of the body, we displace it to the upper part of the body. A woman suffering from some digestive disturbance will usually declare, when questioned about her condition, that she merely has a cold. Instead of telling the truth, menstruating women will very often veil their condition by some such general remark as that they are ill-disposed, or that they have a cold or throat trouble. In other words, they show a mechanism which is well known in symptoms and dreams, namely, the *displacement from below to above*.

If we bear in mind now that the dream simply represented a situation below the waistline, we can readily see its concealed meaning: it was a gross sex wish, the stabbing denoting coitus, a situation which no woman of her type would ever have allowed herself to think of in the waking state. As we have said again and again, it does not matter whether one thinks of these things consciously. Nature demands expression of these powerful emotional and instinctive forces at a certain age in life, and whether we are consciously aware of them or not—particularly if we are not—they manifest themselves in just such ways. We find such an anxiety dream about being stabbed, all because to the average cultured, unmarried woman coitus and everything directly or indirectly associated with it are painted in horrible colors; women are made to feel that it entails very much pain, and particularly if it is illicit, that it represents an experience almost equivalent to death. Those were, then, the feelings that passed through the woman's unconscious mind and found concealed expression in the dream. Thus the dream is not at all so mysterious as we might at first have thought; its deeper meaning becomes clear to us, if we only understand the mechanisms which one has to look for in any unconscious mentation. We said that the dreamer awakened with anxiety and that we dealt with a dream akin to a nightmare. We do not call it precisely a nightmare because it did not contain the amount of anxiety that is usually found in a nightmare, but it was very much like one. Miss W. was awakened by the dream because, although she was asleep, the situation which the dream strove to realize for her organism was too crude for this inexperienced girl. In other words, the mind made an effort to stop this realization by waking the dreamer. Yet the dream did realize the coital wish of which Miss W. never thought when she fancied how pleasant it would have been to be kissed by the handsome lieutenant. The unconscious, or the Id-tendencies of which we shall speak later, recognizes no cultural inhibitions.

Consider with me now the following dream related to me by a patient:

> "*I was discussing some business deal with a prospective partner; I listened in silence and then said: 'You can't put that over on me.' I said that because he put his foot on my knee. I got hold of him by the leg, threw him around and right over my head; he fell on his head to the ground and broke his neck. He was dead. I then went out and found my mother because I was very much afraid; I feared that I would be arrested.*"

Here, of course, there is no difficulty in finding the chief actor; he certainly cannot be the dead man, he must be the dreamer himself. The man who related the dream to me was an officer who had recently returned from the war; he told me that he was seeking new business connections, for his old association was not of the kind that he desired, that he felt that now he was back, it was the opportune time to make a new and better start. With this in mind, he had discussed the matter with different people. The determinant of the dream was a conference, then, with a prospective partner on a new business venture. We find here the clue to the dream. When I questioned him about the action in the dream—throwing the man down and breaking his neck—he replied that he could only recall the following: "When I was at college on the football team I played end. The particular year that I have in mind the other team was much heavier than ours and they beat us very badly. The score was —well, I am ashamed to tell it to you even now—48 to 0." Mark how deeply he felt over the incident, though it was now many years since it had occurred. Then he continued to inform me that the next year they played the same team, and knowing the terrible defeat they suffered at its hands previously, they practiced a great deal and succeeded in beating the rival team. He related how, when the latter began to repeat its old tactics, he was all prepared for them, how he always succeeded in throwing over his opponent, and how he incapacitated one of the adversaries for the rest of the game. In other words, the second year he won; the first year he was badly beaten. I asked him about his mother in the dream and he went on to say that the game was so extremely rough that his mother, who came to see it, was at the very beginning of the game so disturbed and frightened that she had to leave the stand and sat apart crying, fearing that something serious would inevitably result from such a rough-and-tumble contest. As a matter of fact, only three of the original players went through with the game; as for himself, he became delirious and was in such a serious condition when finally brought out after the game that his mother actually had to take him in hand and nurse him back to life, as it were.

The question is, "Why should all these things be bound up with the dream?" As you see, there is a similar situation now: he was in business and considered it a failure; he wanted something new. He is about to go into a new line of work; and the same situation of suffering a defeat before and now taking up something new in which he was to be as successful as in the second football game (or, in other words, in which he was to win) presents itself. He succeeds so well that he "knocks" out his partner at once! "Putting something over on him," as he expressed it, is actually true, it is actually acted out in the dream: "The partner put his foot on my (the dreamer's) knee"; we have an actual picture of it in the dream. Here you see that the whole past associated with the football game is symbolic of the present situation; in other words, he was a failure the first time, a winner the second time. Now the idea in his mind is: "I would like to form a partnership in which I am successful"; and as it is an anticipation dream, he sees himself already win-ning, i.e., acting as he did in the football game in which he was not at all concerned whether he killed his opponent or not, provided he was successful.

The above dream clearly reveals the three temporal strata of every dream—first, the present (trying to get into a new business); second, the past (the present situation becomes associated with a similar situation in the past. We must remember that there are so many experiences that occur in one's life that there is no situation of today that will not revive some similar situation in the past); third, the remote past or infantile. There is no dream, however simple, that does not show these three strata. Your dream today touches, directly or indirectly, something of yesterday; it is absurd to think that we dream merely of some trifle that is only of importance to the immediate present. In the above dream we see how the particular present situation was expressed symbolically by some situation of the past; and when we go further with the analysis, we find that the same tracks, as it were, existed in the person's childhood. At this earlier period he had an older brother who constantly dominated him, "put it over on him," and he was thus prepared, we might say, to meet similar situations later in life. That is why it is so important that you understand these mechanisms; for when, as parents, you find that a child is handicapped in this way, it will be your duty to take a special attitude toward the problem; you must not allow the older child to dominate the younger one. As teachers, you must always see to it that the child who is considerably younger than the average should not be placed in a class of older children, even if he is up to the mark intellectually. Children should mix with those of their own mental and physical stature, and that is usually possible only with those of the same age. The so-called smart child who is put with considerably older children is seriously harmed thereby; when he grows up he is forever harassed by a feeling of inferiority.

I have seen many people who have gone through school by the age of, let us say, fourteen or fifteen, when they should have finished at sixteen and seventeen; they were intellectually precocious, but emotionally they were always handicapped. They were called "Shorty" or "Kid" at school, and it was in such emotional states that they remained throughout life, all because they saw the school situation everywhere, whether it really existed or not; they followed the path of the acquired tendency. As I have reiterated so frequently, certain tracks are laid out from the very beginning and the individual always follows them. In brief, one might say that our present acts, if not exact reproductions of the past, are certainly analogous to it; they are, so to speak, symbolic of the past.

Dreams and Symptoms Analogous

In the beginning of this survey we pointed out that such imperfect analogies, such symbolic expressions as are found in dreams are found also in symptoms. It matters not how bizarre, how seemingly senseless the patient's symptom may be, it has a definite meaning in his life; it bears an intimate relation to his inner problems and conflicts; and it is only by understanding it that we can comprehend and evaluate his attitude toward the world.

Years ago Miss R., a young woman in her early twenties, was brought to me by her mother. The history of the case was that for months she had been very depressed; she ate very little and spent most of her time crying; she suffered from insomnia and thought of suicide. She had been seen by many physicians, some of whom designated her condition as nervousness, others as mental depression. I spoke to the parent before I saw the patient. She talked about the daughter's condition in the characteristic fashion of the grieved and devoted mother, and remarked sadly: "It's too bad, Doctor, such a fine girl! She always stayed at home, never went out with the boys, and was so well-behaved; and now she has been sick so long." When I turned to the girl and asked her why she was so depressed, she began to cry, and upon urging her to speak, she declared that she was unworthy, that she had committed all kinds of transgressions. Upon being pressed for further explanation, she replied that she had drowned some pups; whereupon the mother immediately interposed, "But, Doctor, that happened when she was a little bit of a girl, about twenty years ago, and I am sure she did not do it." However that may be, there was no need for the mother to attempt to exonerate her daughter, for the moment I learned that this incident went ever so many years back, I had all good reason to pause and wonder why a person should cry today over what had occurred twenty years ago, and what, up to a few months ago, had never been given the slightest thought. Moreover, such episodes are rarely impressive to the extent of being taken up again so many years later in life.

A patient like Miss R. may be variously diagnosed: she may be said to be merely nervous; or her condition may be described as manic-depressive psychosis, by which we mean that she suffered from a form of emotional disturbance which comes in certain cycles, periodically, as we said previously; sometimes the patient is manic, sometimes depressed. In this particular case there was no history of any previous attacks, nor was there any family history to justify a tendency to such attacks, as one usually finds in the real cases of manic-depressive psychoses. After observing her for a week I diagnosed her condition as a case of anxiety hysteria with some reactive depression.

When we attempt to help the patient, we must depend in large measure upon his co-operation and treat the symptom just as we treat a dream. Now the dream that one remembers we call the "manifest" dream; in analyzing it we are aiming to get at its "latent" content. The manifest dream may require perhaps just two lines to describe, but when we begin to take down the associations to it, or, in other words, to discover its "latent" content, we may have to write ten pages or even more. The same thing holds true of symptoms. You see a patient in the hospital hallucinating; she hears voices. Ask her who it is that is talking to her and she will inform you that it is "Mr. Brown." Upon investigation you will find that the latter had paid her attention and that she was in love with him; now she is hallucinating, thinking that he is speaking to her. You find the latent content in order to determine the nature and mechanism of the patient's symptom.

I saw Miss R. for a week or two; she would always come with her mother and after each interview the parent would come into my consulting room in the characteristic, apprehensive manner of a mother and would repeat, in passing: "Isn't it terrible, Doctor, that such a misfortune should befall so nice a girl! She never went out with boys, she was always so well-behaved!" I began to feel that the mother was protesting too much, laying undue emphasis on her daughter's being such a "nice" girl. I had no doubt whatsoever that she actually believed what she said and, as for myself, I had no reason to question its veracity, but I was just struck by the emphasis. We say in our work that there is a definite relation between the "noöpsyche" and the "thymopsyche," between the mind and the emotions; they are directly proportional in relation. In other words, if I try to impress you with certain facts, I do not act like a person who would inform you that there is a fire in the building; if I did, the emotional element would be disproportionate to the idea involved. With this key of undue emphasis, then, I began to suspect that there must be something behind the mother's assurance. One could see that the mother in repeating those words to me was really assuring herself; that she undoubtedly reacted to an unconscious doubt about her daughter's proper behavior. So I began to work on this theory, following the paraphrased detective formula, *"cherchez l'homme."* I inquired into the patient's love life, but she was reluctant to speak about it. She simply assured me that she was leading the usual average life. To my question whether she had a love affair she showed an unusual emotional reaction: she burst into tears, and as I was unable to calm her the session had to be ended. The next time she came I began the analysis, and again she cried; but emotions are exhaustible, so presently her tears were spent and she began to talk.

In analyzing her symptoms, I asked myself: "What are the elements that enter into them?" Or, in other words, "Why does this woman cry today over an episode of twenty years ago?" Every emotion that a person experiences must have some reason for its existence, and if you cannot find that reason in the present, you may be quite sure that the affect is displaced to some situation to which it does not strictly belong but with which it has become connected by some direct or indirect association. Now whenever an affect has to be displaced, it simply means that it cannot remain with the original episode but must be transferred to some other situation. There was no reason for the woman's crying over a trifling and insignificant episode that occurred far back in her childhood. One might dislike to witness pups being drowned, but there is no reason why one should continue to wail over it for months, after it was seemingly forgotten for about twenty years. I was urged, then, to the conclusion that the episode relating to the pups was only a concealing memory, it was a memory which she brought to the surface and retained in consciousness simply because a similar episode occurred in the present which had to be concealed.

When we analyze the episode we find that it involves essentially the destruction of young life, pups, by water. That is its intrinsic significance. Now just as in the last dream we considered, the present situation showed a direct analogy to some situation in the past, a business proposition became identified by analogy with a football game, so we have to discover in the symptom some fundamental element that it may have in common with the early childhood reminiscence. The main element in the symptom that one should seek as an analogy would be some form of destruction of life, associated somehow with water, which must have occurred later in this young woman's life, because we are always deeply affected and stirred by some present not by some past circumstance. I told her, accordingly, that I suspected that she had some sexual trouble, that it had something to do with an abortion or some similar experience; whereupon she disclosed to me the whole state of affairs. She informed me that she had kept company with a young man who would regularly call at her home, that when, to her great dismay, she found herself pregnant and informed him about it, he upbraided and repulsed her, accusing her of having had sexual relations with some other man. She pleaded with him and he finally took her to a midwife, who performed an abortion. But that did not end here. Following this, she was compelled to treat herself with douches, and as she did not know how to take them they caused her considerable trouble and worriment. Add to this the fact that the entire affair had to be concealed from her mother and you can readily imagine in what a pitiable plight the poor girl found herself.

When things were settled presently, from a medical viewpoint at any rate, she began to feel the mortification of the past, and it was about six or eight weeks following the painful experience that she had the nervous breakdown. In other words, she could no longer conceal the terrible misfortune that she had to go through; it demanded some outlet, some form of expression. But as she could not openly dwell on it, she unconsciously took some similar situation in the past and endowed it with all the intensity of her actual state of feeling. Shall I repeat again that whatever we experience, no matter whether it be at the age of two, three, or four, is always retained in the mind and recalled on the appropriate occasion? The present episode keeps on revolving in the mind until it falls into the special track that was laid out for it, as it were, from the very beginning, because of some intrinsic element of similarity it bears to the early experience. And when we remember how many and how diverse are the impressions we receive every day, we will not find it hard to see that nothing that happens today cannot find an analogy in something that has occurred in the past. Recall that impression about the drowning pups deep down in the unconscious; here is this powerful, conscious emotion which has to be suppressed because she cannot consciously dwell on it, and naturally, by analogy, it falls into the track of that early childhood experience. The same elements are there: the attributes of both experiences are analogous, that is, attribute for attribute.

I may perhaps make this a little clearer by an illustration from my own experience. One very frosty evening last year I was walking through the street with my dog when his attention was attracted by sounds coming from a paper bundle lying in the middle of the road. I heard a low, moaning sound coming from it and I was naturally interested to know what it could be. On coming up to it I found two little pups that some hardhearted person must have exposed with the hope, apparently, that they would freeze to death or be run over and killed. And here is the significant thing: that very night I had a dream, the latent content of which elicited a little episode that I heard related when I was a boy of surely no more than eight years old. It was about some peasant who was hung because he exposed two of his own babies on a cold, wintry night, thus causing their death, simply to please his second wife, who hated them and would not let them in the house. It was the first time I had heard of an execution and it evidently made a profound impression upon me. But as far as I know, I had never thought of the episode since then. But you see the moment I saw those little pups exposed to the freezing weather, that early childhood experience was unconsciously revived together with all its attending emotions. That is the way the mind works: a present situation may evoke from the past some early impression by reason of the former's intrinsic element of contrast or analogy to the early experience. We may see, then, that in the case of Miss R. the concealing memory simply represented what happened later. It is interesting to mark that the latent content required about three or four weeks to reveal, whereas the manifest content was always on the surface.

The moment the young woman began to grope about unconsciously for a reason why she could cry about her condition in public, that episode from the remote past was revived because of its intrinsic resemblance to the present situation. It was immediately invested with all the affects, and, what is more, she herself did not have the least thought that it was really over the later episode that she was crying. She did not deliberately take up that early childhood memory and wail over it; it was all unconscious on her part. What she really, then, cried over was the immediate past, the terrible anguish and keen disappointment that she recently had to bear. She had, accordingly, typical symptoms of anxiety hysteria with a depression which seemed to resemble the manic-depressive type of psychosis but was reactive to her sad experience. Thus, then, we see that the dream and the symptom show the same mechanisms—both show a definite relation to the inner life of the person, both are incursions into consciousness from the unconscious, and that, in fine, it is necessary to get at what we call their "latent" contents to grasp their essential significance and meaning.

8. Types of Dreams

Anxiety Dreams

WE HAVE DISCUSSED thus far dreams that either represent open wishes, like convenience dreams, or are hidden realizations of a repressed wish. The latter type, of course, is the more usual, and I have given you a number of examples of it. There is another form of dreams which realizes fears, as it were, and which we call anxiety dreams; we say that the anxiety there replaces the libido or the desire. The individual is overwhelmed with a sense of terror, he wakes up terrified and trembling. It is the sort of dream which awakened Miss W. and which is commonly known as a nightmare, and to one unacquainted with the deeper mechanisms of dream formation it does not seem to represent a wish. In order to understand it, it is necessary to understand what we mean by anxiety.

Anxiety[1] or fear occurs in two forms. In the normal form, it is a protective mechanism which is found in every individual. The child is endowed with a certain amount of fear from its very birth. It is needless to say that an animal's life would be seriously jeopardized if it knew no fear. But there is another type of fear or anxiety, manifesting itself in neurotic disturbances, that we recognize as being distinctly abnormal. Take, for instance, the case of a man who is afraid to go out into the street lest he be run over; he realizes too well how absurd and ill-grounded is his apprehension, but, willy nilly, he is afraid to leave the house. Another person may be afraid to go near a window, lest he jump out. Perhaps it is perfectly natural for the average person to experience some sense of uneasiness when standing near a high open window, but he is not going to be apprehensive to the point where he actually fears to go

[1] S. Freud: *Inhibition, Symptom and Anxiety*, 1947.

near it; yet in some nervous disturbances a person will, under no circumstances, go near a window, because he is afraid of falling out. Likewise, some people may refuse to cross bridges: "Suppose the bridge breaks," they will argue. They may be well-trained engineers and realize that it is impossible or most improbable, but they are fearful despite all assurance. Such fears, in other words, are distinctly pathological and are referred to as *phobias*.

When we analyze cases of phobias and anxiety states we find that it is not the immediate particular situation, that, to be more explicit, it is not the perception of the probable immediate danger that is the cause of the fear, but rather some altogether different and basic condition; in other words, we find that the anxiety is merely displaced from a condition to which it properly belongs to an altogether different idea. We have already noted this displacement of anxiety when we spoke about the psychology of the phobia of burglars. It was observed also that this phobia is usually found in women who are suffering from a lack of sexual outlet. We saw that what lies back of it is nothing but the unconscious craving for gross or physical sex; but as the patient cannot harbor such thoughts openly, the repressed craving unconsciously attaches itself to some analogous situation which can be openly dwelt on—an illicit intrusion into her private room for which she cannot be held responsible. It is only a disguised expression of the real craving. The biological demands of life crave for an outlet, but the individual has been so well trained by society, or, in other words, the repression has been carried to such a point that she would not dare even admit the real situation to herself. The craving manifests itself, therefore, in this disguised form.

As I have reiterated so frequently in the past, it matters very little how exacting and scrupulous may be our moral teachings and requirements, the actual biological laws or demands of the human organism are nevertheless of paramount consideration. Biology teaches us that as the individual grows older it becomes more and more patent what his mission in this world is to be—namely, to mate and propagate his kind. This sexual function, as it is generally termed, appears from the very beginning of our existence, and assumes more and more significance and importance with the advance and development of the individual. We use the word "sex," of course, in its very broadest sense, as being synonymous with love, but it may interest you to know that if you trace the origin of the word "love," you will find that it is derived from a word in Sanskrit which denotes "lust"; it is significant that the word for "love" in Hebrew means also "lust." The ancients, apparently, have made no mistake about the meaning of love; to them there was certainly a complete identification of love and what we generally consider, with no little degree of disparagement, as being grossly physical or sensual, or sex. It is only with the advance of Christian civilization that this marked contrast has grown up, that one speaks about sex as something base and ugly and love as that divine fire of which the poet speaks so eloquently.

As a matter of fact, love and sex are one and the same thing; we cannot have one without the other. It is useless to delude ourselves into the belief that one side of the fact is sublime while the other that has to do with the service of propagation is low and degrading. Of course there is just this much to be said—the modern individual cannot use any of his functions in the manner of our primitive ancestors, and our behavior in mating is as different from that of the savage as the function of nourishment in modern man is different from that in his primitive brother. We have learned that certain things are incompatible with our environment. But it would be just as ridiculous to suppose that we can dispense with the natural sex function on that account as it would be to suppose that we can dispense with food, because we do not eat like the savage. The fundamental necessity remains, and no law can be evolved that will eliminate it.

To be sure we had no quarrels with the sex function as long as we considered it beautiful and sacred. We know how much it was revered in early religions. Likewise the child sees nothing ugly or immoral in sex; we know how it shows no scruples in exposing itself naked. But it learns, in time, to control and repress, to conceal what would be obnoxious to its environment. Thus the sex impulses have had to be concealed more and more as time went on. What is more, it was found necessary with the advance of civilization to defer the mating process. Animals begin to manifest the sex instinct at an early age, soon after they begin to walk. The same is found among primitive races. Among the natives of New Guinea many travelers have reported sexual practices among children of six and seven years. The situation is different in modern times: civilization has found that it is impossible to indulge in sex at the time it openly manifests itself, and sexual gratification, therefore, must be deferred for many years. Thus with the advance of centuries of civilization, particularly with the rise and spread of Christianity, the sex instincts have been more and more repressed, so that now the whole instinct is so distorted that it appears to the individual to be incomprehensible and baffling to the last degree, and it is actually necessary to enlighten modern men and women in matters sexual. I say this advisedly. But the fact remains that the urge is there, and whether the individual desires it or not, it always manifests itself.

Hence sex in our sense is only a part of the mating impulse which we include in the general term love. Any manifestation of love, be it in the child or the adult, may be considered as a phase of sex. We may therefore explain on this same basis any phobia or pathological fear even in children, except, of course, that we must bear in mind that here the phobia deals with infantile love. Only four or five weeks ago a little girl of ten was brought to me because she was afraid that burglars might enter her room; she absolutely would not sleep alone. Formerly she was accustomed to sleep in a room all by herself, but now she was so afraid that the only way to quiet her was to take her into the parents' bed, otherwise she would not fall asleep. To be sure this burglar phobia was based on infantile sexuality, in contrast to the phobia of the grownup described before. The cure consisted in just analyzing with the child frankly and simply the basic sexual significance of the situation. I confess that I was a little surprised when the little girl informed me that what puzzled her so much was that her mother told her about childbirth but failed to explain to her how childbirth started. "How does it happen that the child grows in the mother's womb like a flower?" the little girl asked me. The mother had apparently related only part of the story. I explained to the little girl the significant aspects of the problem, and it was really quite impressive to see how grateful she felt for the information. "I learned so much today from Dr. Brill," she remarked. "Why do you call him a doctor? He is more like a teacher." The child was cured after she realized that her fear was nothing but her desire to have her mother and father with her. She had been very much coddled by the parents; her father particularly had been too lavish in his affections. He used to fondle and kiss her altogether too much, and now her emotions could no longer be contained and welled forth overwhelmingly strong. By helping this child to understand this matter and adjusting her love life generally, the phobia disappeared.

To understand better how libidinal demands manifest themselves in the anxiety dream it may be well perhaps to consider with you in some detail the phases of sexual development as propounded by Professor Freud. In his *Three Contributions to the Theory of Sex*[2] Freud uses two terms which should be known to every reader of his works. He speaks of the *sexual object* (i.e., the person from whom sexual attraction emanates) and the *sexual aim* (i.e., the aim toward which the instinct strives). There are many deviations in reference to both sexual object and sexual aim which every psychoanalytic psychiatrist encounters in his practice. Thus the most common deviation from the sexual object is homosexuality (homo here means same), which manifests itself by the fact that instead of craving a sexual object of the opposite sex (heterosexuality) some persons seek a sexual object of the same sex. This inversion is quite common in both civilized and primitive cultures. It has been estimated that from 1 to 3 per cent of the male population is overtly homosexual. And although such people are not mentally deficient, as is often assumed, they nevertheless constitute a socio-psychological problem in our communities. Less is known about female homosexuals, who are usually designated as Lesbians (from *Lesbos,* the home of the Greek poetess Sappho). They, too, exist in large numbers though they are not so notorious as the male homosexuals. There are still other deviations from the sexual object into which we cannot enter here.[3]

The deviations from the sexual aim are also quite numerous and present a problem for the individuals as well as for the community. The normal sexual aim consists in the characteristic act of conjugation which diminishes the sexual tension and temporarily quenches the sexual desire. But even the most normal sexual act offers many possibilities which may lead to anomalies described as perversions which we have discussed above. The perversion represents either a transgression from the bodily regions destined for sexual union or a tarrying long at points which are normally rapidly

[2]Freud's *Basic Writings,* l.c. p. 532.
[3]Those interested are referred to Brill: *Lectures on Psychoanalytic Psychiatry,* Knopf, N.Y., 1947, p. 244.

passed on the way to the sexual aim.[4] Among such deviations are masturbation; the utilization of the mouth as a sexual organ instead of kissing as a preliminary to the act; the substitution for the sexual object of a part of the body which is inappropriate for sexual purposes, such as the foot or hair, or some inanimate object: fetishism. Most of the deviations from the aim are found in patients who were accidentally conditioned to them in early life.

To understand these deviations we have to bear in mind that the sexuality of the child consists of a number of partial impulses and components which function normally up to the age of four to five, that is, in the first or autoerotic phase of childhood. During that period the child obtains pleasure from all senses. Thumb-sucking, touching, looking, tasting, and smelling furnish outlets to the young child. But as he grows older all these partial impulses are gathered into one stream and are first directed to his own body. Between the ages of four and five the child is in love with himself. Freud called this period *narcissism,* after Narcissus, who remained in love with himself. Following this phase of development there is what Freud calls a *latency period* during which the former sexual manifestations seem to be dormant. It is the school period when the child learns to repress and sublimate the infantile sexuality and direct the rest to the genitals for later functioning. The infantile sexuality thus gradually gives way to genitality, which manifests itself at puberty. It is during the narcissistic and latency period phases that reaction formations or dams are formed against the infantile sexuality in the form of sympathy, shame, modesty, disgust, and morality, which keep down the primitive impulses of childhood. We speak of *fixations* or weak spots when any of the partial impulses do not pass through a regular evolution of repression, sublimation, and of leaving a remnant for procreation. Thus some accident may prevent the formation of the dam or reaction formation of sympathy to hold down the aggressive component and the individual may develop into a sadist.

The neurosis represents a conflict in which the component or partial impulse of sex is repressed and then comes to the surface as the negative of the perversion. Thus a fixation in sexual looking results in the perversion of voyeurism or mixoscopia, or in the negative of it as a pain or other disturbance in the eyes. These fixa-

[4]Freud, l.c. p. 564.

tions can take place at any time, but we must bear in mind that it is during the latency period that the child receives most of those impressions which prepare it for life. To be sure the child begins to take on impressions from the very beginning of his existence; but it is in this period, which we may justly call the school period, that he or she actually begins to learn how to adjust to society.

The definite phase of adjustment which we associate generally with education really starts at the latency period when the child begins to go to school. The child has, of course, already a certain adjustment as a result of his home training, and the observant teacher will attest to the fact that he shows even at this early age a very characteristic mode of reaction to his environment. In other words, before entering school the child already has a definite adjustment which is a product of his home development. The teacher, therefore, is not to be blamed for a child's maladjustment, because she is coping with a condition that from the very outset was not strictly normal: If a child has not done well up to the age of eight, he will usually be a ne'er-do-well; if he is defective, his abnormality will become manifest at the outset, and he will not outgrow it, as people generally suppose. A child shows from the very beginning just what the nature of his future adjustment will be.

It is commonly supposed that the latency period shows no sex manifestations. Careful observation, however, points very definitely in the opposite direction. It is a period in which sex is only apparently absent; investigate a little and you will learn from teachers and parents that all kinds of sexual manifestations are in evidence at that age in the classroom and at home. They are, of course, not so prominent; the child does not usually occupy himself with distinct sexual problems. That sexual inquisitiveness of the earlier years seems to have lost its keen edge; we hear no more that insistent query, "Where do children come from?" It either has received its information by the age of four or has been squelched so well that it dare not ask the parents another question.

The period of object love sets in at the age of nine or ten, around the prepubescent age; the boy and the girl now show that they are ready to adjust themselves to the world in a definite way. The child no longer shows the same reactions to both sexes. At the age of puberty one observes marked character changes in both sexes; it is then that the sexual factors become manifest and specialized. The boy develops into manhood and shows an aggressive sexual make-up; the girl, developing into womanhood, evinces a passive or negatively aggressive sexuality. I have collected dreams of children of about the pubescent age, and it is instructive to note how the dreams all showed the definite biological factors which may be observed in the development of both sexes: the boys' dreams always dealt with active aggressions, and the girls' with passivity, with being pursued, caught, or overcome. A number of teachers collected dreams of pubescent children for me, and no matter from what station of life the children came the results were always the same: their dreams all showed the same characteristic biological reactions. It is noteworthy that anxiety dreams are particularly prevalent among girls of fourteen and fifteen, for it is at these ages that the girl becomes aware of the sex urge but cannot as yet place her emotions properly—she has not adjusted herself to the new life.

The pubescent age is also the period when most mental breakdowns start. One of the worst forms of mental diseases, schizophrenia, starts at about the ages of fourteen and fifteen; probably 75 per cent of the attacks occur between the ages of fourteen and eighteen, 90 per cent between the ages of fifteen and twenty-five, the others coming later. Indeed schizophrenia has been designated by many writers as a psychosis of pubescence. As a specialist in mental diseases I may say that if a child successfully tides over his pubescent age, that is, the period from about twelve to fifteen years, then there is no cause for apprehension. If everything goes well at this time, it is indeed rare to find some nervous or emotional breakdown in later years. In other words, an adequate adjustment at that time means an adequate adjustment in the future. In this adjustment, of course, the sexual or emotional factor is of paramount importance, and that is why it may be said that an individual who is not well adjusted in his emotional or erotic life remains inadequately adjusted in every other phase of his existence. *We may posit it as a general principle that one's sex life is always reflected in the general psychic condition of the entire person;* abnormal sex life always interferes with normal functioning in the other spheres of life.

The biologic principles or the direct sex demands manifest themselves all the time. In the dream they appear in the form of anxiety or fear. Let me give you some illustrations. A woman related to me this dream: *A colored man pursued her with a knife, and it was only after a long struggle that she wrested the deadly weapon from him. She awoke terrified, her heart beating wildly.* When I called for associations, I learned that her mother was always afraid to leave her alone at home because of the colored butler, who is a quiet, inoffensive creature. When asked what reason she thought her mother had for fearing to leave her alone with the servant, she replied, "Well, you know I read recently about colored men in the South assaulting white women. Mother reads the same paper that I do and must have read that account also, and so she must be more afraid than ever." The dream is simply a realization of a wish; unconsciously the young woman's own craving for sex manifested itself in this concealed way. The account that she had read in the newspaper the day before only served as a determinant for the dream; the emotions, the unconscious craving were there all the time waiting for an appropriate stimulus to call them into play.

There is, thus, not an event occurring in our world but what calls forth some repressed emotion in the unconscious and acts as a determinant not only for dreams, but for hysterical symptoms and other normal and abnormal phenomena. Perhaps you may remember the time when there was so much ado and excitement about "the poison needle," when women were reported to have been taken into white slavery by the thousands. Some vicious man, it was rumored, would stick a poison needle into a girl, drag her into a taxi when she fainted, and hurry her off to a house of ill repute. It mattered little that scientists protested that there could be no such poison that would render a person unconscious immediately. The police were kept quite active and arrests were made, but as a matter of fact there was not a single authentic case of "the poison needle" throughout the United States. It was quite instructive to me to observe that there was hardly a woman I was treating at that time who did not tell me that she dreamed about being poisoned, attacked, and sold into white slavery.

The unconscious always draws upon the environment for expression; it always utilizes some appropriate situation for the expression of repressed emotions. I know I may shock some of you by asserting that the late war offered an excellent outlet to some people; that is why so many men and women experienced nervous breakdowns after the armistice was signed. I had occasion to see a few soldiers then who had gone through the fighting without receiving the slightest wound but who broke down when they came on board ship bound for home. They were supposed to have been "shell-shocked"; but the real difficulty was that they were cut off from an excellent outlet for their primitive impulses. The same thing applied to those who did not actively participate in the fighting; there were quite a number of women who became markedly depressed as the soldiers returned from overseas and were discharged. There was to be no more prospect of working in canteens, driving ambulances, nursing the sick heroes in the hospitals. We were to have no more of these sadistic or masochistic outlets. And what a terrible void opened up before those women!

In the same way the *Titanic* disaster acted as a marked determinant for dreams. One woman related to me the following dream relating to the catastrophe: *She was on the ship when it was sinking; there were the terrible cries of panic-stricken women and children. Then someone cried out: "Women and children first."* She refused to leave her husband. An officer came up and tore her away from him, despite her loud protests. She woke up crying, seized with terror. I knew this woman's history so thoroughly that it was not difficult for me to see at once the meaning of the dream. When I asked her for associations there was the natural determinant: she had read on the previous day how the wife of a prominent man on board the *Titanic* actually refused to be separated from her husband and bravely met death with him without flinching. In the dream, as you may see, the situation was quite the reverse: she was terribly grieved because she was torn away from her husband. Now the crux of the whole situation was that she was in love with an officer who was stationed right near her; she experienced a great many struggles with herself about the whole affair; that was one of the reasons why she came to me for treatment. Consciously, of course, she would not yield to the officer, but unconsciously, in the dream, she submits and we see her actually separated from her husband. On the one hand, then, we see the wish motive; on the other, the anxiety which is merely the conflict between the two opposing psychic forces, representing the converted libido. Thus the dream strictly had little to do with the *Titanic* catastrophe; the latter only served as the medium through which she was able to give vent to her repressed emotions.

The anxiety dreams, then, show a definite form of unconscious reaction to craving, to unadjusted emotions, in which the anxiety takes the place of the libido. Later on, when we take up daydreaming, we shall see that some women go through these mechanisms without sleeping. They play with the idea consciously; they entertain *Dürnen Phantasien,* prostitution fancies, quite openly. Such women either do not suppress or have sexually emancipated themselves. The others can give vent to their unadjusted emotions through unconscious mentation, and it is the anxiety dream that lends itself to just that type of outlet.

Artificial Dreams and Lying

When we delve into the mainsprings of the dream we find that it is a product of some conscious experience or fancy that the individual invariably represses by reason of its painful and unattainable nature. That is why we find upon investigation that daydreams and fancies which are more or less conscious mental activities show exactly the same mechanisms as the dream and reveal just as markedly a person's character and inner problems. Analysis shows that they are invariably wishes. Thus that spontaneous mental activity known as "building castles in the air" enables us to gain as profound an insight into the individual's deeper striving and desires as the dream itself.

This intimate relation existing between the dream and the daydream is found also between the dream and another type of unconscious mentation which may be designated as "artificial dreams." By artificial dreams we understand those dreams which a person consciously makes up at the request of the physician. The patient is requested to make up a dream by imitating what he regards as a real dream. He is instructed to talk at random without guiding his thoughts. The production obtained in this manner is recorded and analyzed in accordance with the rules. What the patient will produce for you may to him sound very stupid and may seem to bear no relation to his own inner problems, but as a matter of fact you will find, upon analyzing it, that it is just as significant as an actual dream and reveals just as markedly the deeper problems and conflicts in the psychic life. I came upon the subject of artificial dreams in the following manner:

I was treating a physician, an unmarried man about thirty, who was suffering from a rather deep-seated psychoneurotic disturbance. He was one of those patients who claim that they do not dream; after assuring him, however, that it is merely a question of remembering the dream, he came to me one morning and gave me the following dream: *"I was giving birth to a child, and felt very severe labor pains. My friend X acted as accoucheur [midwife]; he stuck the forceps into me more like a butcher than a physician.* Of course," he said, "X is not a physician, he is a businessman." I proceeded to analyze the dream by asking the patient to tell me something about X. "He is a very good friend of mine, but of late we have drifted apart," he replied. I was interested to know the reason for this. "I did not like some of the people in whom X was interested," I learned. "Is that the only reason why you drifted apart?" I continued. "I believe so." The patient then went into details about his relationship with X. I observed finally: "You seem to be jealous of X." "Yes, that is what X claims." "Well," I went on, "but jealousy is perfectly justified only when a person of the opposite sex is concerned, but you are jealous when X talks to other men." He then laughed. "You know, I always thought that this dream business is claptrap. Now I can see it; you asked me to give you a dream and I thought I would make one up. I never dreamed it. I was only fooling you." I must confess I was a little surprised to hear this, but his apparently innocent piece of fabrication revealed to me all the same the very thing I was looking for all the time. A dream such as this could come only from a homosexual, and indeed from the very beginning I suspected that he was an invert. I asked him to go on with the analysis of the dream but he dryly protested, "There's no use; I made it up." I insisted that he continue. He refused and became very angry, whereupon I simply told him my analysis. "You are a homosexual, and in love with Mr. X; only a man who identifies himself with a woman dreams that he gives birth to a child." He left me in quite a sullen mood, but returned very soon and informed me that my diagnosis was correct, but that it was hard for him to acknowledge that he was homosexual.

The case gave me material for reflection. It demonstrated very definitely that one can actually resort to the analysis of artificial dreams to gain an insight into the patient's psychic life. What surprised me at first was that we never seemed to have thought about the matter before, but upon investigating the subject I soon found that Professor Bleuler had touched on it, stating that such artificial productions are not at all impossible. Since that case I resort to artificial dreams whenever a patient fails to bring me dreams, claiming that he does not dream, or whenever a patient suddenly stops dreaming because of some unconscious resistance. Analysis of such a dream usually brings to the surface those factors which were at the base of these resistances, which can then be removed. Of course this is not so easy as it may appear, for it is a significant fact that most people who insist that they do not dream will declare just as strongly that they cannot make up a dream. The same resistances that hinder them from bringing the physician their dreams prevent them also from making up dreams. There is no doubt, however, that with continued urging on the part of the physician they can be led to give some productions. Here are a few that I have reported.

"I do something that meets with my parents' disapproval. I am afraid of my father, as if I were a child." When I asked the dreamer for associations, he replied that he had none, but that he would invent another dream. The latter ran as follows: *"I see an old woman crying. She is evidently trying to decipher shorthand notes."* He began to associate and thought at once of a certain woman, a stenographer, his senior by five years. He had met her in a very questionable environment, while carousing with friends, fell in love with her, and offered to marry her. She soon promised to reform, took up stenography, and through his influence obtained a position in his father's office. When he finally spoke about her to the father, who knew nothing of the woman's past, the latter at first refused his consent, but later showed signs of relenting. It was then that the patient himself began to doubt the wisdom of his contemplated matrimonial venture. Most of his friends knew about the woman's former life, and strongly advised him against marrying her. He knew that he would have to renounce all his social connections and feared lest his father should discover the true facts concerning her past. It was this conflict, coupled with other factors, that revived a dormant psychoneurosis. I may also add that while under treatment he consciously withheld the most important facts in his love affair: he told me nothing about how he met her,

or who she was. He did not think it was necessary for me to know this. Indeed, such things are usually passed over by the patient as being trivial and unimportant; he simply does not deem them worth while to relate.

The first production: "I do something that meets with my parents' disapproval. I am afraid of my father as if I were a child," recalled the patient's early childhood, when he often feared his father's wrath for wetting the bed. The underlying thought was that should he now enter into this contemplated matrimony, he would again soil his bed and be punished by his father. The second dream, "I saw an old woman crying, et cetera," expresses his wish to get rid of the woman. She was indeed a poor stenographer and would have been discharged long before had it not been for his intercession. The dream shows that she leaves voluntarily because she cannot hold a position in his family, i.e., she cannot be his wife.

Another patient, Mrs. C., a young married woman suffering from a mild form of schizophrenia, gave me, after strong urging, the following artificial dream. Patients of the schizophrenic type are usually very inaccessible and the artificial dream is often the only way of entering into their mind.

"I went into a garden where there were many people. One of the ladies fell in love with one of the gentlemen sitting on the bench. They exchanged all sorts of endearing terms until the lady proposed marriage. They married and were very happy."

This dream is quite simple: it shows little distortion, it is a sort of open wish. As Mrs. C. is a married woman the question that naturally suggests itself is: "Who is the man?" Certainly he is not her own husband; there would be no need for that. The dreamer herself apparently is under the disguise of the lady who proposed to the gentleman, in accordance with the well-known principle of dream analysis that the dreamer is always the central figure in the dream. Mrs. C. was a shut-in type of person, extremely inaccessible. Whenever I made any effort to question her about her intimate life, she would say: "I am perfectly happy with my husband. I have nothing to tell you." But when I asked her to tell me the person the "gentleman" in the dream recalled to her, she immediately informed me that it was the family physician; she remembered distinctly that the physician looked very much like him. As she could give me very little further information, I observed: "It would seem that you had an affair with the physician, or that you undoubtedly desired to have one." She admitted that for years she had been very much attached to the doctor. She did not tell me of this before, because she could not see what bearing it had upon the treatment. And yet I must have you mark very carefully, it is the conflict arising from this experience that finally precipitated her mental condition; it was the exciting factor of the disease.

Since my experience with that patient who deliberately attempted to mislead me by making up what he thought a senseless production, I have collected quite a number of artificial dreams. Though most of them are by no means so simple as those I have just given you, they all may be analyzed very readily; indeed they are easier to analyze than actual dreams.

Let me say at this point that one of the objections to dream analysis advanced by some investigators is that the dreamer, in recounting the dream, consciously or unconsciously fills up the gaps which originally existed in the dream and thus introduces elements that strictly do not belong to it; they maintain that the dream you commit to writing is no longer the real dream, a great deal of it is forgotten, and much new material creeps in. But you see how this makes no material difference in the analysis, for whatever the dreamer inserts into the dream bears an intimate relation to his own inner problems: the dreamer consciously or unconsciously will always gravitate toward his own inner strivings.[5]

My experience with artificial dreams led me into quite another field of investigation, the problem of lying. Considerable study and experience convinced me that the lie, like the dream, is nothing but a direct or indirect wish. Every piece of fabrication, whether simple or complex, represents essentially a condition that the person desires to see realized. Frankly, I am sometimes pleased when a patient lies to me, either quite deliberately or unconsciously; he is thereby only giving me another clue to his neurosis. For every lie, even in a normal person, is but an expression of the wish motive, and deals naturally with material of marked importance and interest to the individual concerned.

Lying is one of the defense mechanisms that helps the individual out of difficulties. When done with that in view, the lie is often

[5]Freud: "Interpretation of Dreams," in the *Basic Writings*.

designated as a "white lie." Thus we have a double standard of lying, the "white lie," which is understandable, and the lie made with malicious intent, or done habitually, just for the sake of lying. That the "white lie" is just another mode of self-protection, that it has, we might say, as useful a function as teeth and claws, is well borne out by the fact that primitive people and members of culturally less sophisticated races, like some Negroes and Indians, for example, invariably lie when they wish to get out of some difficulty. The same condition obtains among children. They invariably show a tendency to fabricate. Such a tendency among children cannot be considered pathological. It simply denotes an immature mentality; children, as we know, have not as yet assumed all the necessary ethical inhibitions and therefore follow their impulses. Whenever they find themselves in any difficulty they do not hesitate to get out of it through lying. Thus a boy of four, having broken a dish, insisted that a servant did it; an older boy, having been detected playing truant, asserted that his teacher was sick.

We should always assume a more or less sensible attitude toward lying in children. They should be taught, of course, not to do so, but it is to be expected, and regarded as more or less natural. They should be trained to tell the truth without our resorting to emotional outbursts, for it is certain that we can always accomplish much more with the child by entering into rapport with him, by gaining his confidence and love. How much harm is often done by resorting to marked emotionalism in our attitude toward the child's lie may be seen from the following case:

Mrs. F., a woman of thirty-five, married, complained, among other things, of having a very strong tendency to lie. As far as I could observe, she was perfectly normal mentally, so that one could regard her condition as merely a bad habit. But we know, from psychoanalytic study and experience, that there must be something in the individual's psychic life that feeds that habit, that gives it its motive force. Apropos of the symptom, her history was as follows: At the age of eight she lived in a small locality where, among the very few children who played with her, there was a boy of eleven with whom she associated very much. One day he exposed himself to her, and she played sexually with him. This continued for a few months perhaps, when her grandmother noticed it. The boy got a terrible beating and the girl received a good tongue-lashing, although she was more or less excused, as she was only a little girl. She was not allowed, however, to see her companion any more. Her mother, who was away at this time, presently returned, and the little girl, in an outburst of confidence, related everything that occurred during her absence, not failing to mention the experience with the little boy. Far from being pleased that her daughter voluntarily and frankly revealed to her what transpired between the two children, she flew into a rage and beat the little girl most severely, despite the fact that she had never before administered any form of corporal punishment to the child. She then locked her up in a room and kept her there on bread and water for quite a while. Following this, she continued to remind the girl all the time of the terrible transgression that was committed.

When twelve years old, the girl attended with her mother a funeral of a boy of fourteen who met with an accident and was killed. On her way to the funeral the mother observed: "When you get there, you will see his parents in a state of terrible anguish; they feel heartbroken at the death of their young boy, snatched from them at so young an age. But do you know, I would rather have seen you die than to have you do what you did?" That is how stupidly and deeply the mother reacted to the situation. The grandmother would accordingly remind the girl: "Now you see, if you only had kept your tongue, as I told you to do." That marked a turning point in the patient's whole life. There was a marked change in her relations with her mother and with the world. She now lied frequently to her parent; she actually "kept her tongue," as her grandmother had wisely counseled her. And as she reacted to the mother she gradually reacted to the whole world; what happened was that unconsciously she was constantly trying to rebel against her mother by no longer revealing the truth as she did on that unfortunate occasion. The symptom caused her much discomfort and unpleasantness. Sometimes, for instance, she would be out socially, and in speaking about some book or play would deliberately distort the facts. She was conscious of it, but could do nothing to correct the condition. It was a sort of obsession with her.

Such cases are not at all rare. They are found among people who are normal intellectually and who cannot be considered in any sense psychopathic. The fundamental reason for the symptom may usually be traced to just such an emotionally accentuated occurrence as we have noted in Mrs. F.'s case.

With the advance of age we are expected to tell the truth, and the average normal person can do so to a certain extent. The lies then serve a definite purpose. They are usually well balanced and sometimes even very ingenious and complicated. The same holds true in the abnormal types; the greater the intellect, the more difficult it is to detect the lie. Moral idiots and superior degenerates often make such good impressions that they frequently escape detection for a long time, while it is simple enough to see through the lies of children, of most mental defectives and psychotics. On the other hand, the lowest type, the idiot, is usually incapable of telling a lie. His extreme mental poverty allows him to follow unhindered all his simple desires; he has not enough brains to formulate a lie. He is therefore honesty personified. That telling the truth among normals is considered as something verging on the impossible is shown by the fact that one of the greatest attributes of the father of this country is that he never told a lie. As a matter of fact every normal person tells a lie on certain occasions, and provided certain conditions are fulfilled, it is not counted against him even if he is detected.

To be called a liar, a person must not only show a frequent tendency to fabricate but must also evince a certain weak-mindedness in its execution. Thus a well-bred, apparently intelligent woman had the reputation of being a liar. When I met her for the first time we had occasion to speak of a well-known physician. She remarked that this doctor was much devoted to her. "He kisses me whenever I leave the office," she went on to declare. Noticing my great surprise, for it was indeed an anomalous condition for me to imagine, as I knew the man intimately, she added, "I am just like a daughter to him." I am sure that such behavior was absolutely foreign to him. This woman was psychopathic and was well known as a habitual liar.

A doctor of this same type told me once that he worked in a certain clinic in Europe with which I was very well acquainted. We spoke about the professor who was at the head of the department, and he remarked: "Prof. X thinks so much of me that he sent me the proof sheets of a book he just wrote and asked me to correct them and make any suggestions I deem fit." Every lie, like every dream, must be determined by something. I knew the determinant of this: the professor was about to publish a new edition of the book referred to. "Do you mean the third edition of his . . . ?" I interposed. "Why, I have the book home already; it just came to me." He protested vehemently that this could not be and turned away terribly piqued. Both these individuals (the woman mentioned above and this doctor) are well-known liars among their friends and acquaintances. We have a special name for their malady—*pseudologia phantasica*, pathological lying. People of this type have a constant desire to fill the void in themselves.

I once had a patient who upon coming late would declare apologetically: "Doctor, I am sorry I am late; I just dined with the Duchess of Devonshire." At first I did not know whether to believe him or not. He would go into details about the duchess, inform me who her grandmother was, and relate many other intimate facts. At another time he said he dined with the duke. He kept that up for a week, when I discovered that there was not an iota of truth in what he said. He had ideas of grandeur and tried in this way to realize his abnormal wishes. He thought that he was an illegitimate child and that he came from the nobility. He had made a study of English nobility and was thus able to play his part pretty well. I have no doubt that as time went on he began to believe in the deception himself.

It is a known fact that ordinary liars eventually believe their lies and thus realize their wishes. A few years ago I often heard an acquaintance tell of his interesting experiences in a military academy, where he said he spent a few years. I was very much surprised to find, years later, when I analyzed him, that he never saw this academy. He told me that at the age of ten years he was attracted to a boy, a military student, and entertained a very strong wish to enter this military academy. He took a great interest in military life, and read much about this school, but owing to financial difficulties his ardent wish could never be realized. When he applied for his first position, he boldly stated that he had attended this school, and as the lie remained unnoticed, he stuck to it for years and finally believed that he actually studied there for a long time.

In this connection it is interesting to note that tendencies to fabricate can be produced by exogenous factors. I am referring to Korsakoff's psychosis, a condition found among alcoholics. Here, the poison[6] having destroyed lifelong inhibitions, the patients find it very easy to tell the most fantastic and embellished adventures. They never become embarrassed when brought to bay, because their mental processes are paralyzed. Ask such a patient, who is confined to bed, what he did in the morning, and he replies most cheerfully: "I have been out and walked down Broadway and went into a saloon on Twenty-third Street, met Mr. ——, et cetera." And all the time he was in bed, but he makes the story so specific that one who does not know finds it difficult not to believe him. All we have to do is to give him the slightest suggestion and he has a long story ready. Ask him for some money, and he will at once begin to search for his trousers, though he really has not a cent that he can call his own. There are no inhibitions whatever, everything runs smoothly. Indeed, we may say weak-mindedness due to any cause permits ambitions to run riot, and as the individual finds it impossible to realize them, he makes believe to his fellow being that he has actually accomplished all the mighty deeds. In this respect he resembles the prolific dreamer who has many wishes to fulfill; but whereas the latter, by virtue of ethical inhibitions, can realize his desires only in sleep, the psychopathic liar, who has never fully developed mental inhibitions, puts his wishes in operation verbally in the waking state.

Some lies manifest themselves in very peculiar ways. Thus I knew a patient, a young woman, who suddenly stopped urinating. No amount of urging on the part of the physicians in the sanitarium where she was treated could cause her to attend to this bodily function. Sometimes she maintained that she could not attend to these wants, other times that she simply felt no need for them. And, strange to say, while the doctors were seriously concerned over her ailment she secretly appropriated towels and used them as receptacles for her excretions, which she then threw out of the window. Here the lie was determined by a reversion to infantile eroticisms manifesting themselves in the desire to solicit the doctor's attention to the genitals. This case recalls Professor Virchow's case of Louise Lateau, who refused to take food because she maintained

---

[6]In many cases this condition seems to be the result of nutritional (vitamin) deficiency as well as of the quantity of the ingested poison.

that she was a saint and needed no nourishment. Virchow ascertained that she had regular movements of the bowels and decided that she was secretly taking nourishment. For, he argued, and surely with good reason, that though the Lord created the world out of nothing, no mortal could produce matter out of nothing. Those of you who are interested in cases of this kind will find much interesting material in the police records. These cases make up the classes of international swindlers, charlatans, malingerers, and other psychopaths.

The liar shows a definite relation to the born criminal from whom he differs only in degree. The latter, usually being lower in the mental scale, does not even have to lie; he sees something that he wants and straightway sets out to get it. And that is why, as we have pointed out previously, the criminal dreams considerably less than the average normal person: he actually realizes many more of his wishes than his normal brother.

The liar is also related to the poet, who may be called an artificial dreamer or a convention fabricator. Professor Frederick Prescott, in his interesting study, *Poetry and Dreams,*[7] expresses himself as follows on the origin of poetry: "It represents the fulfillment of our ungratified wishes or desires." The same mechanism is found in habitual liars, and, to a lesser degree, in every normal person. What is the distinction between them? The normal dissatisfied person contents himself with fancy formation which he keeps to himself very carefully. He does not wish to reveal his secret desires because he is ashamed to do so and, what is more, he knows that we will not be interested in them. The liar has never outgrown his infancy, so that even as an adult his fancies, his wishes, are of a childish nature; he is unable to adapt himself to reality, so that he constructs his world on the infantile foundation. His fancies, therefore, are characterized throughout by extreme egotism. He is the hero of every adventure, the *sine qua non* in every situation. That is why he repels us, for we do not like to see another individual behave so all-importantly. The poet or writer overcomes these difficulties by toning down the egotistic character of his fancies. He conceals them under the hero, and that is why his productions give us pure aesthetic pleasure. We are fascinated by the situation

[7]F. C. Prescott, *Poetry and Dreams,* Boston. The Four Seas Company, 1919.

because it offers us the opportunity to put ourselves into the hero's place, and our pleasure is thus derived from deep psychic sources. In other words, the poet offers us an enticing premium or a fore-pleasure, whereby we may release some of our own mental and emotional tension. But the liar, like the child, wants everything and obtains pleasure solely in reciting to others his egotistic adventures.

Typical Dreams

I now propose to take up a class of dreams known as typical dreams. We classify them under that heading because there is hardly a person who does not have them at some time of his life.

One of the most common of the typical dreams is the dream of being naked. As Charles Dickens has so happily put it, it is a dream that everybody has, "from Queen Elizabeth to her most humble gaoler." He describes it quite characteristically: we find ourselves naked in a crowd; though no one seems to notice us or pay the slightest attention, we ourselves are greatly embarrassed. The dream is sometimes also modified. Instead of being naked, the dreamer is not dressed as he should be. With all the others in evening clothes at a ball, for instance, he may find himself in everyday attire; or if he is in the Army, he may find himself dressed contrary to the regulations. Such dreams go back to the earliest period of childhood, when the child is naked and experiences no feeling of shame. Professor Freud declares that this age of child-hood in which the sense of shame is not present seems to our later recollections a paradise, and the idea of paradise itself is nothing but a composite fantasy from the childhood of the individual. It is for this reason that in paradise human beings are naked and are not at all ashamed. When the child grows older, the sense of shame gradually develops; it is then that sex and cultural development begin. The problem of nakedness is not only found in the story of Adam and Eve, but it is quite a dominant theme in fairy tales. You may all recall Andersen's fascinating story of the two rogues who wove that wonderful cloak for the king that only those could see who were truly fit for their positions. You remember that neither the king nor his court nor the populace would admit that nothing was seen; everyone was afraid to confess the truth lest he thus betray his unfitness for his particular position, and so all admired the garment immensely. It remained for a little child to disclose openly that the king was really naked and thus put an end to the ruse. Observe how the unconscious, with which we may identify the child, always tells the truth.

What do these dreams of nakedness represent? According to Professor Freud they are exhibition dreams. We must bear in mind that, despite the fact that we are perfectly reconciled to our ethical criteria, we unconsciously live through many of the infantile states. We still like to walk about naked, as we did when we were children. There is no greater pleasure you can give to children than to allow them to walk about naked; it is quite common for travelers to see children in certain parts of Europe exhibit themselves. Indeed, I have no doubt that Andersen's story itself is a reminiscence of the author's own exhibitionism, of his own unconscious craving to appear naked. We see this reversion to infantile feelings even in the waking state. As you may know, the whole art of dressmaking always aims at one thing—discovering some new way of displaying the woman's body, of rendering prominent those parts of the body which attract men. The décolleté and the evening dresses we see at the opera and at dinner are markedly exhibitionistic despite the fact that they are worn by highly respectable ladies. It is also a matter of common observation that the woman who is not very proud of her physical make-up is by no means eager to display it. Exhibition dreams usually appear when a person is in need to show up to better advantage.

The next typical dream is the dream of the death of relatives. I feel that everybody has had dreams of this nature. The dreamer is usually very much affected by the death and reacts to it in the dream just as deeply as in the waking state. Of course in view of the fact that our dreams are wish realizations, a great many will be shocked and wonder why you should wish your relatives to die. Such dreams usually go back to very early childhood, when the conception of death held no terror to the child, when death merely involved absence. A little child cannot conceive the real significance of the fact; all that he understands is that the father is away on his vacation perhaps, or on a trip. He does not have the same reaction to death that we observe in the adult. The child often welcomes this protracted absence, for he is thus freed from the restraint that his father imposed upon him.

In the same way it may seem strange to dream of the death of
one's sister in view of our fundamental thesis that the dream represents essentially a hidden wish. But we find that if there are two
sisters in the home the older child will usually impose her will
upon the younger one. The younger child is helpless, but in
the absence of her sister she is able to enjoy a degree of freedom
and independence that she could not have before. In one particular case of two married sisters, for instance, the younger one
dreamed that her sister was dead and experienced all the emotions
that go with mourning. Upon analysis it was found that her
dream went back to her childhood, when she was dominated by her
sister. She did not wish so much in the dream that the sister were
dead in the real sense of the word, but that she were away. This
is the basic significance of all dreams of this type; we are dealing
here with a situation representing an infantile wish.

There are a number of dreams, however, describing the death
of a relative in which we find no sadness, no grief, no affective
elements whatsoever. We have here an altogether different situation. Such dreams do not denote death at all. I reported, for example, the case of a man who related to me how he dreamed that
he saw his brother with his head cut open and was by no means
affected by the terrible sight; it seemed quite natural to him to see
his brother in that condition. It is noteworthy that he came to me
some time before the dream and asked me whether I thought there
was any substance in what he read in the newspapers about trephin-
ing a defective boy's head to make him well. I assured him that that
was all nonsense and impossible. His brother was quite a serious
problem to him and the dream, far from expressing the wish that
his brother were dead, expressed his ardent desire that he be cured.

I would have you note also a type of dream in which the sister
dreams of the death of her brother. The relations between brother
and sister are not at all so amicable and harmonious as we generally suppose. Our ethical training enjoins upon us to live har-
moniously, and we realize that we ought to be good and just to our
sisters and brothers. But frankly I have never observed more bitter
enmities than between brothers and sisters. They know how to
hate because they know also how to love. I have analyzed many a
dream which, shocking though it was to the moral principle of the
dreamer, contained, nevertheless, the remnants of this early hatred

between brother and sister. Thus an intelligent cultured woman dreamed that her brother was dead. The situation was that her mother had left some money which her brother was planning to appropriate despite the fact that she needed it far more urgently than he. But I would have you mark very carefully that in reality this woman would rather do without the money than have her brother die. In the unconscious, however, we are living through our childhood, we are primitive and absolutely egocentric, we are concerned with problems solely as they affect us. In the unconscious our wishes balk at nothing: we are ready to dispatch through death or any other means any person who stands in our way.

Very often, too, our secret desires may be unconsciously realized even in the waking state. I have reported the case of a noted physician in New York who was hurriedly called away from his home to the bedside of his sick old uncle. When he arrived he did not take over the charge of the case, because everything possible was done for the patient by his own family physicians. All hope for the patient's recovery was abandoned and his death was expected every day. But despite the many complications, the patient held on to life tenaciously, and days passed without any marked apparent change. His nephew became quite anxious to return to New York as soon as possible, as there was a very busy practice awaiting him, and, what was more, there was illness in his own family. One evening the uncle became very ill, and as the attending physicians were away, he gave him a hypodermic to stimulate his heart. Very shortly the old man died. When he later looked at the vial from which he took the drug, he found, to his great consternation, that instead of giving him strychnine, he gave him hyoscine, a drug that has exactly the opposite action of strychnine. In other words, he actually killed the patient. Consciously, of course, he did not wish to kill him, and in his terrible mortification he consoled himself in the thought that he would have died soon anyway. The physician unconsciously hastened the man's death in his great eagerness to return to his home. He informed me of this years after it happened: he assured me that he revealed the fact to no one; he merely wished to corroborate what I said in one of my psychoanalytic papers. I learned also, that when a boy he had many dreams of the death of this very uncle, and indeed very often actually wished that the man were dead. The boy's father died when the child was very young, and the uncle was unusually severe with him. Though he became more and more attached to him as he grew older, it would seem that the *coup de grâce* did not lack hostile motivation.

In the unconscious, then, our own immediate welfare takes precedence over every other consideration: father, brother, sister, and relative are only of minor importance. Thus an important question to ask yourself in dream analysis is *cui bono,* to whose advantage is the underlying situation in the dream? If it is to the advantage of the dreamer, or, in other words, if it falls in line with his secret inner demands and strivings, then the dream has its significance only in terms of that situation and no other, for the dream always deals with problems of the most intimate personal character. *The dream is always egocentric.*

There is another typical dream dealing with the death of the father that we find particularly among young sons. We have to consider here the primitive state of the human being. There is always a rivalry between father and son for the love of the mother, and this, despite the fact that the father may love his boy very dearly. The son has learned that he receives much more attention and love from his mother, and is treated more leniently in the father's absence. In this type of dream, therefore, we see the desire on the part of the child to get rid of his father. It is really surprising to note how many boys dream openly as well as disguisedly of the death of their father. These dreams are even more common than those dealing with the death of the teacher, for the latter plays a smaller part in the child's psychic life than the father. For one thing, the teacher comes into his life at a later period, and as he is not surrounded with the halo of parental sanctity, hostile feelings against the teacher are generally quite conscious.

We call such dreams of the death of the father Oedipus dreams, because, according to Professor Freud, to whom we are indebted for the name, they bring to light an essentially human situation that has found most fitting expression in Sophocles's noted tragedy of *Oedipus Tyrannus.* You remember the story:

Laius, the King of Thebes, married Jocasta. After years of childless marriage Laius visited the Delphian Apollo and prayed for a child. The answer of the god was as follows: "Your prayer has been heard and a son will be given to you, but you will die at his hand, for Zeus decided to fulfill the curse of Polybos, whose son you have once kidnaped." In spite of the warning the son was born, but remembering the oracle, the child's feet were pierced and tied, and he was delivered to a faithful servant to be exposed. The latter, however, gave the child to a Corinthian shepherd who took it to his master, the King of Corinth, who, being childless, adopted it and called it Oedipus, meaning swollen feet. When the boy grew up into manhood he became uncertain of his origin, and, consulting the oracle, received the following message: "Do not return home, for thou art destined to kill thy father and marry thy mother." In order to avoid the fulfillment of this prophecy Oedipus at once left Corinth and accidentally wandered toward Thebes. On the way he met King Laius and in a sudden altercation with him struck him dead. He then came to the gates of Thebes, where he solved the riddle of the Sphinx, who barred his way. As a reward for ridding Thebes of this scourge he was elected king and presented with the hand of the widowed queen, Jocasta. He reigned in peace for many years and begot two sons and two daughters with his unknown mother, until a plague broke out which caused the Thebans to consult the oracle. The messenger returned with the advice that the plague would cease as soon as the murderer of King Laius was driven from the country. Sophocles then develops the play in a psychoanalytic manner until the true relations are discovered; namely, that Oedipus killed his own father and married his own mother. The tragedy ends by Oedipus blinding himself and wandering away into voluntary exile.

According to Professor Freud this noted Greek tragedy depicts a typical situation found in the psychic life of every individual, that undoubtedly Sophocles wrote the play as a reaction to his own feelings toward his father and his attachment to his mother. Indeed, Freud has pointed out that there are many passages in the play which very definitely demonstrate that it was based upon dream material. We find, for instance, that when Oedipus was so profoundly mortified by the true facts of the tragedy, his mother Jocasta consoles him in one passage thus: "Do not worry over this, because many a man has found himself in his dreams the partner of his mother's bed, but those go through life best who take those things as trifles." It would seem, then, that the author had grasped the full psychological import of what appears to be a universal situation.[8]

Oedipus dreams or dreams involving sexual relations with one's mother or sister are very common. It is noteworthy that when I first wrote a paper on the subject I had collected probably only forty or fifty dreams of this type. But upon its publication I began to receive numerous letters from various people, all of whom had the same story to relate: "I was so shocked by these dreams —I thought I was the only one to have them. But I am relieved to know that they are quite common." That was the general tenor of the communications. We may say, then, that it is everybody's fate, as it were, to be a rival of his own father and have his first love directed toward his own mother. Such a situation has a profound influence upon the individual's whole life. We shall meet it again when we discuss the subject of the only child. It is absolutely necessary to understand it in order to form the proper adjustment to life.

All such dreams are, in the final analysis, a reaction to the tyrannical part played by many a father in the household. The tyranny of father over son is a subject which stands out prominently in folklore and mythology; the struggle between the Greek gods is essentially a conflict between father and son. It is also quite a common theme in literature. I now recall, for instance, that in one year there were no less than five plays running in New York which dealt with the rivalry between father and son. In fact the Oedipus trend is more common in literature than is generally supposed. I have recently read an article by a well-known playreader in New York in which the writer stated that he could not understand why authors should deal so much with topics of the Oedipus character. He went on to assert that many excellent plays had to be rejected because the theme is too delicate; the love between mother and son or sister and brother is too grossly evident. You see, the sister is usually a substitute for the mother.

We shall learn later that when the normal sexual development is retarded through an overindulgence in love for the son on the part of the mother, a fixation on the mother may result. When we say that the man is fixated on the mother or the woman on the father, we do not mean the parents as they look today but as they

---

[8]In western European civilization, at least.

appeared when the children were still infants. At that early age of the child's life the mother and father looked different and also behaved differently. The influence of such a fixation upon the parent is only too apparent in the later selection of the adult. Given a number of women to choose from, a man will invariably select the woman that has been more or less selected for him by the unconscious. That is to say, if everything is normal he will be guided from the very outset by the image of his own mother. If conditions are not normal, however, his selection will be controlled by the reaction formed against it.

Consider, for instance, the case of Mr. B., who informed me that as far as he could remember he was always attracted to women of the Grecian type, tall, well-formed, and well-developed. And though he married a woman of that type, he could not understand why his *grande passion* was for a woman of the opposite type, that is to say, more like the French or the petite type. When we investigated his life we found that his mother was of French descent, and of the French type. The question naturally suggests itself, why should he have been drawn to women of the opposite type or, in other words, to women so radically different from the mother image? Upon first thought we might say that such a condition is only proof of nature's farsightedness in trying to preserve the proper balance, for if like were to attract like we would have, on the one hand, one might say, a race of giants, and, on the other, a race of pygmies. But the explanation is not so simple. In speaking to Mr. B. about his mother, he recalled that he never forgave his father for actually poking fun at his mother on two different occasions because of her small stature, and how deeply touched he felt at some of the disparaging remarks directed at her on that very account by various other people. It is not difficult to see what happened here. Consciously Mr. B was always trying to tear himself away from that particular shortcoming of his mother by seeking tall women. But in the unconscious he gravitated toward the mother image, and accordingly experienced his *grande passion* only when he met the type of woman that approached most closely her type. As you see, then, we are very often negatively influenced by these early attractions.

In normal cases the individual always gravitates toward the parent image, and it is for this reason that husband and wife resemble each other's parents. I have seen numerous cases where the wife resembled the husband's mother or sister to such an unusual degree that one could hardly tell the difference between the two. Thus a New York boy upon the death of his father left his home and went to California, where he was brought up by an uncle. When he married he came East with his wife on his honeymoon, and the moment his mother saw her she declared that the latter looked just like his younger sister Jane. In fact, she insisted that she saw the marked resemblance from the photograph her son had sent her, but she was quite sure. of it now. He walked with his wife on the avenue one day and his sister's classmate, who did not live in New York, ran up to her and kissed her warmly, thinking that she was her friend Jane. People mistook his wife for his sister so frequently that he finally began to become aware of the resemblance himself. I have five photographs, three of his wife and two of his sister, pasted on a cardboard, and I have shown them to quite a number of people, some of whom are artists, and there was only one man, an artist, who could tell the difference between the two women. This he did by resorting to such devices as measuring the angle of the chin and so on. It was absolutely impossible for the average observer to distinguish between the two women. The problem of resemblance has been noted by many students who were not at all working psychologically in our sense. Pearson, an Englishman, for instance, has investigated this subject on a physical basis, studying the color of the hair, stature, color of the eyes, et cetera, and formulated the conclusion that judging from physical resemblances married people look more like first cousins than strangers.

It is because the artists also actually gravitate toward some more or less definite images that we have the different Madonna types. It is unnecessary to say that the various studies of the Virgin Mary are all the products of artists who did not live at the time of the Madonna. Nobody really knew how she actually looked, and indeed if she resembled any type of woman at all, she must have resembled the Jewish type. It is noteworthy that a German artist has recently actually painted a Madonna of the Jewish type. Careful study, however, shows that the Madonnas that we see everywhere are really nothing but idealized images of the artist's own mother. Thus Madonnas painted by Italian artists resemble the

Italian woman, those by Spaniards the Spanish woman, and so on. Study for a moment Leonardo da Vinci's St. Anne and the Child and you will at once observe how much they resemble his own Mona Lisa; they all seem to have that peculiar Leonardesque quality, that enigmatic smile that we hear so much about. In the same way also his John the Baptist bears a marked resemblance to his Mona Lisa, and it is quite common to mistake him for a young woman.[9] We may say that in all these paintings the artist has unconsciously reproduced the image of his own mother. They are all reproductions of the artist's ideal image of his mother. I have ample corroboration of this in the artistic productions of modern artists whose lives I know intimately, but unfortunately material of this character cannot be divulged at present.

[9]Freud: *Leonardo da Vinci,* translated with an introduction by A. A. Brill. Random House, New York, 1947.

9. Types of Dreams *(Continued)*

AS THERE has been considerable objection to dreams of the death of parents, it may be wise to analyze a dream of this type given to me by a patient. It will show you very definitely how even later in life one dreams of the death of parents, though, of course, by no means openly as in childhood, but in a hidden, veiled way.

> *Mrs. B. dreamed that two old people, a man who seemed to be her father except that he looked much older, and a woman who seemed to be his wife and resembled her grandmother, or, more definitely, her mother's mother, were starting for a walk. "I was ill, at least in bed, so I told the people around me to follow them. No one wanted to, so I got up and followed them. They walked through the dining room, passed a pantry, and then came to another pantry which was open. As the old woman seemed unsteady on her feet, I called to the man to hold her back; just then he opened the door and pushed her down and she was killed, as he wished. He turned his head, saw that I was there, and realized that I noticed everything.*

"I wrote down the dream and went back to bed and dreamed the same dream over again, only this time I stepped back so that the old man did not see that I saw him commit the murder."

Mrs. B., a woman of thirty, suffered from a profound psychoneurosis. Her father and mother had been living apart for more than twenty years and were total strangers to each other, and this, despite the fact that they both lived under the same roof. This was as well known to outsiders as to the children themselves, but somehow the parents did not care to separate. What was more, the children knew that the father had a mistress who was his former stenographer; their sympathies were entirely with him, for, from their descriptions, the mother was apparently a paranoiac. They considered her insane and felt that she made the father's life miserable. Mrs. B. even claimed that she had no objection to her father's love affair with the stenographer. She knew the young woman personally and held her in high regard. But she always entertained a more or less deep-seated dislike for her, for she realized that because of her she was being deprived of a good deal of the father's affection; she saw in her a rival for his love.[1] She experienced what we designate in our work as the *ambivalent* feeling, a feeling of contrast: the individual loves and hates, as it were, at the same time. Love and hate go hand in hand. When one loves deeply the more or less disagreeable characteristics of the person will be completely concealed under the love.

A man who is in love will see nothing of that which other persons consider a conspicuous blemish in his *inamorata*. This ambivalency of feeling is a well-known mechanism and we should try to understand it. In ordinary life, of course, we can usually separate the two feelings. "He is a good teacher, but he knows so little about life," you may say about your teacher. "He is a very fine man, but lacks character as far as business is concerned," you may think to yourself about your employer. But when it concerns one whom we love or are supposed to love, we have to hide the disagreeable phase of his character. "He is a fine father, but a despicable man," one cannot say about his father. A mother would never observe: "My daughter is very accomplished, but not quite well behaved morally." We do not see the shortcomings of those we love or are supposed to love. But unconsciously we are well aware of them; though we hide them they keep on growing luxuriously in the unconscious.

Mrs. B. was married to a man whom she had not wished to marry. She had been engaged to him for a number of years, but somehow it was one of those chronic engagements—a chronic engagement never works well. Usually the long-engaged fiancée or her lover marries someone else suddenly, or if they do marry even-

---

[1] Some designate the rivalry between daughter and mother as the Electra complex.

tually, they are rarely happy. It does not at all bespeak happiness in matrimony when the fiancée confidently declares: "I have known him ever so long." We must remember that the love instinct is normally acute and vehement and sees things through at all costs. Anything chronic, even in love, is not good. It is not surprising, then, that when Mrs. B. finally did marry the man, she found she could not get along with him. She would live with him for a few months only to return to her parents again. In a way she imitated the conditions that existed in her own home. This is no accident. Adjustment always begins at home, and the individual always adjusts himself in proportion to the degree of adjustment that existed in the home. Whenever there is quarreling and friction in the family, the child either develops a neurosis, or imitates the home condition later in his life. I can cite numerous cases showing how clear this imitation is. I have cases that go back for four generations, where the same imitation prevailed—unhappy married life, separation, divorce. It is really an unconscious reproduction from one generation to another and is not at all hereditary. Mrs. B. very definitely reproduced the situation that she saw in her own home, except that she identified herself with the father rather than with the mother. But she could not continue this very long. Presently she broke down, and began to have hallucinations, some mild delusions, and various other symptoms.

When I began to treat the patient, there at once came up the problem of her husband. As I do not take any special attitude in such matrimonial difficulties, I left her to decide for herself. It was a difficult problem to solve: on the one hand, she did not wish to stay with her husband; on the other hand, it was hard for her to stay in her parents' home. Her mother would often ask, "What would you do if I were to die?" She was thus but indirectly referring to the fact that if she were to die the father would at once marry the stenographer, and the daughter would consequently have to leave the house. There was considerable truth in this, and the argument struck home, for Mrs. B. always wanted to have the management of the house herself, and she feared the possibility of seeing it pass over entirely into the hands of her father's mistress.

Analysis of the dream revealed that the man in the dream represented her father; the woman appeared to be an old lady, perhaps more than a hundred years old, and resembled her grandmother.

She informed me that her mother resembled her grandmother. Now the latter died at eighty-six and had she lived until the day of the dream she would have been one hundred and one. The slight difference between the woman in the dream and the mother recalled to her the features of the stenographer, her father's mistress. The combined ages of the stenographer, who was thirty-one, and the mother were exactly eighty-six years. In other words, there was a condensation of the two persons, the grandmother representing both the mother and the stenographer.

In the dream, as we see, the father kills them both, and that is indeed the best solution for the patient. She does not sympathize with her mother and would often complain, "There is no use talking about her; she is crazy and does not understand me." As for the stenographer, she liked her consciously and was grateful to her for what she did to help the father. Her objections to her were simply because of a feeling of jealousy. One of the reasons for the friction between her and her husband was that he could not supply her with the little luxuries that she was able to receive from her father at home, whose favorite daughter she was. The only possible solution that she could see was to leave her husband altogether and stay at home. Her father offered to help her husband, but the husband would not accept any aid, though he was willing, however, to live at home with her and thus save rent. But she protested that she married to get away from her home, and that she did not see any need for her husband if she were to remain at home. "Imagine," she declared, "sitting at dinner with a mother and a father who do not talk, the father thinking all the while of the mistress; and you sit there, too, with your husband whom you do not like." On the other hand, the mother was always ready with that powerful argument: "If I should die, you know what would happen to you." We see how nicely the problem is solved in the dream when the father kills both women: the patient would then have the house for herself and her father and not be hampered by a crazy mother and a rival mistress. She did not, of course, formulate such a wish consciously, but you can see how well it fits in with the situation. It is remarkable that there was this condensation, not only in appearance, but also in age. The age of the old lady just equals the combined ages of the two women. This may seem very peculiar to you but it is a common occurrence in dreams.

It is interesting to note the other work of the psychic censor[2] in her dreaming the dream over again. This time she did not wish her father to see that she observed him murdering her mother. The previous day I explained to her the wish as the dream motive and the modified dream, therefore, shows her agreement with what I told her; namely, that every dream represents the fulfillment of a hidden wish. *For a dream repeating something heard shows that the dreamer is in harmony with the thought or sentiment expressed.*

Another common typical dream is the so-called *examination dream.* The dreamer seems to be taking an examination and has the same emotional reaction to it that we usually feel in the waking state; he experiences the same sense of uneasiness and uncertainty that accompany the actual experience. The strange thing is that all during the dream he protests against the idea of being subjected to

[2]The *psychic censorship,* as the term is now used in our work, is nothing but the inhibitions imposed upon the individual by society. Let us recall here Freud's concept of the psychic apparatus. The child comes into the world with an *id* mentality with which every animal is equipped. The id comprises all the primitive impulses inherent in every animal. In order to live, the animal must overcome all difficulties, regardless of whether they are in our sense ethical or unethical. But as the child grows older he or she gradually learns to discriminate between what is good and bad in the outer world. This comes from experiences through the various senses. Thus the child soon learns that a burning candle, though attractive, is hurtful, and that certain things taste badly; and the normal child, that is, one equipped with the average amount of brains, soon learns the difference between good and evil. That part of the id which becomes endowed with awareness of the outer world is what we call the *ego.* The ego is thus only a modified portion of the id which, once developed, prevents the id from putting its blind wishes into operation. Every animal, from the little mouse to the *Homo sapiens,* has a good ego organization which prevents the animal from taking risky chances. However, there is still another grade of mental evolution which is seen only in man which we call the *ideal* or *super-ego.* Unlike the ego, which only keeps the id from hurting itself, the super-ego, which consists of a precipitate of all the commands, inhibitions, and prohibitions originally implanted in the child by the parents, especially the father, lords over the moral standards, the ethical principles of life. Once the super-ego develops, it is no longer a question whether one could accomplish something wrong with impunity but the very idea of doing wrong is immediately stifled. The average person is under a sort of *categorical imperative* where good is done for good's sake and virtue for virtue's sake. Thus a criminal who can plan murder or other felonious crimes may have a good ego but no super-ego, or a very weak one. These three forces of the mind are at the basis of every one of our actions. (Brill: *Lectures on Psychoanalytic Psychiatry.* Knopf, N.Y., 1947.) In the dream when the person is asleep the super-ego sometimes lets some id wishes slip through, but they are usually distorted. Thus in the above dream the distortion was inevitable; the dreamer could not kill her mother even in her dream, hence she was concealed under the composite personality of the grandmother and the stenographer.

an examination: "Why should I be examined in this subject?" he seems to be saying to himself. "Am I not already a doctor?" But the examination nevertheless continues. Another interesting thing to note is that one is examined not in a subject in which one was poor or failed, as might be supposed, but rather in a subject in which one was considerably proficient. Analysis shows that these dreams are typical of individuals who have received the usual academic education at schools and colleges. Upon examining them you find that you have them only at a time when you are about to embark upon some new venture and you experience a feeling of uncertainty and fear as to its outcome. You go to bed with that same uneasy feeling that you had on the day before the examination. "Yes," you may think to yourself, "I know my subject, but I may be asked something that I do not know." So when you retire with your mind uneasy as to the outcome of your undertaking, by association you recall that same emotional feeling experienced in the past on similar occasions, and the result is an examination dream in a subject which you have passed with honors, so that you might be able to console yourself thus: "Now you were afraid before your examination but you passed it without difficulty; in the same way also you will pass this examination. Do not worry, do not fear."

We must remember that what is of fundamental consideration is the emotional element in the dream. If there is any resemblance between the emotional element of today and any emotional element of the past, the dream will conjure up the past in all its vividness. In the particular case it is a *consolation dream;* all uncertainty is to be removed; you are to be consoled. But the psychic censorship which always realizes that you are only dreaming cannot possibly eliminate the element of fear and uncertainty that you experienced on occasions of actual examinations. When the dreamer awakens he feels greatly relieved that it was only a dream. Some of you may recall in this connection the case of the man who dreamed that he was swimming on a board in the bay. We may say that this was a sort of examination dream. In the dream, as you remember, a boyhood experience was revived; we may say that he again engaged in a race, this time, however, not with his young playmates but with a board of directors, and as in those boyhood matches he finds himself again successful.

There is a class of dreams which continue to manifest themselves for weeks and months until the wish they contain is actually realized. They are what are commonly regarded as *prophetic dreams*. A chronic alcoholic showing delusions of jealousy disliked a dog because his wife "was more attached to the dog than to him." He continued to dream at different times that the dog was run over, taken away by the dogcatcher, et cetera, until one day during his wife's absence he really disposed of it. Here the dream ostensibly treated of the future, at least so the wife thought on her return home. "Poor Fido," she exclaimed, "John [husband] dreamed only last week that he was caught by the dogcatchers and now the dream has come true." This is what is designated as the *resolution dream*. The person resolves, perhaps unconsciously, to do a certain thing, and the dream continues to represent it as realized until it is actually accomplished. That is why dreams of this class are regarded as prophetic dreams, "dreams that come true." I have analyzed a number of them, and all showed that the wish always preceded the event in question. Thus one of my patients dreamed that her brother who lived in another city was dead, and after relating her dream to her husband received word that her brother really had died. The analysis showed that her brother suffered from chronic tuberculosis which the doctors months before declared fatal. She was fully aware of the gravity of his malady and often thought he would be better off dead than alive. Her mother lived with her, but owing to her brother's illness, she stayed with him. She was nearing the end of a pregnancy and daily hoped that her mother would return before her confinement. This recalled similar experiences of childhood, when her mother often neglected her for the same brother because he was very delicate and sickly. As a child she often wished him dead, a thing quite common among children to whom the idea of death means simply to be away. The conscious wish "he would be better off dead than alive" became the dream inciter because it succeeded in arousing a similar infantile wish.

The realization of our waking dreams shows precisely the same mechanisms. This can be observed not only in the individual but in whole racial groups. We all know that the leitmotiv of orthodox Judaism is and always has been the re-establishment of a Jewish nationality, the return to Jerusalem. Should Zionism succeed in actually obtaining a part of Palestine under the United Nations, the biblical dreams, the prophecies, could then be considered as having "come true."

Another typical dream is that of *missing trains*. I would not consider this a typical dream if it did not usually have one very important and distinct connotation, despite its many other meanings depending upon the individual case. We observe in this dream a state of anxiety; the individual experiences all the unpleasantness of packing hurriedly to make the train, he meets with all sorts of difficulties and hindrances on the way, and, to cap the climax, he finally misses the train. We have here again a consolation dream; we are told, as it were, not to worry, as there will be no departure. This type of dream is usually a reaction to the fear of death, and recalls to the dreamer some scene in early childhood when his parents were taken from him, sometimes through actual death, sometimes just for a trip, leaving him heartbroken and crying.

We must also not fail to note the important part the train plays in the child's life. Typifying, as it does, motion to the highest degree, the moving train has a powerful hold on his imagination, exercising a fascination over him no less profound than his first sense of awe and terror at the sight.

One of the most typical dreams is the *flying dream*. A man related to me the following dream of this type. He was walking, and suddenly he began to feel lighter and lighter until he could glide over the tops of houses and the whole city looked up to him as to an airplane. Such a dream is usually found among people who have unbounded ambitions, who wish to excel and stand high in the estimation of the world. Very often it is found also among those who are not tall of stature, who by no means relish the idea of having to look up to people when speaking to them. They would rather look down upon others, and the only way they can realize such a wish is in soaring far above them or, in other words, in flying. One man who was under my observation had this type of dream quite often; and it is noteworthy that his most ardent wish was to be taller than he was. He often resorted to mechanical appliances and similar methods to pull his limbs.

It is hard to imagine what an important role in life the wish to be taller plays. I have known a number of people who informed me with all the emotion that usually goes with the disclosure of some very intimate, personal secret, how hard they always tried to be just a little taller. It is difficult to realize how much time, money, and effort men and women spend in their *sanctum sanctorum,* in the pursuit of divers means and ways to become taller.

An unusually interesting typical dream is the *falling dream.* It is significant to note that at certain times in life one has more dreams of this type than at other times. Various investigators in attempting to account for the dream psychologically have offered all kinds of farfetched and amusing explanations. One of the most common of these is that, in accordance with the culture-epoch theory, the dream goes back to prehistoric times, and in this particular case to the period when we were monkeys and lived in the treetops. We are told that when the monkey fell down peradventure from the tree at night, he was immediately devoured by some vicious reptile, and that is the reason why we never strike the ground in the dream. Such a notion is difficult to conceive in the light of the most modern investigations along these lines; surely it is hard to conceive of a monkey falling from a tree and being at once swallowed by some cowering reptile. Moreover, I have known dreams where the dreamer falls and actually strikes the ground. What the falling dream essentially denotes, however, is a repressed pleasure originating from motion, which, as we know, is a fundamental pleasure principle in life. Motion is a passive root of sex, and, as such, has a powerful appeal to young and old alike. Thus from time immemorial, among uncivilized and civilized peoples alike, the way to pacify the child that was unsatisfied with nursing was to rock it. We know that as the child grows older he likes to be taken up by an adult, thrown up in the air, and caught: he experiences a sense of exhilaration and pleasure in the experience. Later on this early emotion repeats itself in dreams, but when that happens we no longer conceive it in terms of pleasure, but, rather, in terms of displeasure. It is now a repressed, a tabooed pleasure. That is why so many men and women have these falling dreams as symbolic of moral falling.

I have on record many dreams of falling given to me by women when they were struggling with the idea of moral falling. I reported a dream of a woman who informed me that she dreamed that she was climbing a staircase and found it very difficult; she was always afraid she would fall down. Right on top of the staircase there stood an old classmate of hers of whom she knew nothing, not having seen her since they left school; she had heard, however, that she was a most unscrupulous, immoral woman. Thus her dream was the result of her struggling with the tabooed thought; she was trying to reach the station of her classmate. The dream being of the anxiety type, she woke up in a marked state of fear. The moral here is very evident: "If you are going to do what you are thinking of you will be just like your classmate"; the classmate standing here as a symbol for moral falling.

There are dreams which you might say are of a *local* character. This is particularly observed when we examine the dreams of Southern gentlemen. The latter invariably have sexual dreams referring to colored women. This would seem strange in view of the degree of aloofness with which the colored people in the South are treated by the white population. But I have never known a Southern gentleman who did not at some time in life have erotic dreams about colored women. The reason is quite apparent: all of these men had Negro mammies and it is to them that they owe their first early impression of the mother. It is well known that many Southern ladies have practically nothing to do with the care of their children, that it is left entirely to the mammy. It is on that account that the mammy is so very often highly esteemed and even considered as a member of the family. But the fact remains that she is colored, and her impress on the child manifests itself in his later erotic dreams. Whereas, then, the Southern gentleman will not deign to be in the same car with a colored woman, he has nevertheless shown no scruples in cohabiting with her in his younger days. This is unheard of in any other place in the United States outside of the South, and it may interest you to know that in investigating the sexual life of thousands of people I have never found a white man with the exception of the Southern gentlemen who by preference would have sexual relations with colored women. But in the South this is quite common even among respectable men. Thus one often learns that many so-called gentlemen maintained colored mistresses and some of them even acknowledged their mixed offspring.

Before leaving the subject of typical dreams I wish to touch briefly upon another class of dreams which we may consider more or less typical—in which *the dreamer identifies himself with some animal.* The dreamer is here hidden under the animal, strange as that may seem. To give you a little more insight into the nature of this identification I wish to cite first the dream of a woman who identified herself with a dog; second, a significant part of a very long dream of a patient who identified herself with a horse. The first dream runs as follows:

> *"Brownie is sick and we give him medicine, or we think he has lived long enough, so we give him poison. Then we regret it and I ring up the veterinarian. I wonder whether the poison is fatal, and as I think about it I realize that it is. 'It is hemlock,' I say to myself, 'and that is what they gave Socrates.' I am very much worried, and I am relieved when the veterinarian arrives and prescribes an emetic of mustard and hot water. My mother is there and she irritates me because, instead of helping, she only wrings her hands and cries."*

The dreamer has had the dog for four years and is deeply attached to him. She is always with him, and never leaves him out of her sight. The dog is a quiet, sober animal and I frequently used to remark to her that "Brownie" appeared very philosophical. Of late the patient continued to fear that he might die, and this, despite the fact that she consulted a veterinarian who assured her that the dog had still four or five more years to live. In the course of the analysis the dreamer recalled a play in which a girl attempts suicide; as soon as she has taken the poison she begins to cry for help; someone appears on the scene and administers hot water and mustard as an antidote. I would have you mark that these are the very medications that the physician prescribed for the dog. She also recalls that on the day previous to the dream she asked a girl at the canteen for something to eat and was told that she could have only a "dog with mustard." The analysis also revealed that she had been very depressed of late and had thought seriously of suicide. In time she began to be concerned over the dog, perhaps he might die, she thought—she thus began to detach some of her own anxiety from her own person to the animal. But she is like the woman in the play who took the poison and straightway called for help: she really does not wish to die. There are so many people who merely like to play with the idea of suicide, because it offers them some form of emotional outlet. In the dream the patient is relieved because the veterinarian gives the dog mustard and hot water, thereby saving his life. The dream thus realizes her wish to live. That part of the dream which speaks about her being irritated by her mother refers to the friction existing between the patient and her mother. Whenever the mother annoyed her she would play sick. The parent, in her great excitement, would then send for the doctor, who would prescribe bromide. In the dream we see the patient picturing herself dead only to revenge herself on her mother. And the interesting thing to observe is that this is all accomplished in the dream indirectly through the person of the dog Brownie.[3]

This identification with animals is often real and profound, as the analysis of the following dream very definitely shows. The dreamer is a noted animal painter, a woman who has always loved animals. One of her greatest pleasures in life is to frolic about in her studio, walking on all fours in imitation of a pony. Her dream runs as follows:

"I am walking in a sort of side path from S——— Station on my way home. My skirt is up and I pass a hard stool like a horse. I look around and see a woman walking some little distance behind, there is perhaps a strip of something across her face, a veil covering one eye. I hope she doesn't see me and ridicule me. Again I pass a hard stool, and turn around and hope the woman hasn't seen me. I am walking with someone, probably my father. I get into the road to drive a horse, possibly an ass. Mr. L. gives me the reins, which are not at all reins, but a single strap attachment without a bridle or a bit. I am driving: I seem to have stopped in the road with the horse, and the cart turned the other direction. I am adjusting the harness at the collar or something; there is a loose sorrel mare which comes up; she is very beautiful, with a delicate head and nose, and slender limbs. She stands right up against my horse, cheek to cheek, as though to make friends with him or me. I slap her on the side of the nose, but she insists upon standing there. I slap her again, and as I put my hand up toward her she bites or attempts to bite. As I resist, I say,

[3]Cf. dream about the two cats fighting—another example of animal identification.

'She bites.' She seems to have gone down under a bridge or
subway. I want Mr. L. to keep her there while I get away with
my horse over the bridge. There seems to be some difficulty.
At last I go down to see how he is managing her, or to assist
him. She is now a young woman, pale and thin, and not in her
right mind. Mr. L. is holding her by a string in her nose—a
piece of wire. I am afraid it will tear and I say so. She comes
toward me with her face near mine and I am greatly frightened;
she has a hairy lip and is much older. I awake in fright."

Mrs. K., the dreamer, is a married woman of twenty-six, who
consulted me originally because she was nervous. As far as the
outer world was concerned she seemed perfectly normal, her intimate friends never knew that there was anything troubling her.
The outstanding factor in her psychic life is a condition that she
had revealed to no one—the fact that she hated to be a woman and
always desired to be a man. This "masculine protest," as the feeling
is designated by Alfred Adler, is not so uncommon a mechanism as
it may seem. The dream is most significant, for it actually reveals the
very mainsprings of her whole psychic development and thus offers
a remarkable analysis of her neurosis.

"Going from S——— Station" refers to the place where she used
to live when a little girl. "Walking with her skirt up"—to this it
was most difficult for her to associate, because she is a very clean-
minded woman. But it goes back to her unusual attachment for
horses. At a very early age she evinced a tremendous interest in
them, at the age of four or five years she always craved to be a
horse, and identified first her father and then herself with the
horse. We can now begin to see the reason for the strange situation—"My skirt is up and I pass a hard stool like a horse." It is
plainly the result of her identification with a horse, it is an expression of her wish to be a horse. We may already see how profound
and deep-rooted is her identification. It is highly significant also
that one of her symptoms is marked constipation from which she
suffered for years. I am glad to say that since the analysis of this
dream the symptom has entirely disappeared.

The woman "walking some little distance behind" is her stepmother, whom she describes as having been just, though critical
toward her. In the dream the patient sees a "strip across her face,

a veil covering one eye." This is a picture of Justice, and she recalls a cartoon of Justice that she saw in one of the local newspapers. The woman became her stepmother when Mrs. K. was five years old, and though she really treated her as a daughter, she has always remained the one person of whom the patient was extremely jealous: Mrs. K. could never forgive her father for marrying her.

Mr. L. is her brother, who represents her ideal type of man, the type of man whom she would have liked to marry. The horse is really herself. "And possibly an ass"—to this she associated her stepmother, thus identifying herself with the stepmother in order to be with her father. We see that she is desirous of taking the step-mother's place.

The analysis revealed also that every time the patient meets a man she experiences a morbid dread that he might "bridle her and put a bit in her mouth"; it is for that reason that she craves to be a man and protests against being a woman. This is the crux of her emotional difficulties. We know that at a certain period of her development almost every girl would like to be a boy. But when the girl reaches a certain age and begins to realize that she cannot do the things that boys do, she gradually adjusts herself to a girl's normal interests and occupations. This is as it should be. As women are biologically different from men, they must be brought up as women, and not as men; we should give them an education that fits them for womanhood. That is why it is so absolutely necessary to guard most carefully against bringing up a girl to be a tomboy. We must remember also to begin training the child to react normally very early, for it will be most difficult for him to give up an abnormal mode of reaction later in life, after it has become a second habit, so to speak.

The dreamer, then, always craved to be a man, her sexual cravings were perfectly normal. She married a man who loved her deeply, out of sheer pity for him, as she maintains. She does not treat him at all as a husband, for it is she herself who desires to be the man; she would be extremely jealous, for example, if he could shoot better than she. Out in the country she once observed him and other men practicing high jumping, and when she found that she could not do it, she practiced for days but without success.

From very early childhood the dreamer always identified herself with her father. She still imitates him in practically everything.

The man was exceedingly fond of horses, and her own love of horses goes back to this source. When she was a little girl he always played horse with her, the practice continuing to as late as nine and ten. It was the little girl's greatest delight. She learned to neigh and romp like a horse. The father, needless to say, fell right into the spirit of the game, encouraging the little girl, and offering her, as he thought, a source of great pleasure.

The mare coming up to her, "with a delicate head and nose and slender limbs," represents her ideal horse. The dreamer has studied and painted horses for years and knows considerable about them. She may be justly considered a second Rosa Bonheur. "She stands right up against my horse, cheek to cheek, et cetera—I slap her on the side of the nose . . ." This refers to a woman who is involved in an affair with a man whom she loves. And as we read on, we find that the mare actually turns out to be a woman.

From the above brief analysis we may readily see that the dreamer retained what we may call her whole infantile sexuality. Her father was to no small degree responsible for this. As nice as it may be to play horse with one's child, it is not quite the thing to do at the age of nine, ten, or eleven; at this time it is altogether too infantile a pastime for father and child to engage in. How much better it would have been had the father taken the child for a walk and indulged in some pleasure appropriate for a girl of that age.

This identification with animals is not at all unusual. We have seen a notable example of it in the case of the young woman who accused herself of having drowned the pups. We saw how real and profound was the identification and the surprising extent to which it affected the young woman physically. We find this mechanism in a more glaring form among the insane. Long before I was a medical student, I remember observing at Blackwell's Island (now Welfare Island) a patient who was known as "Johnny the Horse." He imagined he was a horse, he always pulled a little cart after him, ran, galloped, and behaved in every respect like a horse. I have heard that he continued in this condition until his death. Apropos of this you may recall the biblical story of Nebuchadnezzar, who considered himself an animal when he became insane. Such cases are known to psychiatrists as *lycanthropia or delusions of transformation*. These patients very often imagine themselves to be animals and imitate them in every possible way.

We observe a similar condition also in normal life. A great many people show a marked attachment to animals, and sometimes even take them as substitutes for children, when the latter are denied them. There is also zoophilia, a sexual craving for some domestic animal which is an abnormal deviation from the typical sexual object. There is no objection to animals as pets provided the environment is suitable and the animals are well cared for. They offer a good outlet to grownups and children. I recommend pets especially in the case of an only child. I prefer dogs and birds, animals that can enter into rapport with the human being. I am against such pets as white rats or snakes, because instead of helping the individual to learn to give and take emotions more freely, they actually tend to isolate him; people as a rule either avoid a person who keeps such animals, or else regard him as a freak.

Pets have their purpose as an emotional outlet, and as such fall into the same category with collections; both offer modes of emotional expression. They are valuable, particularly in the case of an individual who lacks the opportunity to direct his affection toward children, family, or friends.

It is a fundamental truth that the human being must have somebody or something to love *all the time;* if he cannot direct his libido toward some human being, he directs it toward some animal or inanimate object, or sublimates it in some intellectual or social activity. It is well known that we become attached not only to a certain locality but to a certain home, a certain room, a certain bed, et cetera. I have actually had to treat a man because the chair in which he sat for thirty years was destroyed. The history of suicides shows very definitely that the individual was led to self-destruction because he had nobody and nothing to love. While there is love, there is life, to paraphrase an old hackneyed saying. I know that some people will never commit suicide no matter in what distressing and harrowing circumstances they may find themselves, for an intimate study of their lives shows that they have some person or object to whom they are deeply attached. That is why we so often hear the well-known formula: "If not for my children . . . If not for my love of art . . . et cetera, et cetera, I would have been dead long ago." I once knew a man who informed me that the only thing that kept him from taking his life was his love for his pigeons. That is why abnormally attached lovers sometimes commit suicide when they are torn away from each other. When they are deprived of the love object they experience a terrible feeling of voidness; they feel that there is nothing left for them in the world; for the moment they cannot take their detached libido and fix it upon some other object, and they commit suicide. When I was abroad in 1905 I read about a couple in Paris who committed suicide because while they were out driving, their cat jumped off the carriage and was killed. There is no doubt that they identified the cat with a child, and when it was gone out of their life they felt that they had nothing more to live for. That is rare.

It is such intimate relationships formed in early childhood between human beings and animals that make for this identification in both normal and abnormal mental life and form the basis for the appearance of animals in dreams.

The Dream Manifoldly Determined

We have noted thus far some of the general principles of dream analysis and now I propose to be more concrete and give you some conception of the dream as it appears in its manifold associations and details. I hope to show you in this way how every detail in the dream is *manifoldly* determined, or *overdetermined*. I have chosen two dreams for this purpose. The first of these reads as follows:

"It was Easter Sunday, and I had been commissioned to bring some buns to my aunts. On my way to their home I saw my uncle on the other side of the street; he was going in the opposite direction and carried under his arm a dog which I recognized as belonging to my aunts. A little farther on I met Miss G., a social worker; she referred to Mr. X, to the effect that he was worth his weight in gold or some baser metal. When I reached the house of my aunts I found the dog there; apparently he had come back. My aunt complained that since Uncle was so fond of the dog, she had consented to his taking him along, knowing that the animal would find his way back. The dog began to play with me. I put my hand in his mouth and said, 'Rover, don't hurt me!' My brother George was there and as he watched me playing with the dog, remarked: 'Make

*believe my little fellow wouldn't like a dog like that to play
with.' At that, someone, I think it was the dog himself, spoke:
'Why, there is a puppy here, Rover's puppy; Rover hasn't
enough milk for it. The poor little thing needs human milk!'
I wondered how Rover came to have a puppy, and my aunts
explained that Rover had met another dog Coucho in the
woods."*

When the person is asked what caused him to have such a dream,
he usually betrays utter ignorance at first, but upon a little reflection soon recalls some incident of the day previous to the dream.
Very often he may even reproduce some situation that happened
long before the dream, *but it is invariably something of the day
before the dream that starts the trend of the associations.* Accordingly the dreamer in question recalled that she had read on the
previous day some notice about a preacher who was going to speak
at a certain church that she usually attends on Easter day. That
very day she also thought of her mother's family; on Easter day
she usually visits her aunts, and that is why it happened to be
Easter day in the dream, though in reality it was by no means
near the spring holiday. When she visits her aunts, she usually takes
buns along, it is a sort of family custom. The uncle is the man who
died a few years ago and whom she often used to meet in her
aunts' home. He was very fond of the aunts, of whom, by the way,
there were three, and also of their dog. The man was considered a
capitalist, and the dreamer states that he was quite wealthy when he
died. As far back as the dreamer could remember, the aunts always
had black dogs.

Miss G., the social worker whom she met, brought these associations: Yesterday the dreamer called on Mrs. B., the mother of
her dead friend; the latter wanted her to call with her on Mr. X
mentioned in the dream, but the dreamer refused to do so. Mr. X
once had a love affair with the dreamer and she hoped he would
marry her; but he married another woman, primarily for the latter's
money. Very few people knew about this old love affair and that is
why she would not call on him with Mrs. B.

Miss G. spoke about Mr. X in the dream and declared *that he
was worth his weight in gold or some baser metal.* This brought
forth the following story: The dreamer read a story in the evening

newspaper the night before the dream about a Negro, Cato Alexander by name, who died in New York in 1832. The account stated that this Negro was originally a slave who had somehow bought his freedom and come to New York, where he opened a tavern. Being an excellent cook, he became in time immensely rich. He had a daughter, and to any white man who would marry her he offered her weight in gold. According to the newspaper, his wish was never realized. Mr. X has been very prosperous since his marriage, and is now "immensely rich." You see in the dream she speaks about his "worth" in terms of "gold" or some "baser" metal, the adjective "baser" having in this connection a distinct and peculiar significance, because she hates him and always thinks of him as "that dog."

As for the dogs, she remembers that in walking to the subway station from her home she saw a lady exercising three dogs. That reminded her of her aunts, who also had three dogs. This recalled a letter that she read in the New York *Times* in which the writer discussed the question whether animals are guided by reason or instinct, and concluded that dogs show considerable reasoning power; he cited the example of a dog who though taken a long distance away from his home nevertheless found his way back, the case allegedly demonstrating a very complex form of reasoning on the part of the animal.

We have here already a great many associations which throw considerable light on the dream. In the first place, it is evident that Mr. X is identified with the dog. The association about the Negro who desired a white man to marry his daughter for her weight in gold is a bit of analogy to Mr. X, who married a woman for her money and whose whole aim in life was the acquisition of money. That is why he was referred to as being worth his weight in gold or some baser metal, and compared to a white man who would marry a Negress for money.

Her brother George, in the dream, she saw in church last on Easter Sunday, and she had occasion to think deeply about him on the day before the dream. The last time she met him, he spoke about Mr. X and made some unkind, caustic remark about him; but she could only recall his saying that Mr. X was "a sucker and a dog." Indeed, that was what the whole family thought of him.

As for having the dog talk—that is not at all impossible in the dream. You may recall, I am sure, the acrimonious buffet of words between the two cats, to which I drew your attention in another connection. In dreams, as in fables and mythology, inanimate and animate things know none of those limitations that they may possess in reality; note, for instance, that we have talking trees in Greek mythology.

To the dog's saying, "The poor little thing needs human milk, et cetera," she gave the following association. She holds a position of considerable importance and she was recently presented with a few liberty bonds in recognition of a charitable deed by the manager; they were given to her with some ceremonial, and in his speech he referred to the dreamer as being "full of the milk of human kindness." And that is exactly what Mr. X needs; he is devoid of all these fine qualities, he is hard and mercenary, he needs a little of "the milk of human kindness."

Please note that the words spoken by the dog were almost an exact reproduction of the words heard before the dream. *A quotation in the dream is always based on something heard or read, but it is usually modified by the dream to fit the situation in the dream.*

The dreamer now returns to her aunts who were four in number, three of whom are living. Their present dog is a male puppy and it is the third they have owned. The former one, called Nellie, died of old age, and it was jocularly remarked in the family that, just like her mistress, she died a virgin; she was never allowed out of the house. Rover meeting Coucho in the woods recalled to her a story by John Burroughs that she had read in the newspaper; it dealt with the mating habits of bucks, how they try to get as many does as they possibly can, that they have a regular "harem." Now, according to the dream, the dog met in the woods another dog called Coucho, although she knew of no such name.

The dream represents the fulfillment of a wish. Despite the fact that at present the dreamer consciously has absolutely no regard for Mr. X and would have nothing to do with him, she nevertheless was in love with him in the past and would have married him, had he so desired; consciously, she entertains no such hope now, but we still see traces of this old attachment in the unconscious. He comes back, as we see in the dream, though he is treated rather roughly and mercilessly; he lacks all the finer qualities; he is base and despicable—a very dog—a man who would marry a Negress for money. He is carried by the uncle, because the latter put him on his feet financially and helped him in every way to become successful; he is carried in the opposite direction, or, in other words, to her home. For indeed the uncle hoped that by helping him, Mr. X would marry his niece; he assisted him because he thought that Mr. X's reluctance to marry her was largely, if not entirely, because of economic and financial drawbacks.

How did this dream come about? Its main determinant was the visit the day before to Mrs. B. who, not knowing what had passed between Mr. X and the dreamer, suggested innocently that they call on him and his wife. Mrs. B even remarked, "It's too bad you didn't care to marry him." The dreamer said nothing in reply, but this undoubtedly stimulated many emotionally accentuated ideas. We have this visit, then, which consciously was just a disagreeable episode; unconsciously, in the dream, it revived the whole past by taking all the associations that were fresh in her mind, particularly the story about the Negro and his daughter whose dowry was to be her weight in gold. "Mr. X is worth his weight in gold, or some baser metal," we learn in the dream, an indirect comparison, of course, between him and the man who was to marry the Negro woman. The unconscious repressed wish still lingers there, and the uncle, who is now dead, and who in the past tried to have Mr. X marry his niece by aiding him financially, is carrying him back to her home. Reading also on the same day about the mating instincts of bucks, she unconsciously thought of what Mr. X had insinuated when he broke to her the news of his engagement; namely, that that ought not to make any difference in their relationship. You see here the indirect analogy to the idea of the "harem." Thus, then, quite unconsciously, because of these episodes that touched certain analogous situations which in reality were very imperfect comparisons, the dream was formed. We may readily see that when she went to sleep, she thought again of her conversation with Mrs. B. and about the significant remarks that the latter had made. But she could not consciously dwell on the situation and pushed it out of consciousness. If she had allowed herself to think of it and all the reminiscences of her sad experiences with Mr. X, she would not have fallen asleep; so she crowded out all thought of him from her mind; and all those episodes of the day, particularly those which showed an erotic accent, were immediately taken up and woven into the dream, for they fitted in with the present situation and could thus realize the wish.

You can now the more readily see what we mean when we say that there are two streams to every dream. The first one is always in conflict with the second; an individual may desire something, but as it is impossible to realize, either because it is not permitted or because it is unattainable, there immediately ensues a sort of conflict in which the mind takes it up and with a few modifications finally realizes it. The modifications are entirely determined by what we call the *psychic censorship* which always stands between these two streams. Instead of allowing the original wish to be realized in its pure form, the psychic censorship modifies it so that you can realize it even in the unconscious without shocking your other self. You remember the dream about Venus and Apollo; it would have been impossible with the dreamer's psychic make-up; so that both characters had to be invested, as it were, with all sorts of disguises. Here, instead of consciously thinking of the mating instincts of bucks, and dwelling openly on the sex question and everything appertaining to it, there was a marked repression, and you have only an allusion to the situation. We learn merely that the dog Rover went into the woods, where he met another dog by the peculiar name of "Coucho"; we thus see in what an ingenious way the essential idea is concealed. The word is a condensation of *couch* and the French *coucher,* to lie.

We must bear in mind that in analyzing the dream it is necessary to ask the dreamer: "What do the elements in the dream recall? What associations do they arouse in your mind?" If the element is an apple, for instance, and the person in question draws it in the shape of a heart and gives you half-a-dozen associations that very definitely refer to affairs of the heart and temptation, then the apple can stand for that group of ideas and that only; it can represent no other, for it arouses in the mind only those associations that refer to love and temptation. In each person, of course, certain elements recall certain associations, and depending upon the nature of the individual's psychic life, you have this or that meaning. But when the associations continually revolve about an element in a certain definite way, then it can denote one thing and one thing only: it only points to some definite and special fact. On the other hand, if the element apple should call forth in the same person's mind associations referring not to love but to taste, such as "sour" and the like, then it would undoubtedly have an altogether different significance. In other words, we cannot categorically declare that an element denotes just one thing and no other; its significance is to be determined only in the light of the situation in which it is found, that is, it must be interpreted through its latent content.

The second dream that I have chosen for our more or less detailed consideration I analyzed with one of my patients, a married woman, who, upon my request, wrote it out with fine accuracy. It runs as follows:

A small tower or room at the corner of a house or barn in the country. A young woman, rather tall and slim, has been shut up in it. I am greatly distressed and immediately I (or my young woman companion or both) determine to break in and save her. We do so out of a sense of profound sympathy for the suffering (asphyxiation and smothering) that she is probably undergoing and with a feeling of deadly shrinking and repulsion from the horror of the sight. I say, to comfort and give us confidence: 'She is dead, she took poison.' We found indeed that she is dead, most parts of the body being dried and brittle like a mummy—the head and the mouth— the latter shaped a little like a turtle, a little like a miter— the mouth through which she breathed her last agony and drank the poison. The hands are broken off at the wrist and hang down from the square stone post or elevated portion in the small room. They are still soft, the flesh on them white as of a fresh corpse. The rest of the body is dismembered and thrown over this raised portion of the room."

The following are the associations that she gave me when she came to see me. "I awoke lying on my back with an uncomfortable feeling in my stomach, perhaps because of the very sandy soft clams I had eaten for supper. The day before I had taken a dose of cascara to get rid of a cold and catarrhal condition that were considerably aggravated by a trip to my brother in Chicago. I associate this with the poisoning in the dream. The asphyxiation may have been suggested by my being too warmly and heavily covered in bed or by my breathing somewhat under the bedclothes. [We thus see the determinant of the feeling of asphyxiation and smothering.] Then I heard Tommy [Joseph's young cat] mewing somewhere outside, as if in great distress. His mother, who was sleeping on my bed, ran out with her ears pricked to find out what was the matter. I slid into my overcoat and rubber boots, for it was raining heavily, and went outside with the lantern. It was 3:30 A.M. Now the mother cat is wont to jump over between two piazza roofs every night to come in through the upper windows, but Tommy, though he can climb the wisteria, has not ventured this jump as yet. So it occurred to me that he might have tried it and failed, and that I should find him hanging by one claw, perhaps afraid to drop. But this was not the case. I located him presently on the garret roof and got him down with the stepladder.

"This episode might have occasioned the dream; Tommy might have mewed and then stopped for a while before I awakened. The thought of going out to rescue a cat in distress that perhaps was entangled in wire, or perhaps was mad, was distinctly disagreeable." Here again, as in the dream caused by the alarm clock to which I drew attention previously, we see that a stimulus, probably of very short duration, produced the whole dream. Added to this there were the other significant factors: she was warmly covered and the room was stuffy; she, too, is suffering from some form of poisoning. The mewing of the cat, then, which undoubtedly brought up in the unconscious all the possibilities that might really have occurred, produced the dream of a mangled woman, smothered and poisoned. In accordance with our well-known principle of dream analysis, she herself was the woman experiencing the terrible death. For no matter what the stimuli are, *the dream is always egocentric;* the individual himself is always taken as the psychic node in terms of which all the stimuli are elaborated.

She continued her associations thus: "I am reminded of an incident a week or more ago when our neighbor who does chores for my aunt killed a large Rhode Island red cock for our Sunday dinner. It was left in the kitchen in a pail. I soon heard the colored girl calling my aunt, 'Miss Fanny, that rooster ain't dead!' My aunt, who found the bird standing up and out of the pail, went upstairs. I ran downstairs, trembling, and wrathy at her for leaving it in that condition, got my hatchet, and finished the job. The cock's head had been horribly mangled but he was far from dead." Here, strictly, were all the elements of the scene she saw in the dream. I am sure you must see by this time how insignificant the manifest content of the dream is in comparison with the vast network of past associations, feelings, and emotions that enter into the latent content. You may compare the manifest dream to a sunken steamer—you see only the very top of the mast, the great bulk of the vessel is submerged, and it is only when you begin to probe at it that you find the whole structure.

"The Italian boy John appeared at the moment when I severed the cock's head and observed: 'Miss Fanny, he's sufferin'.' I told him we had a saying, 'To jump around like a hen with her head off!' But he maintained that when his father killed chickens, they were stone-cold dead and did not move. This reminded me of my drowning the young cats in Edgewater, just before I left there."

I would like you to note the many intimate details that the average person would deem too trifling to relate. And what an unheroic figure the person often presents! There is something ludicrous about the whole situation: here is this young woman taking cascara to purge her stomach, chopping off a rooster's head, and drowning kittens. What mighty deeds! we smile to ourselves.

To return to the associations. "These incidents always made me think of the war and how out of proportion one's distress at pain seems to be when it is visible and when one is responsible for its relief. . . . Now I think of the descriptions of mangled soldiers in *Under Fire,* of the wild girl of the trenches that was lost and accidentally found—a putrid corpse; now of Constance Beverly in *Marmion*—hence the miter, because she was executed by the priests. The turtle mouth: because my father had a turtle for me in a wire cage in the brook when I was a child. During a freshet it became caught in the wire and was held there high and dry after the water went down. We did not visit it for a number of days and then my father released it." It is interesting to note the many and different elements that go to make up the picture of that woman in the dream. We say that each element is *overdetermined,* or *manifoldly determined;* there is no idea that is not determined by more than one association.

But to continue: "I felt my father's pity for the poor animal and was depressed myself. This makes me think how it occurred to me last night that my husband would not have wakened or taken trouble for the kitten, in nine cases out of ten, yet I remembered that in the tenth case he would have been a fine hand at rescue work.

"The girl is shut up as I felt my father confined me, particularly mentally. My female companion is my other self or the female in me, the compassionate, maternal part of me; there is also the ideal part of me that accomplishes the heroic and overcomes horror and fear, the masculine in me that is victorious in the dream. My only comfort is that the girl is dead, and her suffering and distress over. . . .

"I am now thinking of the conversation I had with my brother's wife who recently went with him to the South. I asked her if our family there seemed to be expecting to go on 'peopling the woods of Tennessee.' (I have had three nephews born within the last two or three years.) She spoke as though my sister and sister-in-law were worrying because they feared their children were coming too close together. I observed: 'Then they are following my stepmother in taking them as an unavoidable dispensation of providence. Such an attitude is indeed beyond my comprehension.' "

There now followed a discussion of birth control. The dreamer spoke of the difficulties experienced by Mr. A., her married step-brother, despite all the precautions that he had taken. . . . "I recall his wife's labor and the child's death, the miscarriage, and how most women of her type feel about the whole affair.

"And what would I do if *I* became pregnant?" Observe how personal the dream is, how it always returns to the dreamer's own problems, how the situation is always elaborated in terms of one's self, in terms of one's own inner problems and conflicts. "Is it worth while to run even the shadow of a risk when you do not want children? . . . Probably abstinence is best, but I, for one, become so torpid or so nervous when I practice it long. . . ." The meaning of the dream is now clear. It represents a hidden wish, to wit, not to be pregnant, or, in the event of pregnancy, to have a miscarriage.

From the analysis of the above dreams we may see how the psychic material always revolves around the ego and is elaborated in terms of the individual's inner strivings and desires, and how every element in the dream is *overdetermined* or *manifoldly determined*.

10. Common Forms of Psychoses

THUS FAR I have attempted to show you the psychic mechanisms as we find them first in the normal state and then in the abnormal state, or, more definitely, in the neurosis. I endeavored to make clear how we apply psychoanalysis to everyday faulty actions, to dreams, to neurotic symptoms and other abnormal conditions. Now I wish to give you a brief survey of the most common forms of mental illness.

Schizophrenia

The difference between a nervous disease and a mental disease is very marked in relation to reality; there is as vast a difference between them as there is, we might say, between an ordinary cold and tuberculosis. A psychosis is a deep-reaching mental disturbance. Without any further attempt at definition, for the psychosis is very difficult to define, we may consider an individual psychotic whose actions, whose general behavior, are foreign to his environment. The difference between a nervous condition and a psychosis, then, should be sought in the degree and character of reaction toward the environment.

When we study one of the most common forms of psychoses, schizophrenia, we find that it presents very definite characteristics. It was originally called dementia praecox because it was supposed to be a dementia present in young people. As a matter of fact, it is neither a dementia nor is it confined always to young people, although probably 75 to 80 per cent of the cases are between the ages of sixteen and thirty. It was also designated by some authors as a mental disease of puberty, for it manifests itself in a great many cases at about that age. We may define the disease as a progressive mental disturbance, its main characteristic being an emotional deterioration.

The outstanding characteristic of the schizophrenic is his complete indifference to the outside world. Take, for instance, a concrete case, that of a high-school girl of about fifteen years of age. According to the history given to me by the mother she was perfectly well up to about five months before consulting me, when she became "nervous." She then sat around the house insouciant and listless, did not care to dress, took no interest in school or studies. When we investigate the case more closely we find that there were slight manifestations of the disease long before then, but it was only five months ago that the parents began to realize that the girl was not just lazy but actually sick. The average person usually does not realize the gravity of the condition until a report comes from school that Miss So-and-So absolutely neglects her work and is uninterested and indifferent. But it is a sure sign that there is danger ahead when a girl who has been apparently well suddenly becomes indifferent to the things that interest the average young woman of her age. The average girl likes to dress attractively, is very anxious to appear well in the eyes of others, feels badly when she does not get along in her studies. But the schizophrenics seem not to care about these things.

When the schizophrenic develops into the full condition he presents a rather typical picture. The main characteristic is, as I said, an emotional deterioration; there is apparently no emotional reaction. One of the diagnostic points that I always used to demonstrate to students in the examination of such patients was to take a schizophrenic and bid him put out his tongue, then I would get a long pin and say to them: "Now I am going to stick this through the patient's tongue." And I would pretend to do so. A normal subject, even if he thought I was only joking, would withdraw his tongue, but the schizophrenic sits quite unconcerned, with his tongue out. Indeed he would not object even if one were actually to try to stick the pin through his tongue. And similarly, light a match and thrust it before his eyes, and he will sit quiet and undisturbed, whereas any other person would close his eyes at once. You can singe such a patient's eyebrows and he would not close his eyes. One author declares that you can shoot a cannon near him and he will not move. He is absolutely indifferent to the outside world.

Originally a great many physicians who were not acquainted with the deeper aspects of schizophrenia considered it a "masturbative insanity." We now realize that *masturbation in itself does no mental or physical harm*. It is a very common practice, and most of the authorities who have investigated the subject claim it to be found in 100 per cent of people. In the case of the average normal boy or girl the act is performed usually under cover, in some hiding place. But when the young person becomes indifferent and begins to develop schizophrenia, he will have no scruples in masturbating anywhere, with the result that the parents often catch him in the act. They consider it a vicious habit and try to get the child to break it. Then probably three or four months or a year later, when they are actually convinced that the person is mentally ill, they inform the doctor that they know only too well the cause of his condition: "he has abused himself." But this is far from the truth. All the cases that I have observed that were presumably due to masturbation were really cases of schizophrenia. From the very outset there was a marked emotional indifference, the feelings were dulled, and the patient would masturbate quite openly whenever the impulse moved him. It is because of this accidental relation between masturbation and schizophrenia that some early psychiatrists described the disease as a form of "masturbational insanity." There is no such disease.

Another characteristic of the schizophrenic is that he pays no attention to anyone; he refuses to do what you tell him, and if he does carry out what he was bidden to, he does so in a mechanical way. His handshake is another diagnostic point in these cases. The average person who takes and gives emotions freely gives you a healthy handshake; you feel that he is transmitting his feelings. If a schizophrenic is finally moved to give his hand, he does so mechanically, he extends it stiffly, barely touching the proffered hand.

In the advanced stage of the disease such patients sit in one place for weeks and months. I have observed some of them for as many as four or five years. Every day they would resume their usual position and remain there, going through the same mannerisms. I have seen a man incessantly rub the top of his head as he walked the floor, until he developed a very prominent tonsure. Others will go about and use what we call "verbigerations," stereotyped expressions. They may start with a phrase such as "I don't want to do it," and repeat it without end. When they do this every day for a year there are gradual elisions and only the person who had heard them first begin it can know what they are talking about. The same psychic process is seen not only in speech manifestations, but in various movements and actions, such as peculiarities in gait, writing, et cetera. Then, too, some of them show what we already referred to in another connection as "catatonic" characteristics— they assume rigid attitudes. I have seen a patient of this type imitate the cross, standing in the same position and staring at the sun for hours and hours until he was forced inside for fear of sunstroke. In a similar manner they react toward food and other necessities of life. They gobble their food down as though they were starved to death; often they take such big chunks that they choke to death. I have been called in a number of times to save a patient from suffocation, but sometimes the physician arrives too late to save him. That is why in every dining room in the mental hospitals there are instruments always ready for just such an emergency.

The patients also have certain hallucinations and delusions by which they are constantly controlled. When we delve into their lives we find that these delusions and hallucinations are by no means as senseless and meaningless as the average person would suppose, that there is a cause for them. We find that the patient is living in a world of his own, experiencing over and over again some episode, living through some wish in a delusionary way. To get him out of himself for a little while, to gain entry into his isolated world requires untold strength and endless patience.

When I was in the mental hospital at Zurich I observed the case of an American girl, born in Kentucky, who had been an inmate for years. She had to be kept in bed because she would not keep herself clean. She would sit there in bed the entire day with her head buried between her knees, her eyes closed, in a peculiarly rigid attitude. She had never conversed since she came to the hospital. Occasionally she would say something quite unexpectedly, but no one could find out what she was talking about. Professor Bleuler informed me of a patient whom he had had of that type, a catatonic schizophrenic. He decided once to see if he could influence her to dress and get out of bed without resorting to force; he wished to see to what extent suggestion could be utilized on her.

To the average sane person suggestions can be readily made, but these patients are shut in and practically inaccessible. Professor Bleuler told me that he talked to the patient for hours on end before she dressed and went where he desired. I decided to perform the same experiment upon this woman. I went into the ward one afternoon and talked until I was almost blue in the face. She finally looked up, and I felt highly rewarded considering that she had not done that for years. I said to her: "Aren't you ashamed of yourself lying around like that? Dress, and I'll take you for a walk." I had her dressed, brought to my office, and for two full days she behaved like any normal person. She revealed her whole story to me. I found that she was experiencing symbolically an episode that occurred at her home in Kentucky. From what I gathered, she was reproducing a seduction. She imagined that the young man was there with her in the hospital, talking to her all the time, while she just listened. She talked nicely to me and behaved in a perfectly normal way. But I had had enough experience by that time to know that it was too good to last. On the third day, as I was anxiously waiting for her to be brought in, I received a telephone call to the effect that my patient had relapsed into her old condition, that she was faring just as badly as ever. I dare say if I had had sufficient physical endurance to perform the experiment again, I might have aroused her again for a while.

Any marked emotional affect always tends to arouse such patients from their congealed state, to make them forget, as it were. We see this, for example, when they undergo an operation. I observed a patient of this type in the Central Islip State Hospital who did not talk for almost six years. For two and a half years I fed him by means of a tube through the nose, for he refused to eat. He looked cadaverous and yellow, veritably like wax. One day we examined him and found that he was suffering from an internal inflammatory condition; we felt that it was advisable to operate. I administered the anaesthetic, and it was strange to hear him plead with me not to operate. To say the least I was quite pleased to hear his voice. When he came to from the ether, he behaved like any sane person in a general hospital: he asked me how he was, what his temperature was, et cetera. I remember going into the dining room and imparting the interesting news to some of my colleagues. "So-and-So is normal now." They looked at me in blank wonder. "He is normal like anyone else," I repeated. They talked to him and normal indeed he was. "Look here, why did you act like a crazy fellow and give me all that trouble of feeding you? It is a disagreeable business," I said to him. He did not answer; he smiled. For three weeks he was in bed, recovering from the operation. I informed him that I would soon send him home, and he was pleased. But one morning I came in and, to my profound disappointment, found him in the same old place, in the same posture, with his head down—the same old inaccessible schizophrenic. It was as though the few weeks were completely wiped out of his life. I have seen a number of such cases in which an affect made the patient react. In this particular case, the fear of death and the will to live made him forget his abnormal world. The moment he felt well again, however, he withdrew into his own little world and would not come out again.

Patients of this character are absolutely shut in and their history reveals that they were always more or less so, they never mixed well with their fellows, they never showed any deep emotional rapport. There are many cases of the same type, though of course by no means so pronounced, who show bizarre expressions, who act peculiarly. No one can understand them, they are generally considered "crazy." They are of the schizoid type, but have no fully developed illness. They may have an episode which clears up to a certain extent; its remnants remain, however, and continue to manifest themselves in the person's behavior. I know the case of a man, for instance, who as a boy was extremely precocious. He was far ahead of his class, he performed many an unusual feat. But the teachers were often surprised when all of a sudden he would get up in the class and say something that no one understood. At the age of thirteen he left home and joined a troupe of actors in England. Great things were predicted for him on the stage, but after a while he ran off, tramped about for some time, and then came to the United States, where he worked at all sorts of jobs. Suddenly he disappeared. One day in a café, while discussing the subject of bravery and courage, someone remarked that "to commit suicide requires the higher form of cowardice." He vehemently denied that, and to prove his point shot himself in the head. He was taken to a hospital, where he recovered. If I were to describe to you all that he had experienced by the time I saw him at twenty-eight, we would have a veritable Odyssey. But he never had any direct delusions, he merely had fleeting hallucinations and delusions upon which he acted rapidly. There is no question about his being a rather mild type of schizophrenic, mild in the sense of his reactions to the depth of the symptoms.

The average case of schizophrenia deteriorates mentally, the patient forms his system, and then settles down. Mr. N.'s case is typical. He had been ill for six to eight years; he was very hallucinatory and delusional. He would leave his home and settle down for a time in some out-of-town hotel. I first saw him in a Southern city. I went over to him and called him by name. He did not so much as glance at me, despite the unusual circumstance of hearing his name in a totally strange city. I had to convince the doctors there that the man was psychotic. I asked one of them to bump into him to see what he would do. The doctor was afraid to take the risk, for the patient was quite a husky fellow, and so I bumped into him myself. The man did not say a word; he walked on without paying me the slightest attention. The doctors could not understand how a man could stay in a hotel for years, pay for his board and room regularly, and still be psychotic. But the hotelkeeper declared that he saw all the while that there was something peculiar about the man: he would stay in his room practically all the time, wore the same suit constantly, the same hat, the same pair of shoes, came down to eat promptly at a certain time, and was most methodical in his habits. Such patients are orderly and regular to a point of nausea. Methodicalness is not necessarily a sign of schizophrenia, but we may well think of the disease when we see people who are so extremely methodical.

Manic-Depressive Psychoses

The next variety of mental illness with which I wish to acquaint you, the manic-depressive type, is very widespread. It is designated by that name because, as we have already said on a previous occasion, it runs in certain phases or cycles. Sometimes the patient is excited, exhilarated, restless, manic, and sometimes he is melancholy, retarded in thought and action; depressed. Suddenly a wave of excitement lasting a few days, weeks, or months, usually two to six months, will come over the patient: the emotions run up and gradually down and remain normal for a period. There then may follow another similar wave. If you take the patient's history you will find that during a life of twenty to thirty years he may have had fifteen attacks or more. Sometimes this attack of excitement is followed by an attack of depression; the emotions go down, the patient feels downcast and depressed. Some patients run a different course. They may just begin with a depression, get over it and be a little exalted, just enough to feel well and exhilarated without being regarded as in any way abnormal, and they are perfectly well. Then, probably a few years later, there comes another depression, and so the case continues. When our knowledge of this type of psychosis was rather slight, we designated this phase of the disease as a separate state. This state of depression and retardation was designated as melancholia, which literally means "black bile." The term came from the old Greeks, who thought that a person who was depressed had liver trouble and that when he was purged he became well. It is for this reason that physicians have used purging for such cases. This idea is almost entirely disregarded now.

One very serious danger in this phase of the disease, that is, in the depressive state, is that the patient may commit suicide. You will often read in the newspapers of a nervous breakdown followed by suicide; we are undoubtedly dealing here with a case of the depressive type of manic-depressive psychosis, for there are few other forms of mental disturbances that terminate in suicide. I do not think I am exaggerating when I assert that probably 85 to 90 per cent of all suicides belong to the depressive type of this disease.

There are serious dangers also in the manic state of the disease. When the attack comes in a very mild form, that is, when the patient is just a little exhilarated and feels like one who has had a drink or two, he is liable to jump into all sorts of reckless ventures. I have seen women who married during such a state and were deeply disappointed when they became normal once more. I am convinced that many cases of marital unhappiness are due just to this fact—one or the other of the couple was in such an abnormal state at the time of marriage; when things subsided and became normal, there was a marital upset; husband and wife could not agree. It is like marrying when in a state of intoxication: unless you can continue drinking, matters cannot fare well. I might inform you that I have actually testified in one such case where the marriage was annulled on the ground that the man had had a number of manic attacks previous to the marriage, and we could say with more than a certain amount of probability that he was suffering from an attack at the time he married.

Another danger in this phase of the disease is that of exhaustion. In the extreme cases of excitement, the patient is constantly active; it is necessary to give him the strongest kind of medications and sedatives to keep him quiet. If he is not confined, he very often continues to talk and move about so recklessly and vehemently that he simply develops some intercurrent disease and dies. It is remarkable how many of these cases are at large and are taken for alcoholics. I have met them on the streets and in parks and on a few occasions have had them taken to the hospital. The casual onlooker observes them perform to his delight and amusement and regards them as alcoholics, but the trained observer usually can make the diagnosis easily.

The essential difference between the manic-depressive case and the schizophrenic is that the manic-depressive patient always recovers under general conditions and never shows any mental scar; there is no intellectual disturbance. That is why a great many physicians would not designate the manic-depressive patient as a case of psychosis, unless, of course, he is extreme and delusional; they regard the disease as merely an emotional disturbance. But when the schizophrenic seemingly recovers from the first episode, he always shows to the trained observer the schizophrenic reaction, there is always a mental scar left.

Paranoia

There is one more form of psychosis that I wish to touch upon; namely, paranoia. This is a chronic, progressive form of psychosis which is absolutely incurable. When you examine a paranoiac thoroughly you find that he always presented more or less definite characteristics, he always showed the type of mental make-up associated with the disease. But we usually do not see anything abnormal or maladjusted in his mode of reaction until he is thrown on his own resources or, generally speaking, until he has to come in actual contact with the environment. At the age of puberty we already begin to notice certain distinct peculiarities. First of all, the patient is a sort of quiet, reserved personality, an individual who takes no interest in the trivialities of life. The history from childhood shows that he never played like others, never made friends like others. He may have had perhaps some acquaintances but never a friend in whom he confided. The normal person is always drawn to someone in whom he can confide. Consciously or unconsciously he realizes that it is unhealthy to harbor secrets, for every secret contains something wrong or forbidden. But the paranoiac has never formed any lasting, intimate friendship, he has never learned how to give and take emotions freely. He starts out in life with that all-too-serious attitude; the element of love which manifests itself in childhood in play and later on in friendship and sex either is not developed with him, or its normal development is retarded and it is turned inward upon himself. Upon reaching the period of puberty, therefore, when an emotional outlet is absolutely necessary, he finds himself in a critical position: an emotional wave of puberty comes on, and, unable to place it properly, he begins to find fault with the environment. The young man may feel that he has not received the amount of attention or friendship that is properly due him. The young lady may complain that people are constantly pointing at her in an insinuating way, or that she has been slighted in some way. The situation usually resolves itself into this: "people do not like me."

Of course emotions beget emotions—if you do not like others, others will not like you; if you want friends, you must show friendship. Emerson has put it very well: "Love and you shall be loved." The world is so full of people that no one will worry about an individual who does not come forward himself. The paranoiac projects his own feelings on the outside world, and by an all-too-natural mode of reasoning he finds that the fault lies not with him but with the outside world: "People do not like me"—and since no one likes to depreciate himself, the logical explanation at once suggests itself, "because I am better than they are, therefore they do not like me." As a matter of fact that sometimes may be true, the person may be in a certain respect better than the people in his environment.

And so when the paranoiac reaches an age when he would like to compete, he feels himself too weak or too worthy to do so, and the result is that he is left to himself, his morbid ideas developing all the while more and more. Gradually he begins to elaborate who he is; he cannot admit, for instance, that he belongs to an ordinary plebeian family, he decides that he must be of better stock. Some time ago I observed a typical paranoiac: he imagined that he was an illegitimate son of Louis XIV. His life story was extremely interesting. His father was about thirty years older than his mother, so that when the patient was a little boy the father was an old man. The normal relationship, then, such as one finds between father and son was here impossible—the discrepancy in age was too great. That is why the boy never developed a normal association with his companions. Besides, the father was unusually attached to the child and insisted on having the boy with him all the time. Thus the patient grew up to be a morbid, introspective boy, and as he grew older, he gradually developed and elaborated his delusional system.

Paranoia turns out to reproduce a primitive condition, the individual, one might say, regresses to an atavistic state where he believes that no one is his friend. When we lived in caves, when we were troglodytes, the human being would not dare to put out his head for fear his neighbors would kill him; like animals, everybody worked exclusively for himself, there was nothing in common, there was no sense of mutual interest. Gradually, with the advance of civilization, not only did we make peace with the inhabitants of the neighboring cave, but we got out of caves altogether and began to build houses. Now we can even sleep with our windows open and there is no danger. In other words, we are departing from all those conditions which existed in the most primordial state. It is therefore important to free the child's development of all such primitive tendencies and teach him to give and take emotions freely, for otherwise he is likely either to continue in a primitive state or not know how to place his emotions properly and thus become psychotic or neurotic.

The outstanding symptoms of the paranoiac are these: First,

delusions of reference, by which we mean falsely construing whatever occurs in his environment to refer to his own person. Talk with someone, it matters not about what, for example, and the paranoiac will insist that you are talking about him. He may hear a sermon in church and straightway refer it to it himself by proving that the minister quoted a certain passage from the Bible with which he was only too familiar. In time he begins to develop persecutory ideas, he begins to think that people are against him. Usually he chooses for his target some intimate person in the family. When he fixes on someone, when he actually finds a person whom he likes very much, the attachment usually takes a most violent course for a while, then a violent process of disillusionment sets in: the new-found friend becomes a traitor and is usually taken as the arch conspirator. Gradually the circle widens and widens, the conspiracy becomes more and more involved. At first it may be only a brother-in-law or a classmate, later it is the whole world that is his enemy. It is remarkable how people of this type rationalize a situation. Ask one of them why he knows that detectives were following him from New York to Washington, and he declares: "When I registered, the clerk remarked to another clerk, 'Here he is.' " That was proof sufficient.

I have seen a man who actually went around the world: he maintained that wherever he went, he saw detectives at his heels, heard voices, and saw people watching him. Finally he decided to return to New York to give himself up. He did so, and was sent to the hospital. It took me a few days to take down his history. Only a paranoiac could have gone through all the privations that he had experienced. In the course of time the patient begins to reason why he is persecuted, he begins to elaborate just who he is. And when he finally becomes convinced that he is an emperor or some other great personality, he does not fail to act like one. If he believes himself to be Christ or a savior of some kind, he plays the appropriate role. To the average observer his reasoning is most bizarre, sometimes, though, it is very ingenious.

There are all kinds of paranoiacs. The original ones are, of course, rare; by those I mean the patients whom you have to observe and study for a long time before you can actually decide that they are psychotic. They are often too clever to betray themselves; they realize that they are being examined and are very guarded. You have to be equally clever to get at the proof—you have to hit the right moment to find the clue to the system. It is remarkable how many paranoiacs are taken to court on a writ of habeas corpus and discharged as sane. In one mental hospital that I visited it was interesting to observe that practically every one of the patients had a legal paper drawn in accordance with the legal form, applying for a writ of habeas corpus. Many of the patients thus discharged later commit crimes and homicide. They are so clever that they often elude the average judge or jury; no one but an expert in mental diseases can see that they are psychotic. Thus I had an interesting experience with a classmate of mine, a man of the typical paranoid character as I described it, a typical shut-in personality. When he was taken out on a writ of habeas corpus his mother, wife, brothers, and the principal of the school where he used to teach testified that he was "very insane." No one had any interest whatsoever in keeping him in the hospital. His own relatives and friends, and at least half-a-dozen teachers from his school, who were all sorry for him, all testified to his peculiar actions. After a trial lasting ten days the jury was out about ten minutes and brought in a verdict that the patient "was sane." To a jury of laymen the man's defense seemed altogether plausible, and yet the patient was absolutely psychotic. The man was released, and he might have killed many people and caused irreparable harm during the interval that elapsed between his discharge and his final commitment to an institution.

When a case of this character reaches the newspapers, it is often held up to the public as a very fine example of how "doctors kept an absolutely sane person in the asylum." We have seen an example of this deplorable condition in the case of the B. sisters. These two women were just as ill as any patients of any state hospital. They represent what we call a *folie à deux,* a form of psychosis which affects two people in the same family; sometimes I have seen it affect three people. It is significant that though these sisters were discharged as "insane" to the custody of someone under bond, the newspapers vociferously continued to protest that here were two sisters who were kept in the hospital despite the fact that they were "not insane." The fact of the matter is that the state hospitals are overcrowded; they have 10 per cent[1] more patients than they can accommodate; they are only too pleased to be able to discharge patients. The state hospital in question at that very time actually had a campaign requesting relatives and friends to relieve them of those patients whom they considered well enough to get along at home. On the other hand, the doctors are in duty bound not to discharge patients who are considered dangerous; how can they discharge patients who are distinctly anti-social, who feel that the whole world is conspiring against them? As for those folk who imagine that doctors take malicious pleasure in keeping people in the mental hospital or profit by the patient's confinement, they should be reminded that the physican receives a stipulated salary whether he has one patient or fifty, and that far from taking pleasure in keeping him confined, it is to his interest to see him discharged. In the old days there was the prevailing notion that the patients were killed or poisoned in the "asylum"; today we are doing our utmost to have the lay world realize that the "insane" are regarded and treated as sick people, to be discharged as soon as they are well. Another difficulty is that the lay person usually considers a person "insane" only when he stands on his head and yells nonsense; he considers him perfectly normal if he answers questions and talks more or less connectedly and intelligently, as, for instance, in cases of paranoia. We have been trying for years to have the lay public realize the true facts of the matter. But when a case such as that of the B. sisters is read in the newspapers, all the old stupid prejudices are revived anew. Untold harm is done thereby.

Before leaving the subject of paranoia I wish to outline parts of the history of a paranoiac. I am sure that it ought to prove instructive for, in the first place, it will show you more or less concretely the progress of the disease, how the patient gradually becomes more and more detached from reality; second, what an important part the sex element plays in all such mental disturbances, the patient's history showing a distinct maladjustment in his love affair. The patient is a man thirty-six years of age who at my request wrote out the history himself.

"Bringing up strict, with religious atmosphere, not allowed to

[1] *Patients in Mental Institutions,* 1944, U.S. Dept. of Commerce, Bureau of the Census, p. 29.

play with other children. Was of a somewhat 'sissy type,' but fairly good scholar. Father not at all nervous, but religious and rather strict. Mother extremely nervous. Favors twin brother, possibly because she is interested in medicine, and he wants to become a doctor.

"First vivid impression, quite young, four or five years, used to undress after bathing with brother and sister two years older. Sneaking curiosity as to secondary sexual characteristics of sister, looking at her with pleasure when unperceived. Remember remark of aunt to my mother, 'too old to dress in same room together with sister.' This roused a sense of guilt as to sex, which is still subconsciously retained. My brother also remembers an experience in the bathroom with my sister, each one of the three showing parts to the others. At the age of six or seven vivid remembrance of homosexual experience. About this time experience with the genital; it had to be treated."

He then cites a number of experiences. He dwells at length on his homosexuality which he practiced with his brother and which consisted simply in masturbation. He says:

"We kept that up until six or eight years of age, when we realized its import. I remember arguing with myself, 'This cannot be wrong, because it gives pleasure without pain or wrong consequences.' Later the practice was stopped and I found an intense nervous reaction in looking through cracks of doors at my sister undressing. At school had faint 'crushes' on boys. At college had a 'crush' on a man two years ahead. No sex impressions, but a desire to be of some service to him; liked to be near him."

Here he gives a great many experiences of that type at the age of twenty-two or twenty-three years. Speaking about women he says, "Have been in love only once. The girl was a friend of my sister's, my older sister, the one now in a sanitarium. This sister had 'crushes' on girl friends and teachers; it ended in an infatuation; abnormal girl, subject to attack of insanity. This girl friend has since married and has children. She was normal, but had led a rather repressed sex life; she was a 'nice' girl. I remember that I imagined myself in love with her in this way. She was a twin of two sisters. Had met them when about sixteen or seventeen years old. They appreciated us and we liked them very much. One time driving home from a theater party I noticed her holding hands with my sister. She had a 'crush' on my sister, as other young college girls did. There was nothing wrong in this relationship between the two. I was in a rather soft mood, and I aspired to deserve the same affection as my sister received. 'If she would only hold my hand like that.' And I made up my mind that I was in love with her. There was no sexual attraction. It was a rather sublimated emotion that I felt toward her. Afterward I met her in the subway with my brother. She sat down and I sat down beside her. I think she would rather have had my brother. I had the same rather soft, sublimated, tender emotion at that time, but I was nervous and excited and my heart beat very fast. Later my brother and I were asked out to her home over the week end. Hearing that, I became nervous and excited at the idea of seeing her. The whole thing was in my mind. However, there was no sex feeling. I was inwardly restless, but outwardly I was rather self-possessed while out there. I slept little and felt as if I had fever. I remember walking with her and my brother, and running races also, in which I made a great effort to shine. I tried to talk to her, but her attitude was favorable toward my brother, who liked her in an impersonal way. She did not have any strikingly emphasized secondary characteristics of her sex, which was rather the reason I liked her." What he meant was that she did not look like a big woman, but was more of a boyish type.

"I remember sitting indoors, on a sofa, and her inviting me to sit beside her, as in the subway. At that time I felt that to do so would be dishonest, since she had too much money for me to be happily married to her. My thoughts were socialistic at that time. Yet I had an impulse to do so, and I loved her in that way. I did not see her again, but did not forget her at all, always hoping to see her by accident. One time I actually got the nerve to call, but she was out."

You can see thus far what difficulty this boy had in adjusting himself to his love life.

"Another reason I did not press my suit was that I had heard that another man was violently in love with her. Instead of pressing my suit, I felt no jealousy, as I ought to, but argued that if he was madly in love with her, as he was, and I only in a very spiritual way, I could yield better than he. She married a third man, and it was a great blow to me. My emotion was thus always repressed, and as I appeared self-possessed no one realized it, but altogether I was very much perturbed. I had pneumonia a year afterward, being in a rundown condition. I had two trained nurses but repressed my sex feeling because it would not be sincere. I enjoyed talking to them and was interested in their ideas. I have always clung to the ideal which this girl seemed to fit. I transferred my interest to my studies, and had no friends.

"All this occurred while this homosexual practice was being carried on between my brother and myself. The next incident was that up at a certain lake my brother met a girl toward whom he had much the same feeling in a more transient phase. This period marked the end of our homosexual practice. We were really ignorant of its real import. Altogether we vaguely realized it was wrong. I felt a slight attraction toward this girl, who was beautiful, but rather stood apart, and let my brother do the talking. This time the girl appeared to discourage my brother, and since then I have called on her several times.

"After going through college and beginning the senior part of law, just before examination time my sister, who had been long ailing, suddenly became sick and had to be taken to the hospital." He enters at length into this matter.

"During college and professional school I had formed the habit of watching girls undress by means of field glasses. I did this, sometimes masturbating through an excited imagination. Toward the servants I had no sex feeling. I thought little of sex except with regard to this field-glass habit, which I carried on at intervals. I kept this up till last fall.

"After trying to get a job in vain last fall [the war had affected the situation somewhat] at my brother's suggestion I went to Johns Hopkins University, in Baltimore. I spent two weeks sightseeing, then took a laboratory course. I made efforts to take an interest in girls, flirting with them in streetcars. Baltimore is a small city, and some of the girls flirt very easily. I went to the Lyric Theatre, where the fashionable concerts and plays were given. I lived in a hotel, but did not meet any women at all, except at university classes. I was interested in the Ph.D. courses, and was thinking of taking a degree. I heard that two of the professors at the school were leaders in Baltimore society. Desiring to take for once a real interest in girls, and hoping to meet one I could fall in love with,

I made up my mind to speak to them. I went to Professor B. and told him that there was a case of insanity in the family and gave the impression that it had to do with sex, and also that I would like to get into Baltimore society. He was very nice to me, and when I asked to be introduced to some girls, he said that he would see about it. Apparently I did not show the proper sex interest, for when I next went to him, he said that the roundabout way was best, and also said, 'Go with normal men first,' and smiled, implying sex experience is necessary. He told me to join the Johns Hopkins Club, which I did. At this time I changed my place from the hotel to a boardinghouse, because it was cheaper and the food was better. I remember one story told in my hearing at the club." And then the patient relates some sort of pun which I never could make out.

"The second time upon my return from a game I had a queer experience. I was standing in front of the waiting station, flirting a bit with the girls who passed with 'middies,' when there came out two middies with girls and a chaperon, evidently their mother. One middy carried a suitcase, and as I passed one of the girls nudged me with the case as it brushed by me. I felt an interest in these girls but did not look them over. The mother was evidently a very fine lady and they were fashionably dressed. The light-haired one was rather good-looking I thought at the time. The other one was dark and rather peculiar-looking and had 'sad' eyes. This one sat alone, the mother and the light-haired one on the other side of the car, one seat back. The rest of the car consisted largely of a rather tough crowd. I sat in the rear seat, but sufficiently near to keep an eye on the one who nudged me. The peculiar-looking one seemed to be the object of attention, especially to one man, and the light-haired one evidently became much worried and looked back at me continually. At last, this was before I saw this Professor B., I thought I should not meet any girls on account of insanity in the family. I debated whether to intervene or not. I finally decided upon watchful waiting, but the distress of the three women increased, until finally I was about to get up and look at the man, who got up himself and walked into the smoker."

This idea that the girl nudged him was only imaginary, as well as the situation regarding the man.

"This produced, of course, a great sensation with the girls. I had apparently made a hit. They smiled their thanks to me and I smiled back. Then they took off their hats and wraps and tried to flirt with me, arranging their hair. But I saw no reason for picking them up, arguing that nice girls should not be treated that way. When the electric car stopped to change for Washington, they got out. The light-haired girl's expression was peculiar, as if she had been hard hit. The mother smiled at me rather scornfully, as if to say, 'You'll find out who we are, don't worry,' and seemed half-angry at my attitude. I tried to convey that I would have liked to meet them, but circumstances did not permit. I later remembered that girl on account of the incident and rather idealized her, and thought that she must be in Washington society.

"Evidently in the South it is the custom when one person wishes to meet another, and for some reason cannot, to bring them together at a play or concert. Anyway, shortly afterward I recognized both girls in a crowded audience. The first girl was a girl of German descent, from the remarks I heard at my boardinghouse, which evidently was a secret, for on leaving for the alumni meeting at X they assured me that Baltimore was Germania, with great emphasis. These remarks were made while discussing nationality. I compared this girl with the one I idealized and found I did not care for her.

"A week later I went to a ball game and felt a sort of excitement in my arm. People left hurriedly, and there was a sort of excitement of expectancy. A girl sitting next to me looked all around the bleachers, as if I was to do the same thing as all the others. Finally four or five girls came, and the men behind me began to patter with their feet, as if I was to walk around. I did so, and by careful scrutiny was able to locate my Washington friend. In cold daylight she seemed a different girl. I had seen her at six o'clock, and yet she had the same features and hair. She laughed at me, and encroached her shoulders over as if to call me down from my high horse. After looking her over carefully I returned to my former seat. A man seated near by made this remark, 'Well, well, well,' evidently somewhat surprised at my lack of gallantry. Before this and after this incident people began to look toward Washington when I passed them. I considered this a Southern custom, made to help along matrimony. After this the ball game continued and also they began to turn their heads and indicate unclean fingernails. After a particularly aggravating display of these signs by a rather fashionable party, one of them said, apparently to me, 'This is your last chance.' A lady at the ball game several times touched her mouth significantly, and then stuck her fingers in her glove of the other hand, as if to show what to think of, kissing and the sexual act when I looked at girls, or what to do to be acceptable to society."

You may thus see how nicely these symbolic actions are shown. He interprets everything in his own way, working it out in conformity with his own delusional ideas.

He went to a lecture on physics, but to him it seemed full of hints for him. "Work out these values and then we will go on," which meant, "I am to have sex experience, toil. My inexperience prevented me from getting there. After this I decided to come to New York, as there was nothing else to do in the social line, no one conforming with my ideal. I did so, and called on the girl of the B. L. socially, but did not get to know her sufficiently to make advances."

There is nothing unusual about this case when we bear in mind that it is a case of psychosis. Its most noteworthy facts are as follows: First, it is evident that this young man has had an abnormal love life. The constant struggle between sensuousness and chastity until the patient became psychotic was only the obvious conflict. More deeply rooted difficulties are evident to the trained observer from his story. He began with the autoerotic sexual outlet, masturbation, which he was very anxious to suppress. In this he succeeded for a time but soon returned to it. There then followed the homosexuality with his own brother and a few others. Finally there are his awkward attempts at heterosexuality, his failure in this respect, and the formation of delusions. His whole delusional system was that people were observing him and making remarks about him, disparaging, insulting remarks, because he was unable to do his duty sexually; many girls were interested in him, but he was too slow and not man enough to respond to them. He believed that if he were sexually normal, the women would have liked him; he was not liked because he had had no experiences with them. When the patient was asked, therefore, why he did not go right ahead and have experiences with women, he replied that he could not, that he heard voices telling him that that would be wrong and immoral.

We could continue with the extreme mental cases, the psychoses, for many pages more, but I feel that what I have already told you should suffice to give you a general appreciation of the subject, at any rate as far as our purposes here are concerned. Before leaving the subject entirely I wish to make this one point; namely, that even in the so-called normal person there may be observed some of those traits that I have pointed out in those extreme mental disturbances. That is to say, besides people of the psychoneurotic make-up, the hysterics, compulsive neurotics, et cetera, one also meets in life individuals who are distinctly of the paranoid or schizoid or manic type. A great many writers have thus come to the conclusion that when such individuals ever become ill, they always gravitate toward that form of psychosis that is compatible with their personality. That is, when a person of the paranoid make-up becomes ill, he gravitates toward paranoia, a person of the schizoid type toward schizophrenia. Through careful observation and study of different individuals we may readily discern these types, for we find that individuals show certain characteristic types of reactions which are reflected in their total adjustment and especially in their love life.

11. The Only Child

THAT THERE is really only a difference of degree between the most abnormal and the so-called normal, and that the degree can sometimes be measured in terms of environment, can readily be shown in cases where, regardless of predisposition in constitution, the environment alone impresses a definite stamp on the individual. This can readily be seen in persons who have been subjected to a special environment. I am referring to the "only child." The only child has a special reaction to the world which differs markedly from that of his cousin, let us say, who has sisters and brothers. We also find that the oldest son or daughter differs in many ways from the youngest son or daughter.

The oldest son differs from the others because his position in his environment was such that he had to develop certain characteristic traits. For one thing, he is more aggressive than the others, because originally he was the only child in the home; when the second child came, though only a year later, he already had the advantage over his younger brother, the advantage of strength and knowledge. But usually there is more than the difference of a year. Moreover, the parents constantly urge the older brother to take care of the younger boy. The result is that as time goes on there is the tendency for the oldest son of the family to assume leadership, so that when the father dies or is killed he becomes virtually the head of the family. We see here how the institution of the crown prince developed; it was found that when the father died, the oldest son was more fit to rule than the others by virtue of his standing in the community right in his own home.

And so it is with the only or favorite child; he, too, occupies a special position in the home. Whether willfully or not, parents have always pampered and spoiled the only child. When people love each other they usually enhance the love object; to the man his lady love is the most charming creature in the world; to the woman, her lover is the greatest man on earth. After they have married, a process of disillusionment sets in: the most charming woman becomes an ordinary girl with all the weaknessess and shortcomings of her sex, and the greatest man an ordinary human being. But there is a compensation with the coming of the first child, the gap begins to be filled, there develops a community of interest between husband and wife. To the man there is a compensation in his little girl in whom he tries to realize all those ideals that he found in the woman when he first met her but which seemed to have departed after living intimately with her for some time. The little girl now occupies a special position in the home, the father has a special interest in her, and with no brother or sister to share her father's affection the result is that she becomes spoiled. In a state of nature, the male animal really takes no interest in the young. He leaves them as soon as they are independent enough to seek their own food. It is different with human beings—the marriage institution devolves upon us the duty of living together. Some compensation is necessary, and wherever there is only one child, both parents turn to the child to fill the emotional gap formed because of the disillusionment owing to the original enormous enhancement of the partner.

Another serious factor in the development of the only child is that he meets with no competition at home. Where there are three, four, or five children, as there normally should be, there is constant conflict, they fight one another and thus learn to adjust themselves to the struggle for existence. But take the little one who is kept in the home with no one to oppose his will, whose every wish is gratified and who is always guided and protected most jealously, who is master of all he surveys in the home. What a pitiable sight this weakly brat presents when put out into the world at the age of five or six! The poor thing is helpless. He does not know how to act, he distrusts everybody, he cannot get along with anyone.

One of the most serious handicaps the only child has to cope with is his abnormal attachment to the mother, what we call his fixation upon the mother image. As we have said before, every parent puts her stamp, her image on the child. The child's first impulses of love are always directed to the parent, that is, a little boy's first sweetheart is always his own mother, her image is definitely imprinted upon his mind, so that forever afterward the child is always guided by this image. The same relation exists between the girl and her father. At the age of prepubescence the children normally begin to tear themselves away from the parents; a little boy will no longer even like to be hugged and kissed by his mother, he will feel that it is not quite right, that it is terribly unmanly. He will begin to find other women with whom he will fall in love. The history taken from men often shows distinctly that at eight, nine, or ten years of age they were madly in love. But the only child does not learn to detach his libido from the mother, always guarded as he is by maternal affection. Though he is constantly guided by it in his selection, the child normally tears himself away from the mother image. But in the case of the only child, where the mother had the opportunity to imprint her image on the boy for a much longer time and in a considerably stronger way, the image of the mother becomes fixed so that in later life he is always controlled by it, he cannot trust anyone but his mother or someone resembling her.

It is noteworthy that the woman whom the child first takes as a substitute for the mother is usually of about his mother's age. It is only as he grows older that he begins to be more and more interested in younger women. It is a common observation that the younger the man the older the woman that attracts him. But he behaves very differently when he enters his second childhood; it then seems the other way round—the older the man, the younger the woman that attracts him. As age advances there seems to be a regression to the more or less infantile, so that it is not at all uncommon to find many old men seeking young girls. We see this condition in its abnormal form in cases of *senile dementia,* where the old man in dotage actually attempts flirtations with young girls because of his mental deterioration. In normal cases the man merely evinces a kindly and fatherly interest in the girl.

In transferring this early attachment from the mother to other women, the child is very often a source of much anguish to the parent. Many a mother sometimes has experienced a nervous breakdown when it became evident that the son was tearing himself away from her. It is hard to realize what struggles some women have even later, when their sons finally choose a mate. They never find a single girl of whom they approve. We have here the reason for the mother-in-law theme. This condition exists everywhere, even among savages, and it is because of this one crucial fact: that the mother-in-law either loves her son to such an extent that she does not want any other woman to take him away from her and does not actually find a woman worthy enough of her boy; or, living through her daughter's life, she identifies herself with her and therefore tends to fall in love with her daughter's lover. It thus happens sometimes that the daughter is actually jealous, and I have had many women who have corroborated this from their own experience. Occasionally the press will report the case of a man who courted the daughter and married the mother, and vice versa. We have here essentially the same image, and it is easy enough to transfer its influence from the one to the other.

The only child can do very little on his own initiative, but consciously or unconsciously depends largely upon the mother's influence. I once treated a patient, a last child,[1] who had a domineering mother. It seemed that he was never able to do anything without her. He came to New York to find employment, but could not make up his mind to accept a position, despite the fact that many splendid opportunities were offered him. He would come to me and we would weigh the situation pro and con. I saw no other reason for his indecision and procrastination than his inherent weakness to decide. Finally I discovered that his mother was wont to bid him do something in this manner: "Jack, if I tell you to do it, do it." One day he came to me with the same problem, and I decided to resort to that magic formula. I said to him: "If I tell you to do it, do it." And sure enough, he replied: "All right, Doctor."

The only child rarely marries, and, if he does, his wife is not at all to be envied. As we pointed out, the average boy in a home of four or five children, where the mother has no time to gratify the child's ever-increasing emotional cravings, fixates as he grows older from one woman to another, seeking a substitute for the parent in the person of a teacher, nurse, hairdresser, et cetera. He

---

[1] We must remember that the last child presents the same problem as the only child, particularly the last child who is spaced from the other children by about three or four years.

transfers his emotions to every newcomer in the home. But the only child receives so much attention and love from the parent at home that he does not learn to direct libido toward others, and as he grows older his libido remains more or less fixed upon the parent. Occasionally nature asserts itself and a powerful stream of libido wells forth: he is drawn to some woman and may even go so far as becoming engaged to her. But difficulties soon arise.

It is not at all unusual for an only son to come to me on his wedding day imploring me to do something to stay the marriage. On such an occasion one man expressed to me the fear that perhaps he was suffering from appendicitis, perhaps, he felt, he should be sent to the hospital. I assured him that he had nothing of the sort, and he continued to persuade me, "I really feel a pain, Doctor, maybe I have." I advised him not to marry the girl. I assured him that he would not be rendering her anything in the nature of a favor. But the family physician was terrified at my advice and the mother politely informed me that I was a vicious person. So the poor fellow was led to the ceremony like the proverbial lamb to the slaughter. Now divorce proceedings are going on. How much better to have stopped the fiasco of the wedding; what trouble and mortification would have been saved. I have also observed men of this type suddenly seized with all manner of hysterical aches and pains when the time came for them to keep an appointment they had made with some young lady; they are loath to go. The average normal man is delighted to go out and meet women, play cards, flirt, love, and marry. But individuals of this type are too weak. Some time ago one of these men remarked to me: "If I would not have it so nice at home, I would probably marry, but as it is I do not feel like it." He is of the race of only children and his mother guards him like the apple of her eye. That is the very expression the fond parent used when telling me about her "seven-footer" who is about forty-five years old. When she learned that I advised her boy to marry, she became terribly alarmed and came to me at once and told me just what she thought of me. She felt that although he was strong and healthy now, he still needed Mother's care, for as a boy he was delicate and weak and always had colds.

The only son generally continues to live in his own little sphere, quietly and apparently well, but with the death of the mother he often suffers a breakdown. I have reported the case of a man, the last child, a favorite son, though not an only son. He was really an only child, as there was a gap of about ten years between him and the other children; he was considered by all in the home to be the "kid" in the family. He grew up to be a "fine" man, graduated from college, and became a lawyer. Meanwhile his mother was getting older and older. She was about sixty-seven years old, and her chronic invalidism confined her to the house. One day it occurred to the young man that it was wrong for him to go downtown to the office, stay there all day, and then go out socially at night; he felt he ought to be more with his old mother. He decided to come home an hour earlier each day. Soon he made it two hours, and so he continued to leave the office earlier and earlier until he finally resigned from his position and stayed home all the time.

The father was about eighty, and the son hated him with a terrible hatred. He used to observe: "The only thing my old man does is torture my mother." Finally he resigned from his clubs and the regiment with which he used to drill, and stayed at home to take care of his dear mother entirely. Presently he stopped shaving; he had no desire to leave the house; he neglected his person. The mother and the other members of the family protested against this; they felt there was something wrong. The young man maintained that the children were heartless to let the mother stay alone at home. They offered to stay with her, but he refused; he felt that his sister could not take the care of the poor woman that he did. His fond hope was that the father would soon die and he would be alone with his dear mother. He slept in a room between hers and the father's because for years he was afraid that the latter might come in at night and disturb her, so concerned was he over her welfare. Soon the father died, and a few days later the mother. Her death precipitated the son's complete breakdown. He would go to her cemetery and remain there all day. He desired to commit suicide on her grave. He came home and had delusions of self-accusation. He charged himself with having shortened his mother's life: he cited any number of instances when he could have done things that would have saved her. He also blamed himself for the father's death, and was mortified at his ill-treatment of him. In one word, he began to show glaring symptoms of schizophrenia which he had had for years, but which no one, of course, recognized. Everyone thought that his behavior was just an expression of extreme devotion. Such cases are not at all rare, though of course they are not all so extreme as this example.

It has always been a source of much interest to me to note how many of the so-called confirmed bachelors marry after some serious illness, after they have been operated on, let us say, for kidney trouble or appendicitis. And what is just as interesting is to observe that it is no one other than the nurse herself with whom the devoted son has fallen in love. I confess that before I knew very much about the psychology of the unconscious I was a little surprised at these tricks of *amor*. Now I realize that these men find the mother again in the nurse, the woman who takes Mother's untiring interest in them, administers hot applications to their bellies, and performs all manner of personal services for them. Of course they rationalize their attachment as an expression of gratitude on their part, but fundamentally the affair cannot be regarded as anything other than an unconscious turning back to the mother's influence.

The only child may transfer very readily, but very badly. He quickly forms a strong attachment and just as quickly a strong dislike. This form of reaction can be observed even at an early age. I have a letter that a father of an only daughter sent me, showing the typical mode of transference.[2] It was written by a very precocious girl of eleven to her father, who was out of town, after she had had two conferences with me:

"A wise and all-powerful man has been interviewed, et cetera. At all times the soft pedal was in evidence and he gradually reminded me of Socrates. He was highly pleased when I informed him of my comparison. One more mortal has been added to my following list of ideals: Lincoln, ideal man; Bonaparte, warrior; Shakespeare, author; Caruso, singer; Pavlowa, dancer; Mrs. Vernon Castle, girl and big looker; Fred Stone, comedian; Professor Brill, doctor." But I regret to say that she was so utterly disillusioned in

---

[2] The term *transference* is very often misused by some alleged psychoanalysts. They seem to think that a proper transference requires the patient to fall in love with the physician. This notion causes much harm, and I have seen cases in which it has actually led to scandal, to say nothing of the fact that it renders the whole psychoanalytic treatment absurdly fruitless. Neither Freud nor his school ever advocated such an idiotic idea. The transference mechanism involves a giving and taking of hostile and affectionate emotions alike; it does not mean exclusively one or the other. Every individual's transference is always in terms of the total of his present reactions to the environment. To understand the one, therefore, we must comprehend the other.

me after her third interview that she would have nothing more to do with me. This is a typical example of quick transference, first in the positive and then in the negative direction. There was no more good reason for her strong aversion than for her comparing me to Socrates. The point was merely that at first I may have reminded her of her father by the part I played and she at once identified me with him. But on the second occasion I could no longer fit in with her image, and I was at once struck off her list of the great and elite. We see here a typical only child in the literal sense of the word. She forms enormous likes today and just as enormous dislikes tomorrow.

From what I have said one must not infer that every only child is hopeless. If brought up properly he can turn out to be a very desirable citizen and may very often develop into a leader.[3] He has many desirable attributes which when used in the proper direction place him in the foremost ranks among men. It is instructive to note that what we pointed out regarding the development of the crown-prince institution applies also to such rulers as presidents of republics who depend on the people for their election; or, in other words, that presidents of republics are still only sons, oldest or favorites, and though elected by the people have the same characteristics as those oldest sons who developed the crown-prince institution. This is actually borne out by facts. Washington, Adams, Madison, Jackson, Grant, Hayes, for instance, were the oldest sons; Monroe was an only son, and it is significant that we owe the Monroe Doctrine to him; Van Buren, Buchanan (and he was a bachelor!), and Johnson were also only sons. Lincoln was the second, but really the only son; Harrison, Tyler, and Taylor were the third sons, and it is not surprising that these gentlemen are not outstanding in comparison.

The only child has played a conspicuous part in various fields by reason of his aggressive qualities. It is noteworthy that the first advertiser in the modern sense of the word was an only child. He was Kiselak by name, and was born in Vienna. As he did not wish

---

[3]What I say about the only child holds true also of the oldest child, for in view of the importance of the impressions received during the first few years of life an individual that has been the only boy or girl in the family during that important period will show a great many of the only child's prominent characteristics, though he may not show the latter's typical reaction.

to be a merchant, he entered upon a literary career, but his earnings from that source were so meager that he was compelled to live on the money that his parents had left him when they died. One evening, while in the company of a group of young writers, some of the men began to poke fun at his apparent lack of success and fame in the literary world. He was deeply hurt, and right there and then made a wager with one of the men who mocked him that within ten years his name would be famous all over Europe; no specification was made as to how he would do it. He was twenty-eight years old when he started a tour through Europe to carry out his intentions. He carried the simplest kind of paraphernalia, a knapsack and two cans of paint, one of white and one of red. Whenever he came to a mountain, he would climb up on its most prominent part and there, in huge letters, paint his name in either red or white paint, whichever seemed the more desirable under the circumstances. For six years he continued to do this, until he suddenly died; the name of Kiselak became known to all travelers. Everybody wondered who this man could be; he began to be talked about far and wide. This is characteristic of the only child—he does not give up what he has set his mind upon doing.

I have investigated various activities in life to discover to what extent the only or the oldest child predominates in those activities. Among the great religious teachers I find that Confucius and Paul the Apostle were the first born, Buddha was an only son, William Penn was a first born and his mother's favorite. Cotton Mather was the first born in a family of ten. Martin Luther was a favorite, though not an only, child. Bunyan was the oldest and favorite son. St. Francis was the first born and his mother's favorite. Among men of science, Kepler and Galileo were the oldest sons. Among educators and teachers, Pestalozzi, Bacon, Froebel, and Erasmus were the youngest in the family; Rousseau was the second and last child, but as his older brother ran away as a child and was lost, the noted author of *Émile* was really an only child. This is the briefest possible list, and is intended merely to be suggestive.

One may wonder why so many of the world's greatest teachers were the youngest children of the family. We should bear in mind that the youngest child also occupies a special position in the home. Because the oldest child is the first one to instruct the younger children he becomes especially fitted by his environment to teach.

The youngest child, fathered and mothered as he is constantly by
the others, has his shortcomings pointed out to him so repeatedly
that if he has any worth and virile qualities in him at all, he invariably turns out to be a teacher just to show his brothers and
sisters that he can teach just as well as they.

To give a general idea of the more or less characteristic early
development of the only child, his relation to the parent, his place
in the home, his later problems and conflicts, I can do no better
than to present a dream together with its more or less fragmentary
analysis given to me by one of my patients, an only son, suffering
from what I diagnosed as a mixed neurosis. He is afraid to be out
alone, to ride in subways and over bridges, et cetera; he has also
some obsessive thoughts of the compulsion neurotic type. I must
also add that he is married and that he entered into matrimony
only because he was afraid and found a protector in his wife. He
would have remained single had he not found a woman whom
he could trust. His dream runs as follows:

> *"I dreamed of going on the way to the apartment where I
> live. The sky then became very dark; a storm was approach-
> ing. There were many thunder sounds and some lightning. The
> people were all standing and looking toward the west, from
> which direction this peculiar storm seemed to be coming.
> Gradually it began to rain and storm, and at that time I was
> about at ———— Street, and then it occurred to me that I had
> better go into my mother's apartment. I went to the house but
> decided not to go in. Then I wanted to go in, and so I kept
> on struggling and finally did not go in."*

Here are some instructive facts that the analysis revealed: "I
slept with my mother until the age of six or seven. My mother then
had an illness of some duration. Then I slept with my father
until the age of twelve." It is noteworthy that in practically every
case of this type the boy or girl slept with the parents until a very
late age. I am glad to say that we do not find this practice in
the average home; the child does not sleep with his mother or
father at the age of six or seven. But it is not unusual in the cases
of only children. Such a practice is distinctly harmful to the normal
sexual development of the child; it interferes with his normal
emotional development. Sleeping with the parents involves con-

tact and thus produces a precociousness in the sex life; the child's emotions are abnormally stimulated. If we were savages there would be no harm in having a child sleep with the parents, because we would act as savages upon reaching maturity. But as civilized beings we behave differently upon reaching maturity; in other words, an individual may be old enough to indulge in all kinds of sexual practices, but he is not allowed or supposed to do so until he reaches a certain age.

The patient then continued to relate how unusually attached he was to his mother and grandmother when a boy of five or six. "I recall being told by my mother that when I went to school at the age of six, Mother had to go with me, and that it was only after a few days of staying at the school that I could be induced to stay there alone. I cried and raised some little rumpus."

When I asked the patient what games he played when he was little, he informed me that he was fond of dolls up to the age of seven or eight. He remembered in particular one large doll which he dressed up like a little girl. This is significant, for it is well known that many effeminate men played with dolls when they were young children. Playing with dolls is essentially a feminine game. I have studied the question for a number of years and I feel that the only reason why dolls are liked by little girls is because they appeal to the feminine instinct, the desire for children. As Victor Hugo puts it, "A woman's last doll is her first child." A healthy boy will refuse to play with dolls; the normal boy always gravitates to games of the aggressive type. This is as it should be. Indeed, we should always encourage a boy to engage in those games that help to develop qualities of manhood. On the other hand, I have observed men who were not effeminate though they had played with dolls when they were children. These, however, showed the pernicious effects of the practice in some other way. Thus I recall the case of a big, strong fellow, an only son, brought up by his mother and aunt, his father having died when he was very young. I learned that the only type of woman that attracted him was the woman with yellow hair, of the doll type, and this despite the fact that his mother was not of that type. Analysis showed, however, that as a child he always played with dolls and had a particular attachment to a big doll with which he slept and fondled for years.

From the fragmentary analysis I have thus far given you of

the patient's case, you may readily see that the patient was predisposed to his neurosis, first, by the fact that he was an only child,
second, by the fact that his sex life was stimulated at too early an
age. He had to repress, consequently, very much more than the
normal boy later on in life. As we have already learned, an unusual
amount of repressed libido manifests itself in anxiety, and it is this
anxiety which is at the basis of his neurosis. In the dream we see
him struggling: he really wants to return to his mother but finally
decides not to. This is exactly his problem in actual life. Fortunately,
he made a good selection, but his wife is at the very most only a
poor substitute for his mother. If the latter were strong enough to
help him he never would have married the woman. He had to
have someone take the place of his poor old debilitated mother.
As a matter of fact, he was always seriously thinking whether he
should not give up his profession and stay home with her until
her death. In the dream he realizes his wish not to return to his
mother. This followed our discussion on the subject, as a result of
which the patient began to gain more and more insight into his
condition.

The intrinsic problem of the only child, his fixation upon the
mother, has been noted in literature. I recall in this context a
little conversation in Bernard Shaw's *Pygmalion* in which the author
sums up the situation of the only son most admirably. Professor
Higgins, an only son, speaking with his mother:

Higgins: "I have picked up a girl."
Mrs. H.: "Does that mean that some girl has picked you up?"
Higgins: "Not at all. I do not mean a love affair."
Mrs. H.: "What a pity!"
Higgins: "Why?"
Mrs. H.: "Will you never fall in love with anyone under forty-
    five years? When will you discover that there are some rather
    nice-looking young women about?"
Higgins: "I cannot be bothered with young ones. My idea of a
    woman is someone as much like you as possible; some habits
    lie too deeply to be changed."

How well the author sums up the problem! It is absolutely true
to type.

A few words about prophylaxis: Of course it would be best for the individual as well as the race that there should be no only children. However, when this cannot be avoided by virtue of ill health or death of one of the parents the child need not necessarily become neurotic and belong to any of the categories mentioned above. It all depends upon its subsequent bringing up.

When we read the history of only children we find that only those who have been brought up wrongly develop into abnormal beings; those who are not pampered and coddled have the same chances as other children. As classical examples we may mention Nero and Confucius. The former was a spoiled only child, while the latter was a well-bred only child. An only child should be made to associate with other children who will always teach him that he is not the only child in the world. This should begin at a very early age. I have seen many "nervous and wild" only children who were completely changed after a few weeks' attendance in a kindergarten or public school. But what is still more important is that only children should not be gorged with parental love. Parents should take care that such children should not develop an exaggerated idea of their own personality and think they are the center of the universe. For individuals imbued with such paranoid ideas are bound to come into conflict with their fellow men.

The problem is more complicated when we come to prophylaxis in relation to psychosexuality, and I regret that I am unable to enter here into a long discussion. I shall merely say that proper sex regulation does not imply repression and extermination of all sex feelings, and that the requisites for perfect manhood and womanhood are all the impulses and desires that are normally common to men and women.

The only child is a morbid product of our present social-economic system. He is usually an offspring of wealthy parents who, having been themselves brought up in luxury and anxious that their children should share their fortune, refuse to have more than one or two children. By their abnormal love they not only unfit the child for life's battle but prevent him from developing into normal manhood, thus producing sexual perverts and neurotics of all descriptions.

12. Fairy Tales
and Artistic Productions

THE DIFFICULTIES of adjustment as seen in the only child, which are mainly owing to the fact that the individual cannot live in conformity to the principle of reality, too often lead to neuroses and psychoses. Whenever we study the life history of such a psychosis we find that the patient has been fitted, as it were, by his environment for the abnormal part he is to play. In brief, all cases amenable to examination show that long before the psychosis developed the patient has, as it were, been prepared for his delusions and hallucinations. The only child, living alone, has to imagine himself playing with a younger brother because he is in great need of human companionship; the last child, being dominated and tyrannized by parents and older brothers and sisters, perforce has to imagine himself a hero overcoming them all—a Jack the Giant Killer. Or the sensitive, predisposed child, whose primitive impulses have not been properly adjusted, must dispose the feelings emanating from them somehow in the form of fancies and dreams. Such processes of adjustment have given rise to a literature widely known as fairy tales.

Having their origin in an attempt at adjustment through the creation of an imaginary world after one's own heart, fairy tales are invariably expressions of the wish motive. The individual tries to supplement in the imagination what is denied him in reality. It makes no difference where the fairy tale comes from, whether from Iceland or India, it always shows the wish-fulfillment tendency when analyzed. Lafcadio Hearn's story, the *Nun in the Temple of*

Armida, will serve as a typical example of how the wish fancy motivates the fairy tale.

O-Toyo is patiently waiting with her little boy for the return of her husband, who was for a long time in the service of his feudal lord. She is a very pious and devoted wife and in her anxious expectation she performed many strange ceremonial acts. She offered a miniature meal for her husband such as was offered to the gods, and if steam was formed on the inside of the place which was covered, she was pleased because that was a sign that he was alive. She loved her little boy and occupied herself with him almost constantly. She went on pilgrimages to Dakeyama Mountain with him, where all were wont to go who were anxiously awaiting their beloved relatives. But Anid, her husband, died in a foreign land and shortly thereafter there followed the death of the little boy. After going through a long period of depression she began to collect very small toys; she used to spread out little baby dresses on the lawn and talk to them and fondle them smilingly. This action brought on convulsive sobs. She then resorted to the rite of conjuring up the spirits of the deceased and received the following consoling message:

"Oh, Mother, do not cry for my sake; it is not right to cry over the dead. For their silent way leads over the stream of tears, and if mothers cry the flood rises high and the soul cannot rest and wanders restlessly to and fro." Since that time she stopped crying but refused to marry and showed a liking for little things. Everything seemed too big for her. Her room, her chair, her bed were all too big for her. She made a little baby house and tried to live in places that were toylike. Her parents then advised her to become a nun in a tiny little temple with the smallest altar and Buddha images. She entered the small Temple of Armida and spent her time in weaving very small chairs which, although too small for practical use, were bought by some who knew of her history. Her greatest pleasure was in the society of little children, whom she would imitate in every respect. When she died, a tiny tombstone was placed over her grave.[1]

Here we can see that the mother identified herself with her little boy, trying to realize in this way her abnormal wish. We find this mechanism among primitive men, children, and normal and ab-

[1]Franz Ricklin, *Wishfulfillment and Symbolism in Fairy Tales, Nervous and Mental Disease,* Monograph Series No. 21, New York, 1915.

normal people alike. We know, for instance, how the savage will daub himself to resemble his god. The child, because his greatest desire is to be big, walks on stilts and dresses up like his elder. In our modern times we have spiritualism. People resort to the spiritualist in order to realize their wishes. It is a surprisingly easy matter to detect the whole fraud when we bear in mind that the medium relies entirely upon the suggestions of the audience. When he opens the séance, for instance, with "I see a child, it is looking for its mother," we may rest assured that there is bound to be in the audience a brooding and sorrowful woman who has lost her child who will consequently react to this with apparently marked emotions; her reaction will be such as to tell the medium that he is on the right track. Our inspired friend now has a basis on which to proceed. His messages are not from the departed, they are merely wishes, which he has pieced together as best he could, from the suggestions he has received from the audience. In the same way women wonder how the fortuneteller could know that they are in love; they do not realize that they consulted him because of that very fact. In the final analysis, all such interests on the part of men and women may be reduced to the one fundamental fact—that we always strive to realize our wishes.

The tear motive found in the story of the nun of Armida is seen in many other fairy tales. We find the following tale in Ludwig Beechstein's *Fairy Book:*

Three days and nights a mother cried at the sickbed of an only child, but it died. The mother was seized with terrible pain. She ate nothing and drank nothing for three more days, crying incessantly and calling for the child. Then the door opened noiselessly and the child stood before her. It was now a beautiful little angel and smiled at her ecstatically. In its hand it carried a little pitcher which was almost overflowing. The child spoke the following: "Oh, dearest mother, cry no longer for me. Behold your tears which you shed for me are collected in this pitcher. Only one more tear and it will overflow and I'll have no rest in my grave and no peace in heaven. Please cry no more. I am an angel and have angels to play with." We see here the wish motive most admirably rationalized. The same theme is treated with slight variation by the Grimm brothers.

To grasp their deeper significance many fairy tales must be interpreted symbolically. Here is a typical example:

There was once a man who had three daughters. He was going to the market and asked his daughters what he should bring them home. The oldest daughter wanted a golden spinning wheel, the second daughter wanted a golden reel, and the youngest daughter, Oda, said, "Bring me that which will run under your wagon on your return from market." The father brought the two daughters the things they desired. On his way home he suddenly beheld a snake under the wagon. He caught it for his youngest daughter. He threw it in front of the gate and left it there for Oda. When she came out the snake began to talk to her, saying, "Oda dear, may I not come into the house?" And Oda said, "My father brought you to the door and now you wish to come in?" But she let the snake come in. When he entered the house, he asked to go into her bedroom; when Oda was getting into bed, he wished to be taken to bed. He then became transformed into a young prince, who could be redeemed only in this manner. From what we have already said about dream symbolism it is not hard to see the significance of this story. The snake very clearly represents the male elements, and we have here a simple sexual wish. It is noteworthy that we encounter this particular symbolism also in mental disease. Thus one of my patients in a hospital imagined that a snake lived within her body, and one day she informed me that it was in her genitals. We see here how well the symbolism is carried out.

Fairy tales, representing essentially an abnormal gratification of the individual's inner strivings and wishes, it is not at all surprising to find that they are invariably products of shut-in, seclusive personalities, persons who never came in normal contact with other people and who generally led an abnormal existence. Such individuals resorted to the fairy tale as a mode of emotional gratification. Thus Andersen did not see a single child up to the age of eleven or twelve. In fact, when he was placed in contact with children he could not get along with them. He confessed, himself, that he used to spin phantom children in his brain with whom he constantly played. This is not surprising, for if you take a child who has any desire at all to associate with others and keep him all to himself, he will invariably create some imaginative companion. Thus I have in mind the case of a young girl who continued to fancy that she had a little companion; she would buy various toys for it, save Christmas presents for it, and insist that Mother buy an extra ticket for it when she was taken to the theater.

It is because this performed mechanism of fancying exerts the most pernicious influence in the individual's later life that I am so strongly opposed to fairy tales. Take the case of a patient who broke down when the woman he was about to marry was shot. He was continually obsessed with fancies about her. He would find himself, for instance, unconsciously opening the door of his car to let her in, adding, "Hurry, dear, we have to get there in time." For many hours of the day he would actually engage in imaginary conversations with the woman whom he had lost. It is significant that analysis revealed that the man formed in early childhood a strong habit of fancying. Having learned in childhood to satisfy himself with phantoms, he now found it impossible to resign himself to the fact that she was dead, and lived with her in his imagination. There is no doubt at all that such a tendency to fancy in early childhood is detrimental to the individual's psychic development, for we cannot cope with an inexorably real world if we live in fancies.

There are quite a number of interesting fancies of grownups that I could cite to you which can all be traced to the influence of an early strong tendency to fancy. I shall describe a few:

The scene of one story was laid in the suburbs of one of the principal cities of the United States where families of means and education reside. E. S., who lived here, was a governess in the family of Mrs. L., and had such a pleasing personality that she attracted, in rather an unusual way, the friends of her employer. She was engaged to a rich Englishman who owned an estate. She would read extracts from his letters to her friends, and announced that he was coming to this country. Although Mrs. L. invited him to dine with her there was always the excuse of a previous plan preventing the visit. E. S. would describe to her employer the pleasures she enjoyed with him, and how he would take her to the train and they would talk until it came in. At last the date was set for her marriage to take place at the home of Mrs. L. Owing to the unusual romantic conditions, great interest was evinced by her friends, who all helped with the making of her trousseau. Mrs. L.'s little daughter was to accompany her to Europe for a short visit. A short time before the wedding day word came from Mr. C. that certain conditions had arisen to prevent him from coming over, but he had made proper arrangements for the marriage to take place in his own home. Although this came as a great blow to the governess and her friends, the plans were changed and accommodations secured on the steamer for the governess, child, and rector. They went into the city to spend the night in a hotel because the steamer sailed in the morning. It was in the morning that she confessed that it was a fascinating story that she had woven in her mind. Her relatives were sent for and she was sent to a sanitarium.

There was a somewhat similar case reported in the newspapers some years ago of a woman who continued with her fancies to the supposed wedding day, when she received a telegram that the fiancé had met with an accident in Chicago. She went to Chicago, bought a corpse, and brought back the dead body of her imaginary lover. It was the only way in which she could terminate the fancy.

I have known personally the case of a young lady who would become seriously depressed and ill every time she heard of an engagement or some love affair among the girls of her acquaintance. On a number of occasions she would actually go to the length of writing to the prospective groom informing him as matters of fact what she merely spun in her imagination. She would tell the young man, for instance, that his fiancée had been living with another man for such and such a time; she would give details such as the city in which the woman lived and the name under which she went. Of course she caused a good deal of mischief. In another case a young lady estranged fifteen couples, including her own sister. She always managed to secure data which could be corroborated. Of course when a man is jealous all he needs is the slightest suspicion to build up a powerful case.

Another pernicious result of fairy stories is that they lay the foundation for compulsive symptoms of obsessions. As you know, everything in fairy stories is done by threes, and I have known many people who carried this superstition along with them throughout their lives. Thus my attention has recently been drawn to the case of a mine inspector who began to talk of things in multiples of three. He would get out 600 tons a day, 300 mine cars, and 12 railroad cars; one day he told the shipping clerk that the mine would get out 900 tons, whereas it put out only the usual 500 tons. He applied, for instance, for three more motors and thirty new transportation men; he insisted that the mine was good for 600 mine cars a day and that in three weeks it would be the best mine in the state. This compulsive thinking in threes was also carried over to his home life. When his wife became pregnant, for example, he was sure she would have three children. Analysis showed definitely that the obsession went back directly to the influence of fairy tales.

I have reported the following dream of a woman: *She saw three long-necked bottles. One was almost broken to pieces, the second cracked, and the third contained sparkling champagne.* The dreamer was a widow of forty-two years of age who informed me that as far back as she remembered all her important affairs in life went by threes. Before her marriage she acted toward her suitors in the same way: she never expected very much of the first, regarded with greater favor the second, and expected to marry the third. Her husband had to propose three times before she would marry him. If she accidentally broke a dish, for instance, she had no rest until she broke two more. Indeed, she actually kept on hand a supply of discarded bottles which she could break more economically to complete a series. In the light of her obsession the significance of the dream is evident. The three long-necked bottles are symbolic of men. Her dead husband is represented by the broken bottle; the man who was her lover for years after her husband's death is represented by the cracked bottle; while the third one containing sparkling champagne is meant to represent the man who was paying her attention at the time of the dream. The champagne in the bottle is doubly determined: it symbolizes the quality of the man and is an allusion to alcoholism, to which they were both addicted. Analysis revealed that this number-three ceremonial was determined by the fairy stories she used to hear and read since childhood, especially the following one, which she consciously took as a model. It is the story of a princess whom her father had placed in a castle on top of a steep glass mountain. The knight who succeeded in reaching the top on his horse was to receive her in marriage. The youngest of three brothers finally reached the top of the mountain in the third attempt and married the princess.

Fairy tales are also very harmful to the normal psychic development because they are primitive and archaic modes of expression; and catering, as they do, to the primitive impulse, they encourage primitive modes of thought and action in the individual. Upon analysis, they practically all fall into the categories that we find when we reduce sex to its various components or partial impulses. I have drawn your attention already to the components of sadism and masochism; there are also other components, such as the partial impulse to look, "sexual curiosity," as it is commonly designated, and the partial impulse to touch, both of which components we noted in discussing tendency wit. Fairy tales are based upon these partial impulses, particularly upon the sadistic and masochistic components. They present a state of the most primitive type: the individual either kills or is killed; he actually takes delight in producing horrors. They thus have the most pernicious influence upon the child, for they unfit him for reality by feeding his imagination on modes of reaction that are distinctly out of harmony with a healthy civilization.

Mr. N.'s case, which I have reported, may help you to see to what a surprising degree the individual may be influenced by fairy stories. The patient was considered most peculiar: he often carried a revolver with him, he yearned for those times when everybody carried the dirk and dagger and could kill when offended. He was fascinated by wild animals, especially the tiger, who excited him to a marked degree. He spent much time in the menagerie in front of the tiger's cage, and when unobserved by the keeper, he would tease the animal in order to see him jump and hear him roar. A fancy which often recurred to him was the following: "I am annoyed and angered by someone to such an extent that I run wild and bite everybody that comes in my way, until I bite my way into some person's body!"

Very soon after penetrating into the patient's psychic development I noticed that his symptoms were largely determined by fairy stories, fables, and myths. Thus his sadism and other symptoms unmistakably showed an archaic setting. The associations to almost all his dreams showed how all his inner environments corresponded more to a world as described by Andersen, Grimm, Lang, and others than to our present times. The following dream fragment with its associations will show this:

"On Fifth Avenue with a crowd of people looking at a tiger. Whenever the animal comes my way I fly up to the roof of a neighboring house." Associations: Flying recalled that as a child he often entertained many wishes to fly above the clouds, among the

stars and planets. This recalled his insatiable interest in astronomy at the age of seven to eight years. At about the same period or even earlier he was keenly interested in trees; he was very eager to know where the sap came from. The association then took him back to a still earlier period of his life, when he was interested in the bodily functions and in childbirth. After he had been told that children grew in the mother, he decided that they must come out like a passage of the bowels. This caused him to take special interest in the openings of the body, such as the mouth, nose, and anus. The interest in mysterious openings was later projected to the outer world, so that he was strongly attracted to caves. This unusual interest was facilitated by many fairy stories, especially· the ones concerning the twelve princes who were called One, Two, Three, Four, et cetera, to Twelve, who went down to the bowels of the earth and then became rabbits and burrowed their way up. From very early childhood the patient imagined himself flying and beheading monsters above the clouds, or penetrating to the center of the earth in the form of some wicked magician, all the time passing through the most harrowing experiences. By a process of condensation he fused ancient characters and episodes with persons and actions of reality, but all his fancies usually began with some god or demonlike myth and gradually descended to human beings.

As I went deeper and deeper into the analysis I became more and more impressed with the fact that all his associations were explained by some fairy tale or myth. Thus the flying was not only determined by flying fancies but recalled also the story of Perseus, who undertook an expedition against the islands of the Gorgons.

There is no denying that this is a unique case; but, although I have not seen another psychoneurotic with such a pronounced archaic make-up, I have, nevertheless, observed many persons who showed the same mechanisms in a lesser degree. I have reported numerous cases that very clearly show the direct harmful effects of sadistic and masochistic reading material in childhood. Wanke justly asks: "Of what benefit is it for a child to read fairy stories where there is so much about murder and killing, and where human life is treated in the most careless manner as if it amounted to nothing? What does the child gain by reading about criminal acts which bring no serious consequences on the person perpetrating them?"

Moreover, even those individuals who do not continue with the primitive impulses as far as sex is concerned, who show no algolagnia[2], remain bad dreamers all their lifetime, believing in the unreality of life, unable to appreciate the real value of hard work and persistent effort. Having been imbued in childhood with the omnipotence of the fairy-book heroes, they wish to be like them, and later refuse, or find it difficult, to become plain citizens struggling for existence. Such individuals are constantly wishing for the unattainable that could be gotten only through some of the charms of fairyland, such as magic boots, invisible caps, Aladdin's lamp, and so on. It is, therefore, no wonder that such persons are unhappy as adults and think themselves out of place among ordinary mortals.

That such an attitude of detachment from the actual facts of life is in conflict with the requirements of life and militates against success is not hard to see. No man has ever accomplished anything in life who was not a man of action. This holds true of all fields of endeavor, even of art and literature. Unless the artist or poet is no mere dreamer, he can hope to produce very little. Marshal Foch in his *Strategy of the War* sums up the situation very well when he says, "You can understand that when a man of ordinary capacity concentrates all his thoughts and studies upon a single object, and labors unceasingly to accomplish it, he stands a chance for success. Certain conditions are essential in order to be a force in the world. A man must be objective and not subjective. A man of action must not waste time in dreams. Only facts count; you must stick to facts." And so every man who has made his mark in the world has had to learn to cope with facts, to meet reality face to face. The sooner, therefore, our boys and girls are freed from the influence of fairy tales the better. As for the fear expressed by some people that abolishing fairy tales will stifle and impoverish the imagination, let us remember that there is plenty of material for the imagination in nature and life with which the child can actually come in contact and from which he can derive wholesome pleasure and instruction at the same time.

[2]Algolagnia: sexual feeling connected with causing or experiencing pain.

Artistic Productions

From what we have seen of fairy tales we may say that they represent essentially distorted fancies emanating from archaic modes of thinking. The child with his infantile wishes and desires runs riot, as it were, in the realm of reality. Because he has not as yet learned to value the facts of time, space, and mortality, he operates with invisible caps, magic horses, and other fantastic creations. As the individual grows older, however, reality becomes more burdensome and forces him to repress those archaic mechanisms. He then realizes that only through reality can he attain his wishes and desires, and sublimates those primitive impulses through the various forms of occupations which we shall discuss later. Here, I merely wish to touch more or less briefly upon a form of sublimation as found in the so-called artistic productions.

Every child is an artist in the making. When our little girl drew the picture of the small wagon when she found she could not actually possess the desired toy, she made her first debut into the artistic world. In this simple illustration we see at once the purpose that art fulfills: by its means one is able to realize his inner strivings and desires. Similarly, when a premature thawing of the snow prevents a little girl from trying out her new sled, thus depriving her of her keenly expected pleasure, she produces a picture of children coasting and frolicking on the new-fallen snow which is declared by artists to be a fine artistic production. The drawing represented the desired condition and thus fulfilled the little girl's wish. Similarly, we may say that Pygmalion was in love with Galatea long before he fashioned her out of ivory and that it was the impulse to possess Galatea that caused the talented Pygmalion to chisel her out of ivory. This wish is father to the artistic production, and that every artist is, as it were, a Pygmalion. In brief, *the artistic production, like the dream and the symptom, is a wish fulfillment emanating from unconscious sources.* By virtue of his talent the artist can embody on canvas, or in relief, or in sound, those unattainable urgings which the average individual experiences also but is able to express only through the medium of dreams, daydreams, fancies, and lies. It is well known also that what we would consider impossible feats verging on the infantile or on insanity have been realized by individuals who were able to do so. For example, Nero's Golden Statue is an attempt at his personal deification, and it is significant that Alexander the Great was seriously thinking of making a statue of his own person out of the whole of Mount Athos.

As we have tried to point out elsewhere, the difference between the artistic production and the other modes of wish fulfillment such as dreams, symptoms, lies, et cetera, may be said to lie in the fact that the latter are purely personal expressions having no interest whatsoever for the outside world, whereas the artistic production has a distinct social character and offers a source of pleasure and gratification to artist and audience alike. The symptom or dream is a distinct personal outlet, but through the artistic production the audience becomes identified with the artist, as it were, and partakes of the original source of gratification.

Our conception of the artistic production as an expression of inner strivings and wishes is not altogether new, for we find it embodied in one form or another in ancient and modern literature alike. Thus we at once think of Aristotle's famous theory of poetry and drama as a form of catharsis. In modern times we have a noted representative of this same view in Goethe, who, as Pater says, "escaped from the stress of sentiments too strong for him by making a book about them." The great poet's "Werther's Sorrows" illustrates the point.

It is significant that even individuals who show no artistic talent in daily life suddenly display remarkable ability in such directions when they become "insane." I have in my possession a remarkable collection of artistic creations in painting, sculpture, and belles-lettres produced by individuals who were never known to possess any artistic talent and who, as far as I could discover, never made any attempt to express themselves artistically. Thus I can mention a grocer, who, in his psychosis, wrote erotic poetry of considerable merit, and a cook who, in the same condition, produced embroideries which a number of artists, upon careful examination, considered to be excellent productions of the Byzantine period. To be sure a great many of the insane productions seem meaningless and fantastic on superficial examination, but to one acquainted with the patient's history they are full of meaning and significance. The same holds true of the best masterpieces: to appreciate them fully it is often necessary to have a knowledge of the artist's inner conflicts and problems. In this respect psychoanalytic study is particularly helpful, for it reveals to us the hidden sources influencing the artist.

Sufficient investigation has been done, for instance, to enable us to say that Leonardo da Vinci's characteristic smile which one observes not only in the Mona Lisa, but also in his Saint Anne, Saint Mary, and John the Baptist, is in all probability a vague reminiscence of his mother's smile. In his interesting little book on Leonard da Vinci,[3] Professor Freud has thrown much light on the great artist's inner life and problems. Those of you who are interested in the relation the great painter's work bears to his mother's influence would do well to read it. The intimate relationship that we observe in this particular case between the artist's life and work is seen also in sculpture and belles-lettres. Some striking examples of this are *David Copperfield,* which is a picture of Dickens's own life, and Goethe's "Werther's Sorrows" which describes some of the emotional difficulties experienced by the young author himself.

But the difference between the psychotic production and the sane creation lies in the fact that most of the insane productions are expressions of strivings which are distinctly egocentric. It is for that reason that the average person sees very little meaning in them. He is unable to put himself in rapport with them as it were. On the other hand, when we look at a masterpiece made by an artist, we experience a definite feeling of aesthetic pleasure. There is something familiar in the piece of sculpture, or painting, or literary work, which touches our own experiences. It seems that every great work of art has universal appeal, and that is perhaps why the masters, like Shakespeare, have no limited audience, but are enjoyed to a greater or lesser degree, depending on the individual, by all classes of people. In other words, we may say that the insane production is usually autoerotic, it is of a self-sufficient, self-satisfying, or infantile character; while the artistic production belongs mostly to the object-libido phase[4] of psychic development. The artist projects into the outer world certain feelings and emotions which deal with object love.

It is on this basis of autoerotism and object libido that we may

[3] S. Freud: *Leonardo da Vinci.*
[4] The latter has been termed *alloerotic,* the converse of autoerotic.

explain why most people see nothing artistic in so-called modern art. For some reason or other the latter productions belong to autoeroticism. That is why they seem to most people to be nothing short of insane productions, and as a matter of fact it is often impossible to distinguish one from the other. There is no doubt that if we were to compare side by side some characteristic poem of a representative ultra-modern poet with the verse of some psychotic patient, we would at once be struck by the marked degree of similarity between them. It is thus only by seeing the catalogue that we can know that this particular ultra-modern picture represents a nude descending the staircase, or this one New York, or another a Spanish village. No stretch of the imagination could reveal to one what the artist actually meant to express. Information obtained from the artist himself fully corroborates this view. One artist said that he did not care whether his picture meant anything to the spectator, it represented a source of gratification to him, and that was all that he was trying to attain. In other words, the work was the expression of an artist, but not an artistic expression in the strict sense.

We may thus lay it down as a general principle that all expressions, whether normal or abnormal, such as symptoms, dreams, witticisms, fairy tales, and artistic productions, may be classified as infantile or adult, or as autoerotic or alloerotic. Inherently, there is very little difference so far as the individual is concerned, but conceived socially, we may say that only those productions that have meaning and affect to others besides the artist or producer himself may be considered normal.

13. Selection of Vocations

(*Conclusions*)

IN THE previous chapter I tried to make clear to you that the reason why I object to certain types of fairy tales is because fairy tales are offshoots of archaic thinking originating in antiquity, and because they are products of unconscious wishes symbolically representing those primitive impulses which the cultured being must learn to repress and sublimate in order to fit himself for modern life.[1] Progressive civilization depends on the harnessing and controlling of the forces of nature as well as the forces of the individual, and in directing these forces into socially useful channels. A fairy tale, or a story that stimulates any of the partial impulses or components of sex in children, may impede or arrest the normal control of the individual's energy. Sooner or later every normal human being must give up many of his natural prerogatives and become part of the society in which he lives. He must renounce many of his individual desires and must exert continuous effort for the commonweal. That is, every individual must contribute to society by adding something useful to it. We may designate such contributions as his vocational work.

In the progressive development of culture this mode of activity became more and more complex. At first there were almost as many vocations as men, but as time went on it was found necessary that many persons perform the same kind of work. Instead of one tailor or doctor or musician there had to be many tailors, many doctors, and many musicians. In other words, every individual has been allowed by society to live through some of the pleasure prin-

[1]Brill: *Psychoanalysis, Its Theories and Practical Application*, W. B. Saunders, Philadelphia, 1922, p. 293.

ciples, but he has been forced to adapt himself to the principles of reality. From our psychoanalytic knowledge we recognize this process as sublimation. Every activity or vocation not directed to sex in the broadest sense, no matter under what guise, is a form of sublimation.

Now, is the form of sublimation followed by the individual a matter of accident; in other words, is the selection of vocation a matter of chance, or is it governed by definite laws? The average person seems to consider the selection of a vocation accidental or at least something that is quite impersonal. He usually assumes that, given certain qualifications, physical or mental, or both, a person could undertake any kind of work or vocation. This view is evidently held by parents who usually think they are best qualified to select their children's vocation, and by professional vocational guides who have reduced it all to a sort of mathematical formula. They examine the person, discover some of his attributes, and then feel presumptuous enough to tell him what he is fitted for. Such procedure may be good enough for defective persons whose power of sublimation is poor in any case and whom a certain amount of suggestion can influence, at least for a time. But does a normal person need such advice and does such advice help him? Investigation shows that the normal individual needs no advice or suggestion in the selection of a vocation, he usually senses best what activity to follow, and, what is more, he is invariably harmed if advice is thrust upon him by a person of authority. It is known that all our actions are to some degree psychically determined by unconscious motives, that there is no psychic activity which does not follow definite paths formed in the individual since his childhood. Because work or profession is nothing but a sublimating process in the service of hunger and love we may assume that it also must be guided by the individual's unconscious motives. Investigation has convinced me of the truth of this assumption.

When we ask a person why he follows a certain vocation he usually answers that he does not know, that he just drifted into it accidentally. Occasionally he answers that his grandfather and his father performed the same line of work and that he followed it. On applying the psychoanalytic method, however, one usually finds some hidden reasons for the particular activity. For years I investigated in this manner among patients, friends and strangers, and though my findings are not complete I feel that I can furnish a preliminary report.

The motives which actuate one to take up a certain vocation vary with the person, that is, every vocation is individually determined. My first investigation naturally began with physicians. I asked my confreres why they took up the practice of medicine as a vocation, and from the many answers obtained I shall mention some here.

Dr. W. stated that since his early childhood he had been surrounded with doctors who were endeavoring to cure him of a paralyzed limb, the result of infantile paralysis, and as they could not help him he decided to become a physician and cure himself.

Dr. A. recalled that as a child he suffered from boils or carbuncles and was taken to the doctor by his father. The doctor was very brutal to him, and very inconsiderate, and almost insulting to his poor father. As a child he could not understand his father's humility in the presence of the brutal doctor, for his father's behavior was quite different in his own home. This impression remained permanently fixed on his mind. Whenever he was punished by his father he thought of the doctor before whom his father trembled, and as a small boy he secretly wished he were a doctor. When he became of age he realized his wish.

Dr. B. had no idea why he chose medicine as his profession, but finally recalled a scene from his early childhood. He overheard a conversation between his mother and another woman; the latter, looking at him, asked his mother the month of his birth, and when told that it was the month of October she dryly remarked, "Poor boy, he will be either a doctor, a butcher, or a murderer. He will have to shed blood." As he did not care to adopt the last two vocations, he became a physician.

Dr. C. told me that as a boy he lived near a slaughterhouse and often witnessed the killing and skinning of animals, which greatly fascinated him. Since the age of eight years he had not seen the slaughterhouse, and these scenes entirely vanished from his mind, but when at the age of sixteen the teacher of physiology demonstrated the circulation of the blood in the frog he became very interested and decided to study medicine.

Dr. D. was the son of a horse dealer who was also interested in veterinary surgery. His father urged him to become a veterinary surgeon, which he set out to do, but changed later to human medicine.

Dr. E. was the son of a butcher whose ambition it was that the son should follow his vocation. The latter, however, insisted upon studying medicine and became a learned anatomist.

In all these cases the sado-masochistic components were first accentuated—in Dr. W. through his own suffering, and in the others through early impressions—and later sublimated in the profession.

The woman who associated the doctor (surgeon) with the butcher and murderer was not so far from the mark. All these activities are based on the sado-masochistic components, it is only a question of adjustment. The surgeon and the butcher have both conquered their sadistic impulses and sublimate the same for useful purposes. The former, representing a higher state of mental evolution, becomes a direct savior of human beings, while the latter, not so much endowed mentally or perhaps having lacked the opportunities for further mental development, still helps mankind by butchering the animals which furnish its meat supply.

The professions of prize fighters, wrestlers, bullfighters, warriors, and mighty hunters are direct descendants of pure sadism, and the need for the sadistic outlet is well shown by the popularity of these vocations. Those who witness a prize fight soon observe that the whole audience, and particularly the votaries of the manly art, actually participate in the fight. One of my patients told me that whenever he goes to a prize fight he has to sit apart from everyone, for when the prize fighter who is his favorite strikes, he has to imitate him. He got himself into trouble many a time hitting his neighbors, he simply could not control himself, and to avoid this he has to sit away from the other spectators. Others do not actually strike their neighbors but they shout, yell, and mimic the actors; in other words, they identify themselves with the fighter and in this way give vent to their own sadistic feelings.

Some of the determining mechanisms are quite different. Thus I know three physicians who selected the medical profession because as children they were jealous of the family doctor, who, they imagined, stood in greater favor with their mothers than their own fathers. Quite a number of the sons of my lady patients whom I treated successfully have announced their intention to study medicine and take up my specialty. There is a tendency on the part of the sons to rival their fathers or any other man whom their mother admires. The last mechanism is also observed in other vocations. I know two sons who became real-estate agents in order to outdo the man with whom their mother was in love.

The profession of law is often taken up as a reaction to a dishonest act committed in childhood or early boyhood by oneself, by parents, or by some immediate member of the family, such as brother or sister. Such persons are usually scrupulously honest lawyers and judges, for unconsciously they always feel that they are suspected and that they have something to atone for. Quite often the determinant is an unconscious effort to obtain justice for oneself as a result of an injustice experienced in childhood.

Mr. C., a very prominent jurist, had no idea why he took up the study of law, but examination revealed the following facts: He was brought up in a religious New England atmosphere. His mother was rather nervous, and kept her husband and children in a very repressive state. The *Mayflower* spirit hovered over everything. She particularly objected to smoking, and for years quarreled with her husband about it, until he was forced to give up this luxury. Her two boys were constantly subjected to all sorts of restrictions. One day, while waiting with other children in the dressing room of a dancing school, they noticed a burning cigarette left by the dancing master. The older brother, noticing the burning cigarette, which stood for one of the strongest taboos in his home, conceived the temptation to violate it, and not having the courage to do it himself, he turned to his younger brother and said, "Charles, I dare you to take a puff from the cigarette." "I will take one if you will," answered Charles, and on being assured that the older brother would follow him in this transgression, he bravely inserted the cigarette into his mouth and took the puff.

His older brother thereupon lost his courage and refused to follow suit. And, what is more, in order to atone for his evil thought, he told his parents of what Charles was guilty. One can hardly picture the fear, remorse, mortification, and last, but not least, the sense of injustice experienced by the little boy when he was denounced by his parents. The mother was terrified at the son's "crime," and called him to account for it. Charles was confronted by two alternatives: to confess would be facing his mother's terrible wrath, and to lie would be facing the wrath of heaven. He chose the latter and stoutly denied his guilt. To settle the matter the parents asked him whether he would take an oath on the Bible that he did not commit the crime. Charles hesitated just a few seconds and then stood ready to take the oath. It seems that either the parents suspected that he was guilty, or they feared to use the holy Bible in vain, so that instead of bringing in the holy book they brought in the Bible stories, upon which Charles swore that he did not take the puff. The parents probably soon forgot the episode, but Charles retained an everlasting impression of it. For a long time he felt like a person guilty of an enormous crime against God and his parents, and constantly anticipated some terrible retribution; on the other hand, he felt that a great injustice was done to him by his brother, who first inveigled him into committing this evil act and then betrayed him. In time this episode was forgotten, but the small boy was thoughtful and serious-minded; as he grew older he became a champion of oppressed classmates and gradually decided to become a judge. When he graduated from college he took up the study of law and realized his wish.

What was just related was discovered during the analysis of a stereotyped dream which appeared on two occasions while the dreamer was under an anesthetic, the second time after an interval of twenty years. The dreamer imagined that it was the Day of Judgment, and that he stood before God, who asked him questions; although he knew the answers, he refused to give them and was jeered by the multitude. God in the dream was his father, and being examined on the Day of Judgment referred to the episode just described. The father in the dream as well as in daily life is often substituted by the governor, the mayor, and by God himself.[2] Mr. C., who is now about fifty-five years old, had no conscious knowledge of the cigarette episode and the part it played in his life until his dream was analyzed. When he finished his story I remarked that there was one other vocation that he might have taken up, the ministry, because in my experience this vocation is often followed by persons who unconsciously feel remorse for

[2]Freud: *The Interpretation of Dreams.*

some crime committed in childhood or as a reaction to temptations in later life. He confirmed my statement by telling me that he was in doubt as to which of the two vocations to take up, and if it were not for the fact that his religious feelings underwent a great change during his college years he would have become a minister of the gospel. He was undecided about it until he graduated from college —it was always a question between the ministry and the law.

Unconscious and sometimes conscious feelings of guilt and remorse as a reaction to real or imaginary sins are often the basis of theological callings. This mechanism is clearly seen in such religious groups as the Salvation Army and some of the missions. If one attends such religious meetings one invariably hears confessions such as, "I was a thief and a low sinner until I saw the light of the Lord; two years later I was a backslider, but again I found Him," et cetera. Some of the converts fluctuate all the time between heaven and hell. Here the maladjustment is so marked that sublimation is imperfect or almost impossible; this accounts for the chronic backsliding and the repeated changes from one religion to another. Only a few years ago the daily press reported the case of a clergyman who changed for the third time from one denomination to another.

I know a similar case of a man who fluctuates between fervent evangelism and extreme atheism. He is a morbidly religious person who is making desperate efforts to adjust himself, and depending on the reaction of the time he either preaches the gospel or the non-existence of God. I was also impressed by the number of dissatisfied and struggling homosexuals who follow religious callings.

Sublimation of infantile exhibitionism[3] often impels one to follow the stage, the army, or the vocation of lifeguard. The actor and the professional soldier are sublimated exhibitionists par excellence; the latter is also unconsciously dominated by a strong aggressive component. The aggressive component which under certain conditions changes to sadism is found in the sexuality of most men. "It is a propensity to subdue, the biological significance of which lies in the necessity of overcoming the resistance of the sexual object by actions other than mere courting."[4] This component is

[3]Freud: "Three Contributions to the Theory of Sex," in *The Basic Writings of Sigmund Freud.*
[4]*Ibid.*

seen throughout life in its sublimated form: one notes it in the aggressive businessman, in the lawyer, in the satirical speaker, and in its accentuated form in the soldier. Among the first games of boys one invariably finds the playing of soldier, and the need for such outlets is readily seen in the popularity of the Boy Scout movement and the admiration that has been bestowed on soldiers from time immemorial.

Acting also belongs to the earliest games of children. In fact, most playing of children is acting. It is known that a great many nervous people are good actors; they are natural actors. Hysterical persons can imitate almost anything; they are the best tragedians as well as the best comedians. And if we consider the nature and mechanism involved, namely, the inability to adjust or fix properly one's libido, we can readily understand the psychology of the actor. The actor utilizes this very inferiority as a sublimation. Usually actors are persons who have failed to fix their libido properly. Because of some unconscious disturbance their emotional transference is more or less inhibited, so that they are unable to develop fixed characteristics; they remain more or less infantile and are therefore able to identify themselves with the great characters they represent on the stage; they are still moldable, as it were. That accounts for some of the characteristic traits of the actor. I refer to the sexual maladjustment as evinced in uninhibited morality and marital unsteadiness which have been attributed to stage folks in all lands and all ages. To be rigid or at least regular in the sense of following the dictum of society in one's sex life presupposes a well-adjusted and fixed libido. Now I do not wish to imply that the actor is to be considered inferior because he manifests this maladjustment of his love life; on the contrary, he has the courage to put in operation what the average person secretly desires. That is why we admire the actor, and that accounts for the popularity of plays which deal with the primitive impulses. They offer us a mental catharsis; we cry and laugh at the play because we identify ourselves with the actor, to wit, with the hounded rogue or ideal hero whom he represents. The actor's identification with the stage character is well illustrated by the following story. An admirer of the great actor Booth, after witnessing his wonderful performance of King Lear, asked the famous tragedian to explain the secret of his skillful rendition of this character. Booth, turning very abruptly, responded, "Sir, I am Lear."

It is because of the same mechanism that only few great actors have ever produced original works that could lay claim to individuality. They are so used to identifying themselves with their stage characters that they find no time to develop a steady and fixed character of their own. For the character of a person is nothing but the final total of one's past impressions.

My own investigation with lifeguards convinces me that most of them take genuine delight in their vocation mainly because they love to display their well-developed muscles. Professional athletes and "sport fans" are dominated by the same exhibitionistic impulse; most of the latter, however, unable to exhibit themselves, gain pleasure by identifying themselves with the actors (ball players, fighters, et cetera).

Some of the vocations can be traced to very early infantile sexual traits. Thus I know of a maker of optical instruments, a successful manager of a big camera department, and three photographers who were punished in childhood for evincing a strong curiosity for sexual looking, and although they did not become *voyeurs,* they all manifested a strong tendency for looking. I have reported the case of a man who displayed in early childhood a strong perverted impulse for odors who became a successful perfume dealer after he was a failure in two other vocations. Unconsciously such people take up the vocations that gratify them in a sublimated form. The reader need not be surprised and shocked merely because some people who are doing useful work merged into it through sexual impressions of childhood. There is nothing wrong about it. Some of the most sublime institutions in this world had their origin in sex.

In analyzing a man who became rich from an invention, or rather an improvement of patterns for ladies' apparel, I found the following facts: He was brought up in a small settlement in very poor surroundings. His father was unambitious, apparently not a very strong character, while his mother, to whom he was very much attached, was a very hard-working woman who had a constant struggle to keep the wolf from the door. She was rarely able to save enough money to buy new clothes for the children and herself, and as a little boy he was often moved to tears when she bewailed her sad lot. It was the strong wish to grow up and work for his mother which later guided him unconsciously to occupy himself so assiduously with things relating to women's apparel, through which he made a fortune.

Some selections of professions are quite puzzling. One wonders why some people take up the heavy brass instruments or the bass drum in music. For the information of some it may be said that the players on these instruments usually have as much knowledge of music as any other member of the band. One might ask, therefore, why they prefer instruments that can be used only in conjunction with a band and which offer little if any outlet in any other way. I have not had the opportunity to study many such people, so that I am not offering anything conclusive. I knew two drum players and two horn players.

Mr. T., a drummer in an orchestra, told me that as a little boy of four, five, or six years he was very anxious to have a drum; the neighbor's boy received one for Christmas and he begged his father for one and cried for it, but the latter either did not wish to buy it for him or was perhaps too poor to do so. One evening the neighbor's door was open and no one seemed to be home; he walked quietly into the house and stole the drum. He hid it for a while, but as he could not resist the temptation to beat on it he was soon caught with the goods. The punishment was severe and produced a very strong impression. At the age of seventeen he began to study the violin, and a few years later he joined an amateur orchestra, playing second violin. A vacancy for the drummer's place then occurred and he volunteered to fill it. In a very short time he became such an accomplished player on this instrument that he obtained a lucrative position in a big orchestra.

Mr. X, the other kettledrum player, was very fond of music and studied it for years. He, too, volunteered to take the position of drummer in a band and has played on this instrument ever since. Mr. X came to me for treatment because of bashfulness. He had always been a very seclusive and reserved person, afraid to speak to people. It was impossible for him to put himself *en rapport* with anybody. He became tongue-tied whenever he came in contact with people, men or women. When he first arrived in the city he refused to live in a boardinghouse because he was afraid he would have to sit at the same table with people who might talk to him. Before taking up music as a profession, he lost his position in an office because he was unable to talk to the manager of his department. Here the drum fits in well with his nature; the drum is not an instrument that talks along fluently with the other instruments, as, for instance, the violin or clarinet; though it is a part of the band it is nevertheless more or less aloof in its behavior and it can always be heard when it speaks. In the case of Mr. X it served as a compensation for his enforced quietude.

The players on the heavy brass instruments showed similar mechanisms to the one found in X. One observes that people playing on drums, basses, or heavy brass instruments are not of the same type as those who play the first violin, and are altogether different in make-up from those who lead the band. They are often people who for some reason or other must stand away from the crowd, who are not very good "mixers" but would like to be.

I have spoken to a number of people who were rubbers in Turkish baths. I found that in some cases the vocation went back to the infantile desire for touching, in others it was distinctly pathological, and still others have taken up this vocation because it alleviates their own physical ailments. I have in mind one man who has been a "rubber" for about twenty years. He told me that he suffered from rheumatism and was told that Turkish baths would help him; as his aches diminished through the baths he decided to take up some occupation in the baths and became a rubber.

A few street cleaners have also been examined. Some were seen by me, and a few by former patients who kindly volunteered to assist me. There seem to be two types of street cleaners: some who are quite old or incapacitated to the extent that they are unable to follow their former vocations, and others who select street cleaning as a vocation of preference. The latter are usually clean-cut men of about thirty-five years and one wonders why they should be attracted to street cleaning. Of the few examined, some seemed to have retained the infantile coprophilia and, like children, liked to wallow in dirt. One of my friends brought me a report of a street cleaner, a man of about thirty-five, who described the difficulties he had encountered in obtaining his position—the examinations he had to pass, the political influence he had to get, et cetera. This man distinctly stated that he "loved" his work because "I love to see the water flush the streets and clean them through and through." His whole life seemed to be in his work, as he described it. This man recalls Boitelle of Maupassant, who "made a specialty of undertaking dirty jobs all through the countryside. Whenever there was a ditch or a cesspool to be cleaned out, a dunghill removed, a sewer cleansed, or any dirt hole whatever, he was always employed to do it." Dr. Karpas, from whose interesting paper I am quoting,[5] states: "Boitelle was disappointed in love—he was not allowed to marry a Negress with whom he was deeply in love. Thus his ungratified wish—to marry a Negress who was forbidden him by his parents and by society—found a substitute in the selection of a particular vocation which was likewise dirty and disagreeable to society."

One of the street cleaners who came under my observation presented an almost similar mechanism. He was an able-bodied man of about forty years who could give no reason for selecting this vocation. When asked about it, he said it was "as rotten and dirty as any other—what does it matter, what you do?" He was an avowed anarchist and took every occasion to decry the rottenness of our social system. I heard him a few years ago at a public meeting where he protested against being forced by the Street Cleaning Department to march with a dirty broom on his shoulder. He was fiery in his denunciation to the extent of advocating violence. I was unable to obtain access to his intimate life, but may we not assume that his vocation was an unconscious effort to clean up the rottenness of society which seemed to trouble him so much? I have no doubt that had we been able to enter into this man's life we would have found some infantile determinant in addition.

Besides the specific forms of sublimation, as seen in special vocations, one also notices certain modes of sublimation of a more or less general nature. "Only" children and the first born, who, by virtue of their position in the family, become domineering and officious, usually select the vocation requiring leadership, such as teachers, religious and political leaders; while the youngest child, who was bullied and intimidated by his older brothers, is generally satisfied with a subordinate position in life. I have mentioned only very few examples of the mechanism of selection of vocation that have come under my observation, but these suffice to show the forces that one generally finds behind selected vocations. There is always some psychic determinant which laid the foundation for

[5]Karpas: "Freud's Psychology," *New York Journal,* June 14, 1913.

the later vocation, and if not interfered with the individual is unconsciously guided to express his sublimation in that particular form. It makes no difference whether a man is a financier, preacher, actor, physician, cook, or shoemaker; provided he himself has selected this vocation and was not forced into it by home environments or social conditions, he will find his proper outlet in his work and under normal conditions he will never become fatigued by it or wearied of it.

Most of the failures in life are owing to one's trying to do what one is unfit for or unwilling to accomplish. Incidentally, I wish to say that no one ever suffers a nervous breakdown from overwork. Of course I am not referring to breakdown as a result of physical factors which are seen among workers in factories under unsanitary conditions, but to the so-called nervous breakdown as a result of overwork. Strictly speaking, these maladies do not exist. When one investigates such nervous breakdowns one invariably finds that many of them belong to the psychoses; others represent well-developed neuroses which were brought to the surface by any of the provoking agents one always encounters in such maladies; and in still others one finds that the work or vocation was always accompanied by severe resistances, and that instead of representing a natural outlet it was monotonous drudgery. When one takes the history of such persons one finds that they were always more or less discontented, that they were in constant need of vacations, and were always ailing. Contented workers have to be forced to take vacations. Vacations, as commonly understood, are neurotic fads which adjusted persons don't want and which are of no benefit to those who clamor for them. The fact that most vacations really cause fatigue shows that their alleged purpose is just a blind. The adjusted person works for work's sake—his vocation represents a part of his "cosmic urge" and hence he is unable to stop. That answers those who are puzzled as to why some of our multimillionaires continue to work untiringly. It is surely not for the love of money, as most think. On the other hand, there are cases on record of men who died soon after giving up lifelong vocations.

There are also a great many failures resulting from the fact that some people follow certain vocations for which they are mentally unfit. Such persons are usually defectives who have not enough insight into their own ability and cannot at any time sublimate properly; this is clearly seen in their love life, wherein they evince rapid attachments and just as ready detachments of their libido. They are unable to fix on either the love object or vocation; they are pathological flirts. The other failures are due to exogenous factors; not a few among those were forced into their vocations by some authority, and were then prevented by conscious or unconscious circumstances from changing to something else. Such persons merge in time into a neurosis, which is nothing but a manifestation of their inadequate adjustment, and often enough forces them to give up their work and take up something else. Unconsciously physicians have always sensed this mechanism, and for years it was customary to advise nervous patients to take up another vocation which the former selected for them. Such selections were invariably doomed to failure, as no person of normal mind, even though neurotic, should be advised as to the selection of a vocation. The few attempts which I made to advise patients concerning what to do invariably proved undesirable.

Miss R., a schoolteacher, became nervous and had to be rolled in a chair for a number of years. After being treated for quite a time she finally recovered. She did not wish to return to teaching and I suggested that she take a certain course in the School of Philanthropy at Columbia University; I felt that this would be the desirable thing under the circumstances. She thought it was a splendid idea, and acted upon it at once. I did not see her for a few weeks, when one day she called upon me at my office. She was in tears, and I feared at first that her symptoms had reappeared. After I calmed her, she began to explain that she hated the course; when I asked her why she continued with it, she simply argued: "Well, Doctor, you told me to take it." In other words, here she was struggling along for weeks, unhappy and discontented, because I took it upon myself to advise her. She went on to tell me that though she could not recover all of her tuition fee, she was quite willing to drop the course. When I inquired what she expected to do now, she told me that she would like to make lampshades. I assure you, that was the last thing that would ever have occurred to me. She has been making lampshades ever since, and I am glad to say that she is getting along very well. The point is that she is happy and loves her work simply because it was of her own selection.

I had a similar experience with Mr. S., who was considerably well-to-do and philanthropic. When he was cured, I urged him to enter some occupation, but was at a loss as to what to advise him to undertake. Dr. Putnam of Boston happened to be in New York at that time and he suggested that inasmuch as the patient was charitable and had a regular income it would be a capital idea for him to open up an office and mete out his charitable donations himself. I thought it was a happy suggestion, and I imparted it at once to Mr. S., who was quite enthusiastic over it. After a few weeks, however, he came to me, utterly disgusted, declaring impatiently: "I can't do the damned thing; I hate those people; I'll give them the money, but I don't want to talk to them." When I asked him what he would like to do, I learned that he had been thinking of entering the art business which, he said, he loved and had been interested in for years. I discussed the plan with him and the only counsel I gave him was to go into partnership with a person who was fully acquainted strictly with the business end of the undertaking. He has done very well since then and is now considered a connoisseur in his profession.

As in the selection of a mate, a sensible person needs no advice and wants none in choosing his vocation; and fools will fail in spite of the best guidance, for we can do well only those things that we do with our hearts, with our whole souls. The people who themselves selected their vocations, whose cases I cited, were successful in their various callings because their vocations supplemented or substituted their primitive components. The German expression, *Arbeit macht das Leben süss,* is literally true in cases where the work represents an outlet for the individual. This is true of all vocations. Those of you who have lived abroad and frequented the less-pretentious restaurants remember how proud a French or Italian cook is of his or her special dish, and how pleased the host is when his guest enjoys his meal. One can see they derive genuine pleasure from their work. I feel that the restlessness and dissatisfaction among our working classes, which often results in strikes, is not altogether owing to the causes generally assumed. It is not so much a question of money as of emotion. Because of the many inventions which have gradually transformed manual labor into machine work, the laborer no longer finds the same interest in his work. The shoemaker no longer makes a shoe, but as a hand in the shoe factory he constantly performs one simple thing which is of no interest to him and which soon becomes drudgery. When one compares this factory worker to the shoemaker of yore who took the measurements, selected the leather, and then put his whole personality into the making of the shoe, one can understand why the latter, as we still find him in some parts of Europe, is a much happier man.

On the other hand, I have seen many perfectly normal people who were failures in life simply because they were not allowed to follow their own inclinations. Instead of being prepared for life in general, their parents felt it necessary to accompany and guide them through every detail. Some of them struggled for twenty and thirty years with vocations which their fathers imposed upon them and stopped being failures only after their fathers' death, when they took up something which they really liked.

Thus I have known a man whose father compelled him to study music, despite his resistances. When he completed an excellent education in music in this country, he was sent to Berlin. The teacher declared that he possessed technique but lacked warmth and emotion. The father was obdurate, and insisted that the young man continue his studies. When the son reached the age of twenty-six, however, he took a full breath, as it were, and dropped music; thereafter he turned from one vocation to another, only to be compelled to return to music in every case. He continued to do this until his father died, when he entered the insurance business, in which he is now doing excellently.

Likewise, much harm is often done by parents who take it upon themselves to decide the child's future career. I have seen a boy of about ten or eleven years old brought to me by his father who considered him incorrigible. He informed me that the boy refused to do what he was told, took absolutely no interest in his studies, and flatly insisted on not going to school. I examined the boy and found that he was perfectly normal mentally. When I asked him why he did not wish to study, he said, "Well, I don't want to be a lawyer." "And what would you like to be?" "Oh, well," he quickly replied, "I would like to raise strawberries." When he was in the country, the gardener had told him that there was a good deal of money in raising strawberries; what is more, he liked strawberries exceedingly, and so he decided to make raising strawberries his lifework. I assured him that his father would have no objection to it, but that he would first have to learn how to read and write; upon which he went on to say that if his father would promise him that he might raise strawberries, he would go to school. As you may imagine, the father perpetually kept on dinning into the poor boy's ears that he would have to be a lawyer; every time the child made some error, he would zealously remind him that "he would make a devil of a lawyer." The youngster was already sick and tired of the law at the tender age of ten; and was it any wonder? I then called in the father and after treating him for a little while I had him promise to permit the youngster to raise strawberries in July. The boy did very well following this, and when summer came he at once set about realizing his ideal. He worked with the gardener for half a day, when he grew disgusted and decided to drop the profession altogether. He is now attending college. This boy developed so many resistances to his father and his ideas that he retaliated by simply refusing to do anything. The parents thought that he was vicious and abnormal simply because he revolted against a vocation which his father had selected for him from the very beginning. It is highly advisable, then, that the average normal individual be permitted to select his own vocation.

Conclusion

Postscript

When we look back upon the field we have surveyed in this brief volume we find one fact standing out very prominently. It is a highly significant fact and we find it in one form or another, in practically every subject that we have taken up. Indeed, we may say that it served as the basis and framework for our whole discussion—the fact that *all unconscious mentation is motivated fundamentally by the wish.*

We began with the symptom and we found that in the final analysis it represents the realization of a hidden wish. This we observed to hold true not only in the field of the neurosis but in the field of the psychosis as well. We saw in the very first case that I cited that the hysterical symptom in the arm was a compromise between two psychic streams, the foreconscious and the unconscious respectively, representing the fulfillment of a hidden wish. We noted the patient's mental conflict. She could not accept the young man's failure to propose as proof that he took no interest in her, yet she could not understand why he should not propose. We saw how her state of marked emotional tension was brought to a climax when the young man pressed her arm on the night before he left, and how it was this emotionally accentuated incident that she wished to retain in memory. For it was then that she expected he would say the long-awaited word. Analysis revealed that it was this marked mental state that became converted into the pain, that the hysterical symptom was but a concrete expression of her inner wish.

We see the same conversion in the psychoses. But here the process is much more far-reaching and more violent in reaction; in order to attain his wish, the individual is compelled to tear himself away from reality altogether. We tried to make this clear by citing several cases. We saw in the instance of the tailor who had been maltreated by the farmer and his sons at first an attempt at a solution of the problem through the regular channels of social justice. But when this failed, he tore himself away from reality altogether, realizing his desire for redress in his hallucinatory condition. We saw a more marked example of the same condition in the case of the young woman who developed delusions of reference, when she realized that she had lost the man in whom she was interested. Here, the rationalizing process, which was quite unconscious, is noteworthy. Forced to the conclusion that she lost the man because she was too reserved and moral, the patient attempts to readjust herself to the new condition by imagining that she really is immoral. "He left me because I am immoral": that is how she realizes her unconscious wish.

The psychopathological action—the slip of the tongue, the various "little" mistakes we make from day to day—all follow the same wish tendency. When the young man wrote "maternity" instead of "fraternity," there is no doubt at all that he expressed in that way what was uppermost on his mind: his ardent wish to enter upon matrimony. *The unconscious never lies.* When a young woman writes: "From now on I am going to be running back home," when she should have written: "From now on I am *not* going to be running back home," we may be sure that she wishes to return, and, other things being equal, that she will. This is borne out by the facts. The young woman in question was experiencing many conflicts in her work as a salesperson for a publishing house. The letter in which the above slip occurred was written directly upon arriving in her field, which she had left as many as three times, only to return again on the persuasion of her field manager. The letter was intended to assure the manager that she was no longer experiencing any mental conflicts regarding the work, but her mistake showed clearly her real state of mind, for a week later actually found her back home again.

The examples given in our discussion of wit show conclusively the wish motive. This was particularly shown in tendency wit, where the hostile or sex wishes always show themselves. When we come to dreams, the wish motive becomes more and more evident. The latent content of the dream invariably expresses a hidden wish. The individual craves for something, but as he cannot attain it in reality, it is realized for him in the dream. I am not going to stop to give any examples; the numerous dreams we have cited all show the wish tendency very clearly.

In collecting manias, and in a more highly sublimated form, in the selection of vocations also, we have the same wish tendency in evidence. Fairy tales, too, as we saw, follow the same trend: they are poetic productions containing some wish which the individual was unable to realize in reality. And, finally, all normal and abnormal artistic expression is no exception to our rule, for in the final analysis the artistic production is nothing but a wish compromise emanating from the unconscious mental activity of the individual endowed with talent.

In brief, we have demonstrated what Freud[6] discovered: that the neurotic symptom has a definite and logical meaning (psychogenesis), that it results from a repression of a disagreeable and painful past occurrence to which the patient could not at the time react adequately, that this repressed material—the idea with its concomitant affects—remains unconscious but dynamic, and that in due time there is a failure in the repression and the old episode works its way to the surface by some devious path in the form of pains, obsessions, phobias, anxieties, delusions, or hallucinations.

[6]A. A. Brill: "Reflections, Reminiscences of Sigmund Freud; *Medical Leaves,* Vol. III, 1940, pp. 18–29.

Freud also established the fact that sex, or, as he called it, libido, follows a definite course with various fluctuations in both the normal and neurotic person from childhood to adult life.

What is most important to note is that in studying patients by the method of free association (psychoanalysis) Freud wiped out the putative line of demarcation between the so-called normal and abnormal mental processes. He removed the stigma of *dégénéré* from the neurotic and showed that the only difference between him and the so-called normal is one of degree.

Psychoanalysis revolutionized the theories relating to normal and abnormal psychic life by showing how one readily merges into the other, that the reactions in both are the same, and that their various manifestations depend altogether on constitutional and environmental factors. All this is demonstrated in the psychopathology of everyday life, in dreams, in wit, and in all human activity. The normal civilized individual cannot express himself in ordinary speech and actions, but must often resort to devious ways. The neurotic symptom is a symbolization or dramatization of the conflicts between the primitive self, what Freud calls the Id, and the ethical self, the super-ego. The same is true of the lapses in talking, writing, or handling, which are so frequently seen in the actions of normal people. Wit, which is a specific creation of civilization, uses the same distortions as the neurotic symptom, and the everyday mistakes express those thoughts which are forbidden by culture. Wit permits us to obtain pleasure from forbidden sources. The dream serves the same purpose in so far as it permits the individual to get rid of that tension which accumulates during the day because of unattainable and prohibited desires. To accomplish this purpose the dream again makes use of symbolization and dramatization. For our ego or rather our ideal or super-ego tends to guide the average person in the straight and narrow paths laid out for him by the *mores* of his environment.

Psychoanalytic investigations not only led to the childhood of the individual but to the childhood of the race; it involved not only ontogeny, but phylogeny. For in solving the meaning of dreams which Freud called the *via regia* to the unconscious, he also found the meaning of myths, fairy tales, and folklore. Thus the *Oedipus complex,* which represents the first struggle between the son and his father which is found in the analysis of a person's dreams, leads directly to primitive history. Every neurotic symptom is based on some early trauma, but the study of the reaction to such traumas often enough shows that they do not strictly refer to the individual's own experience, but fit far better into some phyletic model and could generally be explained only on the basis of such an influence. This is especially noticeable in tracing the reactions to the *Oedipus* and *castration complexes,* in the study of animal phobias, and in the phobia of being eaten by the father.

After noticing this state of affairs for many years and in many different persons, Freud finally bridged the behavior reactions of modern man to those of prehistory. There is a remarkable resemblance between the psychic lives of neurotics and savages. However, the struggle between father and son, or the Oedipus complex, came to a different issue in prehistoric society. In our times it shows itself in death wishes against the father, which are manifested in dreams of the father's death, whereas in prehistoric society this wish was actually effectuated through the slaying and devouring of the primeval father by his rebellious sons. Indeed, Freud traces religion and other moral and social institutions to that earliest of all dramas. He describes the psychological basis of monotheism[7] on the scheme of a traumatic neurosis in the individual. The sum and substance of this ingenious and great work is that, as in a traumatic neurosis, one can recognize in religion the same historical and emotional background. In Freud's own words: "Mankind, as a whole, also passed through conflicts of a sexual, aggressive nature, which left permanent traces, but which were for the most part warded off and forgotten; later, after a long period of latency, they came to life again and created religious phenomena similar in structure and tendency to neurotic symptoms."

Though this prehistorical survey leaves many gaps, there is considerable evidence for his assumptions. Some are historically proven and "others have survived in remarkable replicas." As an example, the rite of the Christian communion, wherein the devout symbolically incorporate the blood and flesh of their God, and thus reproduce the inner meaning of the totem feast. There are numerous other survivals of our forgotten early history found in the

[7]*Moses and Monotheism,* translated by Katherine Jones, Knopf, 1939.

legends and fairy tales of people and in the analysis of children. In the traumatic neurosis one can say that memory traces of the traumatic event continue to exist in the individual's unconscious and can be brought to life again. The masses, too, retain impressions in the form of unconscious memory traces—that is to say, the psyche of man consists of not only personal experiences but also of what he brought with him at birth. In other words, the mind contains also fragments of phyletic origin, i.e., an *archaic inheritance,* which is made up of certain dispositions which are common to all living beings. And as experience shows that men differ in their mode of reaction to stimuli and impressions, we can say that the archaic inheritance contains these differences, which may be recognized as the *constitutional* elements in the individual. *The archaic heritage thus consists of not only dispositions, but also ideational contents, or unconscious memory traces of the experiences of former generations.*

Psychoanalysis recognizes the direct path from ontogeny to phylogeny. The individual begins with the lawless Id psyche, which, as a result of struggles with the outer world, gradually becomes molded into a conscious ego and later into a super-ego. The race which constitutes an aggregate of individual beings is subjected to the same trials and vicissitudes and reacts to stimuli in the same manner, and with the same results as the individual. The super-ego, the highest evolution of man, plays the same part in both. In the individual it is the precipitate, or the representative of the earthly father, while in the race it represents the heavenly father, or the ideals and traditions of the race. Conflicts between these psychic forces produce neuroses or psychoses in the individual and psychic upheavals in the race.

The dictum of science that ontogeny is a partial repetition of phylogeny is equally true in the psychic realm. Briefly, every civilized boy today goes through the same struggle with his father as his prehistoric brother did in the dimmest past. In prehistory the struggle was unabated and inexorable until the father was slain, while in the modern boy, because of his long cultural heritage, everything must be hidden. Unless he is a defective, he simply dreams that his father died. As Plato puts it—the virtuous man contents himself with dreaming of that which the wicked man does in actual life. By a virtuous man we mean, of course, one who is influenced by his mores, especially by religion, and by a wicked man, one who is incapable of assuming such restraints. Be that as it may, the continued existence of such dreams definitely points to the link between the present and the past, between the individual and the race.

List of Books for New Reader

Basic Writings of S. Freud, tr. by A. A. Brill. Modern Library, N.Y., 1938

General Introduction to Psycho-analysis, tr. by Joan Riviere. Garden City Publishing Co., 1943

Psycho-analysis for Teachers and Parents, Anna Freud. Emerson, N.Y., 1935

Freud's Contribution to Psychiatry, A. A. Brill. W. W. Norton & Co., N.Y., 1944

Psychoanalysis and the Social Sciences, ed. by Geza Roheim. Int. Univ. Press, N.Y., 1948

Index

Abreaction, 8, 9, 32
  definition of, 7
Absent-mindedness, 44, 65
Actions, psychopathological, 41, 43, 44, 282
  symbolic (*See* Symbolic Actions)
Actor, psychology of, 272
Adam and Eve, story of, allegorical significance of, 57, 178
Adjustment, abnormal, 33
  to environment, 16, 28, 137, 237
  normal mode of, 35
  to sex life, 25, 164, 228–34
Adler, Alfred, 201
Aggression, hostile, wit of, 111–13
  sexual, 110, 112, 115
Aggressive component, 271
Agoraphobia, 37
Alcohol, 13, 23, 176
Alexander the Great, 262
Algolagnia, 260
Alloerotism, 263, 264
Alphabet and symbols, 55
Ambivalency of feeling, 190
Amnesia, infantile, 60
  post-hypnotic, 13
Anaclitic relation, 136
Andersen, Hans Christian, 178–79, 254
Animals, identification with, 198–205

Animism, 104
Anxiety, definition of, 157
Anxiety dreams, 146, 157–67
Anxiety hysteria, 37, 151
Aphasia, 43, 58
Aphonia, 35
Archaic inheritance, 286
Aretaeus, 1
Aristotle, 262
Artificial dreams, 167–71
Artistic productions, 260–64
  wish motive in, 261–62, 283
Associations, revived by impressions, 10, 124–25
  trend of, 206, 210–14
Augustus Caesar, 103
Autoerotic phase of sexual development, 162
Autoerotism, 263–64
Automatism wit, 102–3

Baudesson, Captain, 74
Beard, G. M., American physician, 4
Beechstein, Ludwig, 253
Bell, Sanford, 60
Bernheim, 13
Beziehungswahn (*See* Delusions of Reference)
Bible, Wicked, 82
Bleuler, Eugen, 24, 45, 54, 76, 169, 219

Booth, Edwin, 272
Breuer, Josef, 6, 7, 33, 34
Burglars, fear of, 86–87

Castration complex, 285
Catatonia, 2
Catatonic characteristics, 218–19
Categorical imperative, 193
Catharsis, 262
    mental, 272
Cathartic method, 6–20, 33
Cathexis, 35
Censorship, psychic, 193, 194, 210
Cerebral hemorrhage, 42, 58
Charcot, Jean Baptiste, Professor,
    5, 6
Charnwood, Lord, 114
Child, early impressions of, 16, 61
    mental evolution of, 50–55, 136
    oldest, 244
    only, 237–49
    primitive impulses of, 12
    sexual life of, 18, 28, 60, 162–
    63
    youngest, 27–28, 149, 240
Christian communion, 285
Christmas, 57
Civilization, 22, 25, 27, 111, 138,
    265
Collecting manias, 87–95
    in children, 91
    psychological meaning of, 93
    in psychotics, 91
    symbolic actions in, 93
    wish motive in, 283
    (*See also* Fetishism)
Comparison, expression by, 51,
    53–54
    symbolic character of, 58
Complex, definition of, 10
Complex readiness, 76, 77, 83
Compulsion neurosis, 37
Concealing memories, 58–64, 152
    encroaching, 59
Condensation, 107, 145
    in dreams, 100

in wit, 98–100
Confucius, 249
Consciousness, organ of percep-
    tion, 13
Conversion, of past emotion into
    physical pain, 9
    of psychic energy, 9–10, 34
Crying spells, 26, 90

David Copperfield, 263
Davis, Jefferson, 80
Daydreaming, 167
Defense mechanism, lying as, 171
Degenerates, mental, 21
Delirium, 35
Delusions, 3, 218
    definition of, 32
    of grandeur, 32
    of persecution, 32
    of poverty, 91
    of reference, 39, 226, 282
    of sex, 24
    of transformation, 203
Dementia praecox, 3, 46
    symptoms of, 23
    (*See also* Schizophrenia)
Dereism, 54
Devil, nicknames for, 74
Dickens, Charles, 84, 178
Displacement, 59
    from below to above, 146
    in dreams, 107
    of psychic accent, 101–2
    retroactive, 59
Displacement wit, 101–2
Disraeli, Benjamin, 98
Distortions of memory, 58
Dostoevski, Feodor, 84
Double-entendre, mechanism of,
    129, 131
Doubts, 37
Dream analysis, 14, 171
    difficulty in, 129–33
Dreams, 19, 141, 284
    abstract ideas in, 129
    absurdity in, 107

anxiety (*See* Anxiety Dreams)
artificial, 167–71
condensation in, 100
consolation, 194, 196
convenience, 127, 131
of death, 179–87
definition of, 126
displacement in, 107
distortion mechanism in, 133–34, 140
egocentricity of, 182, 212
emotional element in, 19, 194
examination, 193–94
exhibition, 179
expression through opposite, 107
of falling, 197
of flying, 196
function of, 119–55
as guardian of sleep, 128
identification with animals, 198–205
indirect representation in, 107
internal and external stimuli for, 120–25
interpretation of, 128
latent content of, 211, 283
of local character, 198
manifest, latent content of, 151, 155
manifoldly determined, 205–14
meaning of, 119
of missing trains, 196
motive of, 119–55
of nakedness, 178–79
nature and meaning of, 125
Oedipus, 182–84
overdetermined, 205–14
past situations in, 149
prophetic, 195
quotations in, 208
resolution, 195
and symptoms: like mechanisms of, 155; like symbolic expressions in, 150; types of, 157–214; typical, 178–87;

wish motive in (*See* Wish Motive in Dreams)
and wit: differences between, 117; like mechanisms in, 107; similarity of, 117
Dumas, Alexandre, 29

Easter, origin of, 57
Education, 137
Ego, 35, 193, 286
Electra complex, 190
Electricity, therapeutic value of, 5
Ellipsis wit, 104
Emerson, Ralph Waldo, 224
Emotional deterioration, 23, 216
Emotional outlets, 29, 31, 200
collecting manias, 90
Emotionalism, 11, 84, 172, 174
Emotions, 44, 152
past, converted into physical pain, 9
strangulated, release of, 10, 21
Empathic index, 144
Environment, 17, 165, 284
Epileptic, psychic, 46, 49
Erb, Heinrich, 5
Ethical self (*See* Super-ego)
Examination dreams, 193–94
Examinations, physical and neurological, 3–4
Exhibition dreams, 179
Exhibitionism, 108–10, 273
infantile: 109; sublimation of, 271–72
Experiences, painful, and the unconscious, 10–11, 29
Expressions, alloerotic, 264
autoerotic, 264
by comparison, 51, 53–54
symbolic, 9, 41, 56
therapeutic value of, 7
wish (*See* Wish Motive)

Fairy tales, 178, 251–60, 265
pernicious influence of, 255–60
wish motive in, 251–60, 283

Fancy, tendency to, 255
Fear (*See* Anxiety)
Fetishism, 92, 162
Fixations, 162, 184–85
Foch, Ferdinand, 260
Folie à deux, 227
Folie du doute, 37
Folie raisonnante, 38
Foreconscious, 12
Forgetfulness, organic, 43
Forgetting, 35, 41, 43–44
  typical case of, 45–50
  wish motive in, 43–44, 67
Forgetting names, psychopathol-
  ogy of, 65–75
Free association, 14, 34, 46, 48–
  51, 53, 284
Freud, Sigmund, 1, 3–7, 11, 13,
  14, 17–20, 24, 25, 33, 34, 40,
  43, 45, 48, 49, 59, 61, 84, 94,
  109, 121, 135, 161, 178–79,
  183, 263
  concept of psychic apparatus,
  193 (*See also* Id Psyche)
  concept of sex (*See* Sex and
  Love)
  The Interpretation of Dreams,
  19
  psychology of, basis of, 41
  *The Psychopathology of Every-
  day Life*, 20
Fugue (*See* Poriomania)

Gain, morbid (*See* Morbid Gain)
Galen, 1
Goethe, Johann, 262, 263
Grimm, Jacob and Wilhelm, 253–
  54

Hallucinations, 3, 39, 151, 218
  definition of, 32
Hearn, Lafcadio, 251
Heine, Heinrich, 107
Heterosexuality, 161
Hippocrates, 1
Homosexuality, 161, 168, 229

Hunger and love, 26
Hypnotism, 5, 13–14
  hysterical symptoms through, 5,
  7
  and psychoanalytic method, difference between, 14–15
Hysteria, Studies in, 7
Hysteria, 6, 13, 26, 33
  anxiety, 37, 151
  and crying spells, 26
  pathogenesis of, sexuality in, 34
"Hysterical Phenomena, on the
  Psychic Mechanisms of," (report) 33
Hysterical symptoms, 5, 7

Id, 284
Id Psyche, 193, 286
Id-tendencies, 147
Identification, with animals, 198–
  205
  psychic mechanism of, 121–22
Illusion, definition of, 32
Impressions, in early life, 16
  reviving associations, 124–25
Inheritance, archaic, 286
Inhibitions, 22
Insanity, 2
  pretended, 30
  (*See also* Psychosis)
Insomnia, 26
Interpretation of Dreams, The, 19

Jean Christophe, 72
Jefferson-Jackson dinner speech,
  78
Joke, obscene, 108, 110, 114

Karpas, Dr., 276
King David, 115
Kiselak, 244–45
Korsakoff's psychosis, 176
Kraepelin, Emil, 2, 3, 23, 24

Lamar, Mrs. Walter D., 79–80
Language, symbolic, 41
  in the unconscious, 16

Lapsus linguae, 19, 78–81, 97–98
(*See also* Talking, lapses in)
Latency period, 162, 163
Lesbians, 161
Liar, and criminal, relation between, 177
and poet, relation between, 177
psychopathic, 176
Libido, 18, 24, 109, 239, 241, 272, 284
object, 263
repressed, as manifested in anxiety, 248
Libido theory, 18
Lincoln, Abraham, 80, 114–15
Locke, John, *tabula rasa* of, 16, 61
Losing, keys, 86
symbolic action of, 85–87
wish motive in, 85–87
Love (*See* Sex and Love)
Lycanthropia, 203
Lying, 98, 171–78
as defense mechanism, 171
double standard of, 172
pathological, 175
psychopathic, 174
and the unconscious, 282

Macmillan, Professor, 127
Madonna types, 186–87
Malingerers, 30
Mania, 2, 23, 24
doubting (*See* Folie du doute)
reasoning (*See Folie raisonnante*)
(*See also* Collecting Manias)
Manic-depressive psychosis, 151, 221–23
and schizophrenia, difference between, 223
symptoms of, 24
Masculine protest, 201
Masochism, 143, 258

Masturbation, 162, 217, 229, 234
and schizophrenia, relation between, 217
Maupassant, Guy de, 131
Melancholia, 2, 23, 24, 222
Memories, concealing (*See* Concealing Memories)
Memory, distortions of, 58
lapse of (*See* Forgetting)
and pain, 8–9
Mental analysis (*See* Psychoanalysis)
Mental catharsis, 272
Mental deterioration, 91
Mental diseases, borderline cases of, 3
history of, 1–6
Mental retardation, 43
Meyer, Adolf, 3
Michelangelo, 15
Mixoscopia, 162
Monotheism, 285
Montaigne, Michel, 119
Morbid gain, 9, 29–31

Names, deliberate changing of, 73–75
forgetting, psychopathology of, 65–75
Napoleon, 144
Narcissism, 162
of small differences, 80
Nero, 249
Nervousness, 1
Neurasthenia, 4, 13, 23
Neurosis, 24–26, 41, 68, 69, 162
compulsion, 37
mixed, 246
morbid gain from, 29
and psychosis, difference between, 22, 38
and sex life, 17, 24
symptoms of, 21, 29
traumatic, 285–86
Noöpsyche, and thymopsyche, relation between, 152

Object-libido phase, 263
Obsessions, 35, 37, 173
  compulsive symptoms of, 256–57
Oedipus complex, 284–85
Oedipus dreams, 182–84
Oedipus Tyrannus, 182–83
Only child, 237–49
Ontogeny, 286

Pain, physical, past emotion converted into, 9
  psychic, 7
Panic, 87
Paralysis, 35
Paranoia, 23, 77, 223–35
Paroxysms, physical, 46
Pathology, 2, 41
Perceptions, false (*See* Hallucinations)
Persecution, ideas of, 226
Perversion, 16, 110, 161
Phillips, Wendell, 113
Phobias, 35, 157–58, 160
Phylogeny of race and psychoanalysis, 286
Pinel, Philippe, 2
Pleasure principle, 136
Poet, modern, and psychotic, similarity between, 264
"Poison-needle" case, 165
Poisons, 23, 176
Poriomania, 47
Post-hypnotic suggestion, 13–14, 125
Prepubescent age, 18, 27–28, 59–60, 136, 138–40, 163
  (*See also* Child, mental development of)
Prescott, Frederick, 177
Primitive self (*See* Id)
Projection, 39, 122
Prostitution complex, 39
Prostitution fancies, 167
Pseudologia phantasica (*See* Lying, pathological)

Psychiatry, 2
Psychic accent, displacement of, 101–2
Psychic apparatus, Freud's concept of, 193
Psychic censorship, 193, 194, 210
Psychic energy, conversion of, 9–10, 34
Psychic epileptic, 46, 49
Psychic equivalent, 46
Psychic manifestations, 11
Psychic mechanism, of identification, 121–22
  value of knowing, 94
Psychic pain, 7
Psychic streams in conflict, 35–37
  (*See also* Symptoms)
Psychoanalysis, 3, 4, 15, 40, 284
  definition of, 1, 14
  literature on, 20
  as prophylaxis, 17, 40
  and sculpture, similarity in materials of, 15
Psychoanalytic psychiatry, 42
Psychogenesis, 283
Psychoneurosis, 12, 168
Psychopathological actions, 41, 43, 44, 282
Psychopathology of Everyday Life, The, 20
Psychopathology of everyday life, 65–95, 284
Psychosis, 24, 25, 30, 32, 41
  alcoholic, 32
  definition of, 215
  folie à deux, 227
  forms of, 215–35
  functional and organic, 23
  Korsakoff's, 176
  manic-depressive (*See* Manic-depressive Psychosis)
  and neurosis, difference between, 22, 38
  and sex life, 24
  wish motive in, 282

Pubescent age, 13, 18, 164
Pygmalion and Galatea, 261

Reaction formations, 162
Reading, lapses in, 75–83
Reality, principle of, 136–37
Religions, early, 56–57, 159
Repression, 11, 12, 34, 35, 50, 61,
    87, 90, 111, 112, 135–36,
    138, 158, 162
Resistance, 35, 110–11
Revue Philosophique, 121
Roosevelt, Franklin D., 79
Roosevelt, Theodore, 77, 79

Sadism, 258, 268, 271
Sado-masochistic components,
    267–73
Sanctis, Santo de, 135
Schiller, Friedrich von, 26
Schizophrenia, 24, 164, 170, 215–
    21, 242
    and manic-depressive psychosis,
        difference between, 223
    and masturbation, relation be-
        tween, 217
Sears, Lorenzo, 113
Self-preservation, 26
Senile dementia, 239
Sensation, intensity of, relation of
    stimulus to, 124
Sex, and love, 17–18, 24–26, 158–
    60
Sex impulses, 25
    control of, 159–60, 165
Sex instinct, 18
Sexual aggression, 110, 112, 115
Sexual aim, 161
    intermediary, 109
Sexual curiosity, 62, 109, 257
Sexual development, autoerotic
    phase of, 162
Sexual excitement, 108–9
Sexual factors, 163
Sexual function, 158–59

Sexual life of child (*See* Child,
    sexual life of)
Sexual needs, control of, 22, 27,
    90
    (*See also* Repression)
Sexual object, 161
Sexuality, infantile, 160, 162, 203,
    273
    in pathogenesis of hysteria, 34
Shaw, G. B., 143, 248
Snake, symbols of, 56–58
Sophocles, 182–83
Speech disturbances, 68
Spiritualism, 253
Stammering, 68–69
Studies in Hysteria, 7
Stuttering, 70
Sublimation, 162, 266, 276
    of infantile exhibitionism, 271–
        72
Suggestion, post-hypnotic, 13–14
Super-ego, 193, 284, 286
Suppression, 35
Swett, Leonard, 114
Symbolic actions, 83–87
    in collecting manias, 93
    of losing, 85–87
Symbolic expressions, 41, 56
Symbolic language, 41
Symbols, 52, 55–58
    and alphabet, 55
    barber's pole, 55
    colors, 55
    definition of, 50–51, 58
    ethnic, 56
    of moral falling, 37, 197
    sex, 56
    of snake, 56–58
Symptoms, 2, 6, 7, 14, 35, 173,
    281
    causes and development of, 7
    hysterical, 5, 7
    neurotic, 21, 29
    origin of, 15
Syphilis, 23

Tabula rasa, 16, 61
Talking, lapses in, 41, 65, 81
Talking cure (*See* Cathartic Method)
Tear motive, 253
Tendency wit, 111, 258, 283
Thackeray, W. M., 84
Thymopsyche, 152
Titanic disaster, 166
Transference, 243
Transformation, delusions of, 203
Traumatic neurosis, 285–86
Truman, Harry S., 78–79

Unconscious, the, 10–12, 16, 20, 165
    actions guided by, 12–13
    and conscious, distinction between, 34
    language in, 16
    and painful experiences, 10–11
    protective mechanism in, 11–12, 16
    psychology of, 34
    wish motive in, 281
Unconscious manifestations, 65
Unconscious mentation, 55–56, 146–47
Unconscious motives, 95
Unification wit, 103–4

Vacations, 277
Van Dyke, Henry, 93
"Verbigerations," 218
Vinci, Leonardo da, 14, 187, 263
Virchow, Rudolf, 2, 176, 177
Vocations, selection of, 265–87
    mechanism of, 267–78
    sado-masochistic components in, 267–73
Voyeurism, 110, 162. 273

Wallace, Dr., 123
Wanke, 259

Weber-Fechner law, 124
White lie, 172
Wish motive, 39, 141, 167, 171, 180, 193
    in artistic productions, 261–62, 283
    in collecting manias, 283
    in dreams, 19, 126–28, 139–42, 179–82, 193–208, 283
    in fairy tales, 251–60, 283
    in forgetting, 43–44, 67
    in losing things, 85–87
    in lying, 171–75
    in psychosis, 282
    in the unconscious, 281
    in wit, 283
Wit, 284; automatism, 102–3
    condensation in, 98–100
    displacement, 101–2
    and dreams: difference between, 117; like mechanisms in, 107; similarity of, 117
    ellipsis, 104; harmless, 107
    of hostile aggression, 111–13
    main function of, 113
    nonsense, 104
    outdoing, 106
    purposeful, 107
    repartee in (*See* Unification Wit)
    representation through opposite, 105
    sense in nonsense, 105
    through similarity, 107
    technique of, 97–117
    tendencies of, 107–17
    tendency (*See* Tendency Wit)
Writing, lapses in, 19, 65, 75–83
Wundt, Wilhelm, 2

Yoni lingam, 56

Zoöphilia, 204
Zurich school, 10